Clarity and Coherence in Academic Writing

T0386476

This book presents a lively, rich, and concise introduction to the key concepts and tools for developing clarity and coherence in academic writing. Well-known authors and linguists David Nunan and Julie Choi argue that becoming an accomplished writer is a career-long endeavor. They describe and provide examples of the linguistic procedures that writers can draw on to enhance clarity and coherence for the reader. Although the focus is on academic writing, these procedures are relevant for all writing. This resource makes complex concepts accessible to the emergent writer and illustrates how these concepts can be applied to their own writing. The authors share examples from a wide range of academic and non-academic sources, from their own work, and from the writing of their students. In-text projects and tasks invite you, the reader, to experiment with principles and ideas in developing your identity and voice as a writer.

David Nunan is Professor Emeritus of Applied Linguistics at the University of Hong Kong; and President Emeritus, Distinguished Research Professor, and Director of the David Nunan Institute, Anaheim University. He is also a former president of TESOL International. He is well-known internationally through his many academic and English Language Teaching textbook publications.

Julie Choi is Senior Lecturer of Education at Melbourne Graduate School of Education, Australia. She is the author of *Creating a Multilingual Self: Autoethnography as Method*, and co-editor of *Plurilingualism in Teaching and Learning* and *Language and Culture: Reflective Narratives and the Emergence of Identity*.

Clarity and Coherence in Academic Writing

Using Language as a Resource

David Nunan and Julie Choi

Routledge
Taylor & Francis Group

NEW YORK AND LONDON

Designed cover image: © Getty Images

First published 2023
by Routledge
605 Third Avenue, New York, NY 10158

and by Routledge
4 Park Square, Milton Park, Abingdon, Oxon, OX14 4RN

Routledge is an imprint of the Taylor & Francis Group, an informa business

© 2023 David Nunan and Julie Choi

ISBN: 9781032015590 (hbk)
ISBN: 9781032013824 (pbk)
ISBN: 9781003179092 (ebk)

DOI: 10.4324/9781003179092

Typeset in Goudy
by codeMantra

To our students
past, present and future

Contents

Acknowledgments

We would like to thank our graduate students and teachers who contributed their writing and learning experiences to this book, sharing their insights, and raising with us questions and concerns about how best to guide their own students' writing development. Special thanks to Kailin Liu, Tharanga Kalehe Pandi Koralage, Xingyi (Sean) Wang, Francesca Lo Presti, Xiaotong Zang, and, in particular, to Catriona Mach who not only assisted us in revising each chapter but also provided insightful comments on the text along the way. To Routledge Senior Editor, Karen Adler, who embraced the project when it was first suggested, and whose encouragement and enthusiasm sustained us at those times when our own begin to flag. Olivia Powers was invaluable in guiding through pre-publication editing stages. Last but not least, we are grateful to Debra Myhill for graciously agreeing to write the foreword. Her influence on our own approach to teaching academic writing will be evident throughout the book.

Foreword

At its heart, this book is about understanding academic writing and understanding yourself as a writer. What it is not is an instruction manual on academic writing. And this is its strength. The authors invite you as readers to engage with how academic texts are crafted, to consider how you tackle the process of writing, and to reflect on your own writing. The book is about being a writer, as much as it is about academic writing.

For me, as an academic writer myself, as a journal editor, and as a supervisor of doctoral students, there are two fundamental messages underpinning the book which resonate powerfully with my own experiences. The first concerns the role of grammar and knowledge about language. The authors recognize the inseparability of form and content and emphasize a Hallidayan functional view of language, where grammatical choices shape meaning and effective communication. Writers need to understand how texts work and how different grammatical forms function to establish meaning. The authors stress that this is not about *knowledge* which is learned then routinely applied, but about *understanding* which supports and informs authorial decision-making and writer agency. The second fundamental message relates to the writing process, shifting the gaze from the academic text to the academic writer. This foregrounds the key processes of planning, drafting, and revising but, crucially, disrupts the rigid notion of first, you plan, then you draft, then you revise. Instead, the recursive and messy nature of writing is described, and particularly that writing and thinking co-occur. The process of writing itself generates new ideas or new problems not anticipated in initial planning, and equally the process of writing is one of constant rewriting and 'shuttling' between phrases, sentences, and paragraphs.

In developing their argument about understanding language and understanding the writing process, the authors do not avoid difficult concepts or challenging issues, but address them head-on, without adopting dogmatic stances. For example, Halliday's metalanguage is explained clearly, using examples (in contrast to the conceptual density of some of Halliday's own explanations!). The problematic concept of 'voice' is considered from multiple perspectives and with rich complexity and not simply reduced to superficial discussion of first and third-person pronouns. There is recognition that 'academic writing' is not a genre, as implied in so many resources for academic writing support, but is a term which groups together a range of written genres, including, for example, theses, journal articles, reports, and applications, and which varies across academic disciplines.

The title of the book is enacted in the way it is written. The writing is a model of clarity and coherence, with chapter topics providing both a clear structure and supporting the development of a clear argument. Throughout, the voices of the authors are strongly present, sharing their own experiences and understandings of being an academic writer, and offering direct invitations to readers to think, reflect, and act. This book will not tell you the top ten steps to writing success: instead, and much more importantly, it will open up how you think about the academic texts you write and about yourself as a writer. Confidence and success as an academic writer is not about *knowing* what you should do, but about *understanding* the infinitely creative possibilities of language as a resource.

Debra Myhill
University of Exeter, UK

Introduction and overview

This book is a collaborative effort between two experienced writers. There were times in the course of writing the book that we wanted our individual voices to be heard. We have made these occasions evident within the text. We also wanted to engage you, the reader, in the ideas presented in the text. We have done this by inserting 'Making Connections' boxes into the text. These consist of tasks and questions to help you relate what we have to say to your own context and experience as a creator of academic texts. As we worked on the book, we also sought feedback from emergent writers. We were fortunate in being able to enlist a group of young graduate students who read earlier drafts of the manuscripts, and posed many questions, challenging us on points that were not clearly or adequately articulated. We have added a selection of these, along with our responses, at the end of each chapter. Their enthusiasm for the project sustained us during difficult periods in the writing process.

David's voice: how the book was born

This guide was born out of a conversation I had one evening with Julie who is a Senior Lecturer in Education (Additional Languages) at the Melbourne Graduate School of Education where I have given many face-to-face and online seminars. The conversation had turned to the topic of academic writing, and Julie urged me to produce a guide to good, clear academic writing. Flattered, but also puzzled, I asked why.

"My students like your books. I'm constantly told many of the standard texts in the field are extremely challenging, but yours are clear. What's his secret?" they want to know. "Most of them struggle to express their own ideas. This is true, not only of the second language speakers, but

---

DOI: 10.4324/9781003179092-1

the first language speakers of English as well. If you could share your insights, I'm sure the students would find it helpful".

She challenged me when I commented that learning to write by reading a book or article was akin to learning to drive by watching a video.

"Of course, you can't spare them the blood, sweat and tears, but if you can share with them your insights, it will give them concrete ideas they can try out to improve their own writing skills. Telling them 'this isn't clear', or 'this is garbled', or 'I haven't got a clue what you're talking about here', isn't helpful. It might indicate where the problem lies but tells them nothing about how to fix the problem".

Julie's suggestion reminded me of an incident that occurred about ten years into my academic career. At the time, I wasn't desperate to scramble up the academic ladder. However, one day a colleague forwarded to me an advertisement from a well-regarded university for a position a grade or two above the one I currently occupied. From the criteria for appointment, it seemed my experience, qualifications, research record, and publications were a good match for job. I applied, was shortlisted, acquitted myself well at the interview, and waited for a phone call from the Dean to inform me that the position was mine. The phone call never came. Eventually, I received a proforma letter thanking me for my interest in the position and expressing regret that the university was unable to offer me a post at that time. Resisting the urge to write back saying that any time would do, I consigned the letter to the dustbin.

At a conference some months later, I bumped into a member of the interviewing committee. I accepted his invitation to have a drink. After a second drink, I asked him what had been lacking in my application.

"Well, I supported you", he began. (*Yes, they all say that*, I thought.)

"Unfortunately, a majority of the committee didn't. The burden of their objection was that your books and articles were clear and accessible to their students. One of the members said that even some of his undergraduates understood your work".

Even some of his undergraduates? Goodness! That's the nicest thing anyone has ever said about my work. I couldn't help smiling.

He was surprised at my reaction. I told him that I saw clarity as a virtue. I have never subscribed to the notion that if academic writing is comprehensible it must be superficial. While there are profound works that should carry a health warning, there are others that are only profound in their incomprehensible triviality. So, significance and clarity are not to be confused. You owe it to yourself, but more importantly, you owe it to your reader to strive for clarity while at the same time presenting often complex ideas in a non-trivial fashion. It's called showing respect.

Although flattered by what Julie's students had to say about my books, I hesitated about taking up her suggestion. To offer advice on how to write is to invite criticism. Fashions, practices, and standards of acceptability change over time. Take the case of *The Elements of Style*. The first edition was written and privately published in 1918 by William Strunk before being commercially published in 1920 (Strunk, 2018). The book was a best-seller. A second, expanded edition was produced by E. B. White (Strunk & White, 1959) after Strunk's death. In 2011, *Time* magazine named this edition one of the 100 best and most influential books of the previous century. Now in its fourth edition, the book continues to sell well. It has been highly praised by celebrated authors such as Dorothy Parker and Stephen King, the latter arguing that it should be read by every aspiring author. It has also been trenchantly criticized. Pullum's (2009) main criticism is that while Strunk and White dish out a great deal of advice on grammar (avoid the passive voice), their own knowledge of English grammar is either misguided or just plain wrong.

> Some of the recommendations are vapid, like "Be clear" (how could one disagree?). Some are tautologous, like "Do not explain too much." (Explaining too much means explaining more than you should, so of course you shouldn't.) Many are useless, like "Omit needless words." (The students who know which words are needless don't need the instruction.) Even so, it doesn't hurt to lay such well-meant maxims before novice writers.
>
> (Pullum, 2009, p. 32)

After thinking about Julie's suggestion for a week, I decided to accept her challenge. However, I'd do so on only one condition. We met for a lunch, and she was delighted with my decision. "But what's the condition?" she asked.

"That you co-author the book with me", I replied.

Defining academic writing

Academic writing has been defined as any formal written work produced in an academic setting. While academic writing comes in many forms, the following are some of the most common: literary analysis, research paper, and dissertation (or thesis) (Valdes, 2019). The serious business of producing pieces of written work that can be characterized as 'academic' usually begins in junior high school and, for many students, continues all the way through senior high to undergraduate study at university and, for some, on to graduate school. In the book, we deal with a range of academic writing genres, although our focus will be those of concern to our primary audience (see below), most particularly academic assignments and dissertations.

At this point, we won't elaborate on the definition provided above. The characteristics, conventions, and controversies over the nature of academic writing will emerge as your read the book and complete some of the application activities along the way. You may be surprised at the notion that academic writing stirs controversy. It does. This is particularly the case in those disciplines concerned with qualitative inquiry such as the social sciences, education, and the humanities. In our final chapter, we devote the first section to revisiting and elaborating on the controversies touched on in the body of the book.

Audience

The primary audience for this book is graduate students. As our own fields are applied linguistics, education, and the teaching of English as an additional language, it should come as no surprise to find that many of our examples are drawn from these fields and directed to readers who plan to become teachers. However, we hope the book is also useful for those from allied disciplines as well as undergraduates and even those who are in senior high school.

In developing the materials, we followed our usual practice of trying them out with our students as well as getting feedback from those who had recently graduated. From them we learned that the material should appeal to a wider audience, including undergraduates. It should help teachers in a range of disciplines developed their own writing skills as well as giving them insights into how they might improve the writing skills of their own students. The notion that every teacher is a language/literacy teacher has been around for many years. In the United Kingdom the Bullock Report, officially called A *Language for Life*, recommended that every school should develop a language policy for language across the curriculum in which there is a dual focus on language skills and subject knowledge. The prevailing notion that developing academic language skills was the sole responsibility of language/literacy teachers was challenged. In secondary school, memorizing content and mastering procedures in subject areas such as science, history, or geography was only part of the learning process. Students also needed to master the language of history and learn to think as an historian. The same was held for other subjects. Teachers of these subjects had a major responsibility for teaching the language of their subject. Unfortunately, most were ill-equipped to do so. The point is that language and subject content are inseparable. You can't think and communicate without language, and you have to think and communicate about *something*, be it content related to everyday life or specialized subject matter. This is not always appreciated by subject specialists. We often encounter lecturers from other disciplines who argue that our job is to teach students language so that they can get on with the (more important) task of teaching science, law, or mathematics.

In the rest of this introduction, we provide a synopsis of the chapters to come along with brief overview of the concepts and principles you will encounter in the rest of the book. The book falls naturally into two parts. Chapters 1–3 address questions that underpin the rest of the book:

- What fundamentals of language should writers, teachers, and students should know about?
- What linguistic tools are available to writers to enhance the clarity and coherence of their writing?
- What are the intended outcomes of the writing journey and what processes do writers deploy along the way?

The remainder of the book deals with practical issues and techniques, including the use of figurative and academic language, knowing one's audience, finding one's voice, dealing with feedback, and revising/redrafting initial efforts. As you embark on this challenging, but hopefully rewarding journey with us, you would do well to keep in mind what the author and broadcaster Clive James had to say about the art and craft of writing: that expressing yourself clearly is the most complicated thing there is.

Chapter 1: What every writer should know about language

The proposition we put to you in this chapter is that a basic knowledge of the English language will help you become a better writer. The proposition probably raises several questions in your mind: What counts as 'basic'? What aspects of the language should I know about? and how can this knowledge help me become a better writer? In this chapter, we introduce you to the elements of grammar, vocabulary, and spelling that you should be familiar with. We also introduce you to functional grammar, describing what it is, how it different from other models of grammar, and why we favor this model over its competitors. Succeeding chapters will look at other key aspects of language that you should know about such as language relating to discourse, figurative language, and voice. We also give you an example of how explicit knowledge can help you make informed decisions about revising your written work rather than relying on intuition.

Chapter 2: Only connect

In Chapter 2, we move beyond sentence-level aspects of language to longer stretches of text. At the paragraph level, we examine resources of thematization, given/new structuring, and cohesive devices for improving coherence between and across sentences within the paragraph. In the course of the discussion, we discuss the concepts of cohesion and coherence: the differences between the two concepts and the relationship between them. We also look at signposting, informing the reader at the beginning of a chapter of the section of terrain to be covered and reminding them at the end of where we have come. We elaborate further on functional grammar and give examples of how we can use functional grammar to make connections between grammatical form and communicative meaning.

One of the biggest challenges in creating a clear and coherent text is representing real and imagined worlds in print. These worlds are populated by ideas, entities, events, actions, states of affairs, and so on. In the experiential world these phenomena are interrelated in intricate, multidimensional ways. Texts on the other hand are linear. The line of print marches on, one word at a time. The challenge for you is to capture in sequential lines of print, the complexity of the multidimensional world where phenomena interrelate and overlap. The resources we describe and illustrate will help you represent a non-linear world in a linear form that makes sense to the reader.

Chapter 3: Product and process approaches to writing

Writing can be seen as both a process and a product. Writing as a process involves initial drafting of ideas, revising and redrafting, incorporating new content that arise during the writing process, inserting new ideas as a result of feedback from a teacher or critical friend, dividing a complicated sentence into two or more sentences, combining two or more sentences into a single sentence by turning them into clauses and phrases, shifting sentences and even whole paragraphs around, and so on. In this chapter, we'll describe and give examples of these different processes. The end result is a product: a report on the state of the economy, a set of instructions on how to conduct a science experiment, a short story, a discussion on how to improve an academic essay. Beginning writers are often advised not to put a finger on the keyboard until their ideas have been thought through and formulated. This advice is misguided. Thinking and writing go hand in hand. It is through writing, and rewriting, that we discover what we think. In this chapter, we introduce two important concepts: register and genre. These are part of systemic-functional linguistics, the approach to language we have drawn on throughout this book.

Chapter 4: Audience and purpose

Audience and purpose are fundamental to the writing process. They will have a powerful influence on the linguistic choices you make when you write. The two questions you should keep firmly in mind throughout the writing process, from planning, through draft and revising are: Why am I writing this? And who am I writing for? In the beginning, your purpose may be vague, or you may have several competing purposes in mind. The process writing approach we discussed in the last chapter may help to bring the main purpose into focus. Similarly, the audience may not be clear to you. If you are a student, your audience will probably be restricted to your teachers or perhaps an examiner. This doesn't mean that the audience will be unproblematic. Some teachers, you'll know well, and you'll be able to tailor your piece to their interests and perspectives. Others, you may not know well. In this chapter, you will read an academic conversation between David and a recent graduate. In it the graduate discusses the complexities and problems she encountered with audience and purpose in writing up her thesis and then turning it into an article for publication. We then present a view of writing as problem-solving when tailoring a piece to a particular audience and purpose and give an example from our own writing in relation to the construction of a single paragraph. We discuss the importance of the register variables of field, tenor, and mode in relation to purpose and audience. We also reintroduce the 'linearity problem' when making choices about selecting and structuring content for particular purposes and audiences.

Chapter 5: Toward active voice

Traditional approaches to academic writing insist on objectivity. This insistence betrays their roots in the positivist research paradigm. By objectivity in writing, they mean that the author's hand must remain invisible. We challenge this perspective. We are not the first or the only ones to do so. Times are changing. Even many in the hard sciences admit that their research does not proceed according to the procedural tenets of the scientific method, and that storytellers should have a presence, albeit a modest one, in the narratives they spin. The two pivotal concepts in this chapter, voice, and identity are complex ones, and we warn you this at the outset. To help you grasp them, we present definitions and examples from scholars who have written extensively on the subject. Linguistic devices enabling you to 'add voice' to your writing are many and varied. These include person choice, sentence length, active voice, and vocabulary choice. A particularly powerful tool is storytelling. Even small vignettes can make your writing memorable. They will help the reader form a view of who you are as a writer. However, they should not be inserted gratuitously, but be relevant to the subject at hand. By the end of the chapter, you should have clarified your understanding of voice and identity and be prepared to experiment with some of the techniques presented in it.

Chapter 6: Using figurative language

Figurative language, or figures of speech (we use both terms synonymously in this chapter), is the use of terms or phrases whose meaning differs from the literal meaning as defined by the dictionary. We've chosen to deal with this aspect of language because it's ubiquitous in both speech and writing. This is as true of academic writing as any other genre. While there's a wide range of figurative language, we've chosen to deal with six of these: similes, metaphors including personification, idioms, colloquialisms, clichés, and slang. A thoughtfully chosen simile, metaphor, or idiom can add color and drama to your prose. Commonly used idioms, colloquialisms, and clichés should be treated with caution, while slang expressions should be avoided. These expressions often indicate confusion, laziness, or imprecise thinking, revealing to the reader that you're unsure of what you want to say. If you're in any doubt about a particular expression, then leave it out!

Chapter 7: Seeking and providing meaningful feedback

The phrase 'meaningful feedback' may seem oxymoronic, but we've seen in the course of the book that it's anything but. Like beauty, 'meaningful' is in the eye of the beholder. In Chapter 4, a graduate student, Kailin Liu, reports on her M.A. thesis in which she looks at the concept from the perspective of her informants – graduate students like herself. In the same chapter, Julie tells of spending an inordinate amount of time providing meaningful feedback to students on their assignments. She notes that many students have low expectations when it comes to meaningful feedback. In this chapter, we interrogate the question of meaningful feedback from the perspective of both students and teachers. Meaningful feedback is crucial to producing quality writing. This is as true for professional authors as it is for students. Regardless of one's experience and expertise, we are writing from the 'inside out' and are usually too close to our own work to have an independent perspective on it. We suggest that meaningful feedback will contain both critical but also positive comments but will also offer advice to the writer on how they might improve problematic aspects of their text. From interviews we learn that meaningful feedback has an important affective dimension for students: it tells them that their work is taken seriously and valued.

Chapter 8: The power of revising

Writing is hard work. We don't say this to discourage you, but to remind you of a fundamental fact. Regardless of what you do, you'll be constantly challenged by the demands of everyday life. If you're a student, in addition to these demands, you'll have classes to attend, extensive reading lists to work through, and assignment deadlines to meet. Most likely, as the end of semester approaches, more than one assignment deadline will compete for your attention. You'll be distracted by the easy affordances of the Internet: Facebook, Twitter, emails, and Google searches. Unless you can resist these temptations, the evening you've set aside to complete a writing assignment will have evaporated. Submitting a hastily assembled first draft is unwise. In this chapter, we describe the journey we take from first to final draft. We point out that producing a first draft is qualitatively different from producing subsequent ones. The first draft provides an opportunity to be as creative as you like, to write without self-censoring. In subsequent drafts, you progressively refine your project. In our own work, we enjoy the creativity afforded by the first draft and then the opportunity to craft tighter and more parsimonious drafts. We know there's no such thing as a perfect final draft, but at a certain point, often dictated by a looming deadline, we are forced to admit that enough is enough.

Chapter 9: In a nutshell: ten thoughts to take away

The book introduces what we consider to be the fundamentals of academic writing. In this final chapter, we pull together the themes that have emerged into the course of the book and summarize the suggestions that have been made by us and others on improving the clarity and coherence of your writing. While interrelated, they provide different perspectives on the theme of language as a resource for writing. They are not presented in any hierarchical order of importance, although the first point, that a detailed and explicit knowledge of language is fundamental to good writing, underpins the others. The second focuses on the relationship between language and thought. A great deal of confused and confusing prose reflects confused and confusing thinking. The writer has published prematurely rather than using the writing and rewriting process as a method of discovery. This process can also help you clarify and refine your purpose and audience.

A fundamental problem is representing the non-linear experiential world in linear form. Resources such as cohesive devices and thematization can help us solve this problem. As we say, solving problems is at the heart of the writing problem. Also important is receiving meaningful feedback and using this in the rewriting process. Through this work, and with the judicious use of other resources such as figurative language, you will find your own voice and your identity as a writer will emerge.

Two other themes we highlight in the final chapter are the fact that academic writing is no one's native tongue. This leads to the issue of standards, and who gets to adjudicate on which standards should apply.

References

Pullum, J. (2009). *50 years of stupid grammar advice*. The Chronicle of Higher Education. https://www.chronicle.com/article/50-years-of-stupid-grammar-advice/

Strunk, W. (2018). *The elements of style: The original 1920 edition*. Suzeteo Enterprises.

Strunk, W., & White, E. B. (1959). *The elements of style*. Macmillan.

Valdes, O. (2019). An *introduction to academic writing*. ThoughtCo. https://www.thoughtco.com/what-is-academic-writing-1689052

1
What every writer should know about language

In this chapter, we will tell you what you need to know about the English language to improve the clarity and precision of your writing. We focus on those aspects of language that are relevant to the writing process, in particular, the sub-systems of grammar (technically referred to as morphosyntax) and vocabulary (technically known as lexis) (Nunan, 2013). In addition, we will have something to say about punctuation, which is also important, particularly in its association with grammar. If you are aiming to enter a profession where advanced proficiency in English language and literacy are essential (which are, or should be, most) the basics of English grammar and vocabulary we describe in this chapter are an absolute minimum requirement. You'll certainly need them to understand the more complex aspects of language we deal with in the subsequent chapters.

For students planning on a career as a language teacher, it's possible to register for graduate programs in TESOL with little or no knowledge of the basics of language. This is not the case for programs preparing students to teach science or mathematics where prerequisites will usually include having majored in the subject in your bachelor's degree. The lecturers will assume that students have the requisite content knowledge and will focus on *how* to teach the subject. In the case of English, the assumption is that if you can speak the language you can teach it. If there are prerequisites, they are menial, such as having done a semester of a foreign language as an undergraduate. A semester of German or Japanese will not equip you to write or teach academic English writing (or any other aspect of the language, for that matter). While the audience for this book is broader than aspiring language teachers, we know that many readers will plan on entering the profession. It's for this reason that we make this point.

Many years ago, in the preface to his play *Pygmalion*, the Irish author George Bernard Shaw famously wrote *It is impossible for an Englishman to open his*

DOI: 10.4324/9781003179092-2

mouth without making some other Englishman hate or despise him. These days, 'hated' or 'despised' for the way you speak may be too strong, but people will make judgements about you. They may not voice their opinion to your face, but they will have formed one just the same. When you speak, certain people will make judgements about your nationality or social class based on your dialect and accent. If you mispronounce a word, they will make judgements about your level of education and possibly even your intelligence.

The same holds for writing. Grammatical errors, poor vocabulary choices, as well as punctuation and spelling mistakes will be held against you. It's for this reason that some people are unwilling to show others their writing. What you write and how you write reflects your voice and identity as a writer.

This chapter introduces linguistic terms that might be unfamiliar to you. If you do encounter a term that is unfamiliar, you'll find a glossary with explanations and examples at the back of the book. Although we have treated grammar, vocabulary, and punctuation separately, in reality, they are not so easily segmented. In fact, many linguists integrate the description and analysis of grammar and vocabulary under the single label of lexicogrammar.

Grammar

Answering the question, what is grammar?, in a paragraph or two is an audacious undertaking, when entire volumes have been devoted to the task. Here, we provide a basic definition which we'll elaborate on in the rest of the book. Most definitions see grammar as sets of rules for forming words, phrases, and clauses and specifications for arranging these to form meaningful sentences (see Harmer 1987; Richards, Platt & Weber, 1985). We follow a linguistic model known as functional grammar. This model describes the systematic relationship between grammatical form and communicative function. Fundamental to the model is the notion of choice. Debra Myhill (2011) draws an analogy between the tools of a mechanic and the grammatical tools of the writer.

> Both have to create products from the materials available, be that physical materials or linguistic resources; both have to test things out to see how they work, both have to make choices and decisions about the purpose of their work.
>
> (p. 81)

In the course of the book, we show how you can use linguistic resources to make informed choices and solve problems in creating clear and coherent text.

David's account of what writers should know about grammar

At a recent seminar, I made the point that all teachers should have a 'reasonably comprehensive' knowledge of grammar regardless of the subject they teach. A member of the audience raised his hand and asked, "What do you mean by 'reasonably comprehensive'?" When I wanted to bone up on my knowledge of grammar, I did an Amazon search for books on grammar. I didn't want anything too complicated and came across a book that had the ideal title *A Short Introduction to English Grammar*. Before ordering it, I looked inside and found that it ran to over 200 pages!

In a little book on teaching grammar (which runs to only 178 pages!), I argued that at the very least, teachers should be familiar with the word classes in English, the grammatical roles they play, and the clause types they are used to form. In English, we have the common word classes of nouns, verbs, adjectives and adverbs, and less common (closed classes) such as articles and prepositions. Within the sentence, these word types have five grammatical roles: subject, verb, object, complement, and adverbial (Nunan, 2005).

Traditional grammar recognizes seven different clause types made up of these basic building blocks.

Table 1.1 Seven basic English clause types (Nunan, 2005, p. 4)

Clause type	Example
Type 1: Subject + Verb	Maria sang.
Type 2: Subject + Verb + Object	William saw a UFO.
Type 3: Subject + Verb + Complement	I became wary.
Type 4: Subject + Verb + Adverbial	I've been in the office.
Type 5: Subject + Verb + Object + Object	Malcolm bought his wife a diamond.
Type 6: Subject + Verb + Object + Complement	We think traditional grammatical analysis rather pointless.
Type 7: Subject + Verb + Object + Adverbial	We had to take our children home.

This knowledge can be helpful when it comes to making choices as you pro-duce successive drafts of your writing in order to achieve greater coherence and clarity. Revising and refining can be done intuitively, of course. But we find it useful to be explicit not only in terms of our own writing but also when giving feedback to students on their own writing. It enables us to go beyond vague generalities such as "this isn't clear", or "this is garbled", or "I haven't got a clue what you're talking about here".

We advocate a functional approach to grammar which accounts for gram-matical structures in terms of the communicative acts they enable us to perform through speaking and writing. Functional grammar demonstrates the choices available to us when we are constructing our sentences. By thinking in terms of 'meaningful chunks' (word groups that form around a head word), we can see "how these words work together to make mean-ing or how different shades of meanings could be made through author choices" (Derewianka, 2011, p. 11). Writers can change the order of the groups depending on their purpose or intentions. Consider, for example, the sentence 'A golden ray of sunlight was shining through the leaves'. In this sentence, the writer may be drawing attention to the 'who' or the 'what' by starting the clause with a noun group. If the author wrote, 'Through the leaves, a golden ray of sunlight was shining', she/he is draw-ing our attention to the physical environment by starting the clause with an adverbial of place. Drawing our attention to a sentence element (word or group) by placing it at the beginning of the sentence is called the-matization. We'll elaborate on this process in the next chapter. In the following table you can see how the simple sentence 'Sunlight shone through', can, in Derewianka's words, be given greater elaboration or shades of meaning by inserting additional elements to the head word (see Table 1.2).

Table 1.2 From word class to word groups (Derewianka, 2011)

Word	Sunlight (Noun)	Shone (Verb)	Through (Preposition)
Group	A golden ray of sunlight (Noun Group)	Was shining (Verb Group)	Through the leaves (Adverbial Group)
Function	Naming 'who' or 'what'	Naming 'action'	Naming 'where'

Grammar offers us tools for thinking, creating, and crafting meaning in ways *we* want them to be communicated. It can help us to create dramatic effect in telling a story which enables us to become more compelling and expressive storytellers. Writers can also take greater control of their writing – they can influence the reader to read for particular messages or details depending on their purpose and we begin to develop a sense of the writer's 'voice'. Julie recalls how learning about functional grammar well after her formal education allowed her to develop much more appreciation of texts and allowed her to read and write more critically. Later in the chapter, we elaborate on the benefits of studying grammar. (For a detailed discussion of functional grammar in relation to academic writing, see Caplan, 2023.)

Assessing your own knowledge of language

How detailed or sophisticated is your own knowledge of linguistic terminology? Presumably you know the different word classes of English (nouns, verbs, prepositions, determiners, etc.). Do you know the difference between an object and a complement or why we have a passive voice in English? We think it would be useful for you to take an inventory or 'snapshot' of what you know of the language you are currently studying, teaching, or proposing to teach. There is a range of online instruments which are designed to help you carry out such an inventory. One we would recommend is the Cambridge Teaching Knowledge Test (TKT).

The TKT is a comprehensive set of self-study modules through which you can assess and improve your knowledge of English vocabulary, grammar, language functions, and pronunciation. As it's aimed at aspiring language teachers, it also includes modules such as first and second-language acquisition and techniques for presenting new language items. If you have no plans to become a language teacher, you can ignore these modules. Both print and online versions of the test are available.

Here are two sample items from the online version of the TKT. This version contains free, downloadable practice tests. Having completed one of the tests, you can download the answer key and check their answers. The site also contains a glossary of terms, which the teacher can consult if he/she is unsure of any technical terms. On the site, it is also possible to purchase support materials which include coursebooks and practice tests. These also exist in both print and digital forms.

Making connections

Example 1: Knowledge of lexical/grammatical terms

Instructions

For questions 8–13, read the text. Match the underlined words or phrases in the text with the lexical terms listed A–G. Mark the correct letter (A–G) on your answer sheet. There is one extra option which you do not need to use.

Lexical (and grammatical) terms

A   phrasal verb
B   compound noun
C   word with negative affix
D   compound adjective
E   word family
F   verb and noun collocation
G   noun with affix

Text

During his career, Sean Connery made over 70 films and became very rich. However, as a child (8) growing up in Scotland during the Great Depression in the 1930s, he was poor. He and his family were not (9) unusual in living in a two-roomed flat with no (10) bathroom. Sean left school at 13 and did a variety of jobs to (11) make money including being a milkman and a (12) builder. Eventually he began acting and his role as the first James Bond made him (13) well-known all over the world.

Example 2: Knowledge of language functions

Instructions

For questions 20–25, match the underlined parts of the email with the functions listed A–G. Mark the correct letter (A–G) on your answer sheet. There is one extra option which you do not need to use.

Functions

A   expressing ability
B   making an offer
C   making a prediction
D   expressing intention

E   expressing possibility
F   making a request
G   expressing preference

Email

Dear Juan,

Thought I'd let you know (20) I'm planning to come to Chile next year and I'm hoping to visit you there! (21) January is my first choice, but I might stay with Mum then, so (22) it could be that I'll visit you in February instead.

Anyway, (23) I'd be really grateful if you could share your knowledge. What's the weather like in February? How much can I see in two weeks? (24) I know how to check all this on the internet, but it would be good to speak to someone who knows the country. By the way, (25) would you like me to bring you anything special from Britain?

Speak soon, I hope.

Frank

(Cambridge Teaching Knowledge Test, 2020)

We like this resource from Cambridge for a number of reasons. First, it is amenable to a range of instructional contexts, from instructor-guided classroom use to self-study. Second, the online version is easily accessible for students regardless of where they happen to be living and/or studying. Third, source texts, such as the ones in the samples we have provided, are either authentic or simulate authenticity. (What Brown and Menasche (1993) refer to as 'altered', i.e., adapted from authentic sources.) Finally, many of the test items make explicit the links between linguistic form and communicative function.

Making connections

Click on the following link to access the Cambridge TKT free online practice modules. Complete several of the modules.

- How useful was the activity?
- How good is your knowledge of English grammatical terminology?
- What areas of grammar do you need to improve on?

https://web.archive.org/web/20220717062756/https://www.cambridgeenglish.org/teaching-english/teaching-qualifications/tkt/prepare-for-tkt/

David's example of putting grammar to work

Here is an example of how knowledge of grammar can help us go beyond intuition when redrafting our initial writing efforts. It consists of the first draft of a paragraph from an anecdote I'd been writing up followed by a 'think aloud' piece in which I talked about my concerns with the draft. Finally, I present the second draft resulting from my critical self-evaluation.

Draft 1:

The genesis of this piece began one evening when a friend and colleague with whom I had just had supper suggested (in fact, urged) me to write something on writing clearly. Slightly flattered, but also puzzled, I asked her why. My friend is a lecturer at a prestigious graduate school of education.

"The final sentence doesn't follow coherently from the preceding sentences, but I want to get that information in. I'll demote it from the status of a sentence in its own right to a relative clause. Having supper is irrelevant – drop it. 'The genesis of this piece…' Hmmm, don't like this. By beginning the subject with the noun phrase 'the genesis', I'm thematizing its origin, but that's putting the cart before the horse. I'll re-thematize the subject giving 'the piece' the status it deserves. I'll also add the prepositional phrase 'in a conversation'. 'The conversation' will be instantiated as the subject of the second sentence. The indefinite article 'a' becomes a definite article because the reader knows which conversation I'm referring to. Creating this anaphoric link also improves the coherence of the paragraph. In the second sentence, I'll drop the 'slightly' because it's wishy-washy. 'Be hard on yourself when it comes to adverbs and adjectives!' I remind myself. (Advice I give my students, but don't always follow myself.) Oh, I'll also delete the possessive adjective 'her'. It's cohesive but redundant".

Draft 2:

This piece had its genesis in a conversation I had one evening with a friend who is a lecturer at a prestigious graduate school of education. The conversation had turned to the topic of academic writing, and my friend suggested (in fact, urged) me to produce something on writing clearly. Flattered, but also puzzled, I asked why.

Of course, it's perfectly possible to revise drafts of your writing without possessing a detailed knowledge of grammar. The majority of writers probably don't possess such knowledge. They revise their text intuitively until it 'feels' right. However, knowledge of grammar provides you with a tool for knowing *why* the revised version feels better. It also provides you with vocabulary for talking about your text.

The status of grammar within the curriculum

For many years, in western educational contexts such as the United Kingdom and Australia, the teaching of grammar in schools has been controversial. The traditional way of teaching grammar was dry, decontextualized, and lacked creativity. Students spent hours parsing and analyzing sentences that had no obvious applications beyond the classroom. (The same could be said about many subjects in the curriculum.) As a result, the anti-grammar brigade won the battle.

In her investigation into the empirical evidence for the explicit teaching of grammar, Myhill (2016) makes the point that the debate over whether or not grammar should be explicitly taught in schools has been highly politicized for decades. Politicians, and policy-makers, conflate grammar with accuracy and correctness and tend "to equate mastery of grammar with standards, including moral standards" (p. 36). She gives the example of a London newspaper (the *Daily Standard*) which attributed street riots across England in 2011 to the fact that rioters couldn't speak correctly. The notion that forcing young protesters to use the "Queen's English" might quell civil unrest is clearly ludicrous, but not uncommon. Recently, a conservative Minister for Education in Australia pronounced that poor literacy in schools could be cured with explicit instruction and a good dose of phonics (Tudge, 2021). We have no argument with either explicit instruction or phonics. Phonics is one of a number of tools that can assist young learners to make the often painful transition from spoken to written English although it has major limitations. (For one thing, that 26 letters in the English language have to represent almost twice that number of sounds. For another, it will be of little assistance to the beginning reader when it comes to words such as 'through' and 'tough'.) In addition, use of the singular noun 'literacy' is problematic. The terms 'multiliteracies' and 'multimodalities' are prominent in the educational literature (see Vinogradova & Shin, 2021). This has been prompted by globalization and technology which have transformed the ways in which we communicate and created new, hybrid, communication modes.

Educators opposed to the explicit teaching of the sub-systems of language including grammar, in particular, argue that such a focus cripples creativity and stifles freedom of expression. This may be true, if the focus is restricted to the decontextualized manipulation of grammatical forms isolated from the communicative functions they exist to serve.

Myhill's research demonstrated that the explicit teaching of grammar had a positive effect on learners' writing when it was taught from a functionally oriented perspective in which connections were made for the learners between "grammatical choices and meaning-making in their own writing" (p. 42). She concludes that "there is a clear emerging body of research signaling real benefits of explicit grammar teaching when the teaching is grounded in meaningful language learning contexts" (p. 44). In a recent call for putting grammar in its (rightful) place, David echoed this view:

> I'm not arguing for a return to transmission teaching accompanied by the dreary, decontextualized parsing and analysis exercises to which I was subjected as a schoolboy - although through such exercises, I did develop a thorough understanding of the structure of English, along with the metalanguage to talk about it. ... A detailed, contextualized introduction to the fundamentals of language underpinned by a functional model of grammar, can be taught through the scaffolded, inductive procedures promoted by Bruner all those years ago.
>
> (Nunan, 2023, p. 18)

Although the status of language in general, and grammar in particular, is beginning to change under the influence of Myhill, Jones et al. (2013), and other proponents of functionally oriented perspectives, the influence is scant in some educational systems and non-existent in others. In this book, we try to show how knowledge of language in general, and grammar in particular, can assist you in your efforts to become a better writer.

Vocabulary

Making effective vocabulary choices also has a significant impact on the clarity of your writing. In this regard, lexical collocations are particularly important. Lexical collocations are pairs or groups of words that naturally or commonly co-occur. The development of corpora (singular, corpus), massive, computerized databases of words, and the linguistic contexts in which they naturally occur, enable linguists to "identify patterns, principles, regularities and associations between words that would not be apparent from a casual inspection of language samples" (Nunan, 2013, p. 219). Corpora that researchers, publishers, textbook writers, and so on include the British National Corpus which consists of over 100-million word samples taken from a wide range of spoken and written sources. Unlike a dictionary, these corpora can answer questions such as *What are the 100 most common words in English?* and *What are the other words and phrases with which they collocate (co-occur)?* Dave Willis, an applied linguist and textbook author, was one of the first writers to use a corpus (COBUILD) to guide decision-making about which words to include in the course and when to include them. He points out that a number of important words such as *problem, solution, idea,* and *argument* are often omitted from most English language textbooks. He goes on to say:

> A particularly striking example is the word *way*, the third commonest noun in the English language after *time* and *people*. The word *way* in its commonest meaning has a complex grammar. It is associated with patterns like:
>
> ...different *ways of* cooking fish.
>
> A pushchair is a common *way to take* a young child shopping.
>
> What emerges very strongly once one looks at natural language, is the way the commonest words in the language occur with the commonest patterns. In this case the word *way* occurs with *of* and the *-ing* form of the verb and also with the *to* infinitive.
>
> (Willis, 1990, p. vi)

For second-language writers, mastering lexical collocations is particularly challenging. The difficulty is that pairings are often metaphorical and can't always be deduced from context. In the following examples, the writer's intended meaning is clear, although readers who are familiar with the collocations may find them odd.

"She likes to drink **powerful** coffee" (strong coffee)

"John has been a **large** smoker all his life" (heavy smoker)

"I need to go out and **achieve** money" (make money)

While effective writers select the best lexical option from two closely competing alternatives, the truly accomplished writer will make creative, and

Making connections

Listen to the following webinar in which Professor Mike McCarthy talks about the use of corpora to inform the analysis and development of academic vocabulary and answer the following questions. Go to YouTube and enter the following: Using corpora to inform the teaching of academic vocabulary.

https://www.cambridge.org/elt/blog/2016/04/08/using-corpora-inform-teaching-academic-vocabulary/

- What types of analysis did he use to analyze the words in the corpus?
- What is a key word?
- Why don't we think of single words but word chunks?
- What's dispersion of academic language? Why is it important?
- What does he say about the most frequent words in academic English?
- Why are nouns and noun phrases significant in academic English?
- Do a search of one of your assignments for the existence of four-word chunks. How many of these chunks appear in your text? Which do you think you might like to include in your writing?

Making connections

Are the words in bold acceptable to you? Which (if any) would you change and why?

- The small sailing boat battled through the **hilly** waves.
- Technology **makes** a pivotal role in students' learning.
- Jane is **celebrating** a party for everyone on Tuesday.
- Don't **lose** time.

sometimes surprising choices that express their own attitudes toward the subject at hand. The late author, poet, and broadcaster Clive James (2007) was a master at surprising the reader with choice of words and turn of phrase. In an essay on Auden, he refers to the English poet as "the achingly modern Auden". That single, inspired adverb says what it would have taken a less accomplished writer a paragraph to articulate his attitude to Auden. Similarly, in his critique of narrowly focused, experimental research, the American educational researcher, Terry Denny (1978) critiques academics who come up with "nifty solutions" to problems that teachers never pose. Most dictionary definitions cast the adjective in a positive light: a 'nifty' person or an action as skillful or effective. It is also a colloquial word and used to describe the writing of one segment of the academy is a clever put-down on Denny's part. The alliterative collocation with 'shifty' is also no accident.

Punctuation

Punctuation has a number of important roles in written language. One role is to tell the reader when to take a breath and how long the breath should be. In advising young writers to learn punctuation, Dillard (2005) put it most eloquently – poetically, you could say.

> Learn punctuation: it is your little drum set, one of the few tools you have to signal the reader where the beat and the emphases go. (If you get it wrong, the editor will probably throw the manuscript out.) Punctuation is not like musical notation; it doesn't [only] indicate the length of pauses, but instead signifies logical relations.
>
> (p. 5)

The mention of logical relations brings us to the second important role played by punctuation. (We would have used 'grammatical relations' rather than 'logical relations', but we won't quibble about terminology here). In many respects, punctuation can be seen as a part of the grammatical sub-system of language. Let us give you an example. Consider the following sentences:

1. My sister who lives in Atlanta is visiting me in Melbourne.
2. My sister, who lives in Atlanta, is visiting me in Melbourne.

The only difference between the two sentences is the addition of a couple of commas. It may seem that an additional comma here or there is inconsequential. However, they signal an important difference in meaning. The implication in sentence 1 is that the writer has more than one sister, and the function of the relative clause 'who lives in Atlanta' is to specify or define which of the sisters she is referring to – the one who lives in Atlanta, not the one who lives in Toronto. It provides essential additional information and for this reason is known as a defining relative clause. In the second sentence, the information in the 'who' clause is incidental, and the commas mark the fact that this is so. For this reason, it is referred to as a non-defining relative clause. The implication is that the speaker only has one sister.

If you think that punctuation is a dry subject, albeit a necessary but mechanical aspect of the writing process, we urge you to read Lynne Truss on the subject. Here is the introduction to her marvelous little book on the subject. Interestingly, in light of our discussion above, she begins the book by recounting a personal anecdote about the misplaced apostrophe.

> Either this will ring bells for you, or it won't. A printed banner has appeared on the concourse of a petrol station near to where I live. "Come inside," it says, "for CD's, VIDEO's, DVD's, and Book's." If this satanic sprinkling of redundant apostrophes causes no little gasp of horror or quickening of the pulse, you should probably put down this book at once. ... For the stickler, the sight of the plural word "Book's" with an apostrophe in it will trigger a ghastly private emotional process similar to the stages of bereavement, though greatly accelerated.
>
> (Truss, 2003, p. 1)

Questions from readers

Q: As a non-native speaker of English, it is really difficult to grasp collocations. Do you have any advice on how I can learn collocations?

A: Yes, collocations, idioms, phrasal verbs, and other forms of figurative language are particularly challenging for second-language learners because they have no 'logic' and have to be learned individually. Native speakers 'pick up' collocations as they acquire other aspects of their native language. Several resources can help you increase your knowledge of collocations. For example, dictionaries such as the *Oxford Collocational Dictionary for Students of English* is available in both print and online versions.

Q: Am I correct in thinking that a functional approach to grammar focuses on 'meaning' rather than prescriptive 'rules'? If the meaning comes through, does it mean we don't have to worry so much about correcting grammar?

A: The notion that functional approaches to grammar focus on meaning rather than form is not correct. In fact, grammar is fundamental. Functional grammarians seek to establish principled relationships between form and meaning. In 'traditional' approaches to grammar, learners are taught grammatical forms with little or no reference to meaning. For example, when the passive voice is taught, learners are shown how to transform active voice statements. (*"The boy broke the window"*.) into the passive voice (*"The window was broken by the boy"*.) They are then drilled until they are fluent in the new form. They might be able to make statements in passive voice, but have no idea how, when, and why to use it. Functional grammars not only teach the form but also meaning and use of a particular grammatical item.

Summary

The main message of this chapter is that a knowledge of language can make you a better writer. The level of detail is a matter for conjecture. We've set out what we believe to be the bare minimum. Knowing terminology, particularly grammatical terminology, is a useful tool and can provide a shortcut when it comes to discussing your writing with a teacher or other writers. Identifying instances of grammar in action within texts and being able to see how accomplished authors are able to put grammar to work to communicate their ideas effectively will be important steps along your path to doing the same. In this chapter, we cite research supporting the contention that an explicit knowledge of grammar has a positive impact on the quality and effectiveness of writing if it is learned functionally. In other words, if you can experiment with and see the different meaning-making or communicative effects that result from making different grammatical choices within and beyond the sentence, this will help you be a better writer. This experimentation is not a technique that, once mastered, can be applied to automatically to your writing. Like us, every time you sit down (or stand up) to write, you will have choices to make and problems to solve.

We've covered a lot of ground and introduced some difficult concepts in this chapter. For many readers, this will be difficult to digest. To help you develop and refine your ideas on function grammar, we have recommended six books. We don't expect you to read all of these from cover-to-cover. However, consulting one or two that appeal to you will help to consolidate the ideas we have introduced here.

In the next chapter, we build on the ideas introduced in this chapter and will explore other linguistic tools such as thematization and cohesion. These tools will also help you improve the clarity and coherence of your writing.

Further readings

Derewianka, B. (2011). *A new grammar companion for teachers*. Primary English Teaching Association.
This is an accessible reference book for people interested in learning more about systemic functional grammar, an approach that many schoolteachers use in Australia as it was written in response to the new Australian Curriculum.

Derewianka, B. (2020). *Exploring how texts work* (2nd ed.). Primary English Teaching Association.
For people interested in how language and text work particularly within the curriculum, this book will be the perfect introduction.

Humphrey, S., Love, K., & Droga, L. (2011). *Working grammar: An introduction for secondary English teachers*. Pearson Education Australia.
This is a professional resource book for teachers seeking an introduction to teaching systemic functional grammar. It provides many exercises to try for those interested in this approach to grammar.

Thornbury, S. (2001). *Uncovering grammar*. Macmillan Heinemann.
This book takes the view that grammar is not a 'thing' to be studied, but a tool to be used. It contains a wealth of ideas for the practicing teacher as well as providing valuable insights into ways in which teachers can guide students to 'discover' grammar.

Truss, D. (2003). *Eats, shoots & leaves: The zero-tolerance approach to punctuation*. Profile Books.
An insightful, and very funny introduction to English pronunciation.

Webb, S., & Nation, P. (2017). *How vocabulary is learned*. Oxford University Press.
An extremely accessible introduction to the nature of vocabulary and how it is learned by two of the most authoritative figures in the field.

Willis, D. (1991). *The lexical syllabus*. Collins ELT.
A clear and accessible introduction to collocations, corpora and concordancing. Although aimed at language teachers, it is a useful text for all those who want to know more about the patterns of vocabulary in texts.

References

Brown, S., & Menasche, L. (1993). *Authenticity in materials design* [Conference presentation]. TESOL International Convention, Atlanta, GA, United States.

Cambridge Teaching Knowledge Test. (2020). *Teaching knowledge test*. Cambridge University Press. https://web.archive.org/web/20220717062756/https://www.cambridgeenglish.org/teaching-english/teaching-qualifications/tkt/prepare-for-tkt/

Caplan, N. (2023). The grammar choices that matter in academic writing. In E. Hinkel (Ed.), *Handbook of practical second language teaching and learning* (Vol. 4, pp. 466–479). Routledge.

Denny, T. (1978). Story-telling and educational understanding. *Case Study Evaluation: Past, Present and Future Challenges, 15*, 41–61.

Derewianka, B. (2011). *A new grammar companion for teachers*. Primary English Teaching Association.

Dillard, A. (2005). Introduction: Notes for young writers. In L. Gutkind (Ed.), *In fact: The best of creative nonfiction*. W. W. Norton & Company.

Halliday, M. A. K. (1975). *Learning how to mean: Explorations in the development of language*. Hodder Arnold.

Harmer, J. (1987). *The practice of English language teaching*. Longman.

James, C. (2007). *Cultural amnesia: Necessary memories from history and the arts*. W. W. Norton & Company.

Jones, S., Myhill, D., & Bailey, T. (2013). Grammar for writing? An investigation into the effect of contextualised grammar teaching on student writing. *Reading and Writing*, 26(8), 1241–1263.

Myhill, D. (2011). Grammar for designers: How grammar supports the development of writing. In S. Ellis & E. McCartney (Eds.), *Applied linguistics and primary school teaching* (pp. 81–92). Cambridge University Press. doi:10.1017/CBO9780511921605.011

Myhill, D. (2016). The effectiveness of explicit language teaching: Evidence from the research. In M. Giovanelli & D. Clayton (Eds.), *Knowing about language: Linguistics and the secondary English classroom* (pp. 36–47). Routledge.

Nunan, D. (2005). *Practical English language teaching: Grammar*. McGraw-Hill.

Nunan, D. (2013). *What is this thing called language?* (2nd ed.). Palgrave Macmillan.

Nunan, D. (2023). The changing landscape of English language teaching and learning. In E. Hinkel (Ed.), *Handbook of practical second language teaching and learning* (Vol. 4, pp. 3–23). Routledge.

Richards, J., Platt, J., & Weber, H. (1985). *Longman dictionary of applied linguistics*. Longman.

Truss, D. (2003). *Eats, shoots & leaves: The zero-tolerance approach to punctuation*. Fourth Estate.

Tudge, A. (2021). *Roaring back: My priority for schools as students return to the classroom* [Speech transcript]. Ministers' Media Centre: Ministers of the Education, Skills and Employment Portfolio. https://ministers.dese.gov.au/tudge/roaring-back-my-priorities-schools-students-return-classrooms

Vinogradova, P., & Shin, J. K. (Eds.). (2021). *Contemporary foundations for teaching English as an additional language: Pedagogical approaches and classroom applications*. Routledge.

Willis, D. (1991). *The lexical syllabus*. Collins ELT.

2
Only connect

Creating a coherent piece of writing involves making decisions about where to place information in a text so that it makes sense to the reader and to make connections between the different pieces of information in the text. In shorter pieces of writing such as essays and reports, this involves making decisions across paragraphs, within paragraphs, and within sentences. Making choices at each of these levels, the text, the paragraph, and the sentence will influence and be influenced by the other levels.

In the case of longer works such as theses and books, connections and choices have to be made about the placement of content across chapters and even the location of individual chapters within the work. For example, if you are writing a book-length research report or doctoral thesis you need to decide whether to locate your research questions at the end of your literature review or at the beginning of your research methodology chapter.

In this chapter, we describe the resources available to writers to help them craft coherent sentences, paragraphs, and texts. For the sake of convenience, we will look at each of these elements separately. However, the act of writing requires constant shuttling between the sentence, the paragraph, and the text as a whole. We begin with the sentence, describing and illustrating the concept of thematization. However, in order to provide a satisfactory account of thematization, we will have to stray beyond the sentence and into the paragraph. In examining the inner workings of the paragraph, we will introduce the important concepts of cohesion and coherence. What are these concepts? How are they related and what differentiates them?

Another concept introduced in the chapter is signposting. The word signposting is used metaphorically. Through it, you indicate to your reader the terrain you plan to traverse in the paragraphs and pages ahead. At the end of a section, and also at the conclusion of the chapter, you can remind the reader of the main points you have covered.

DOI: 10.4324/9781003179092-3

In the final section of the chapter, David shares with you an exercise he carried out with a graduate student. The exercise is introduced to illustrate how the various tools and techniques introduced in the chapter can be mobilized to make connections and strengthen the coherence of your writing.

Thematization

The first resource for making connections at the sentence level is thematization. We will describe the phenomenon before showing how it can be used to improve the clarity and coherence of your writing. We will also give you an application exercise. In keeping with our philosophy, we won't simply provide tricks of the trade and formulae to follow but will give you insights into how and why the procedure works. As we mentioned in Chapter 1, you'll be introduced to unfamiliar terms and concepts. Learning any new subject, skill, or discipline always entails learning new vocabulary and the concepts they represent. Some academics liken it to being initiated into a new discourse community. In a sense, you'll be learning academic writing as a foreign language.

Thematization concerns the choice you have to make when writing a sentence: which word or word group do you select as the point of departure for your sentence? This word or word group is the theme. The choice you make will direct the reader to the element they should focus on and how they are to interpret the sentence. Although it is a sentence-level phenomenon, it has important implications for the sentence that follows, and the one after that, through to the end of the paragraph. This underlines a point that we'll return to constantly throughout the book. Choices at the sentence level will have implications for the paragraph, and choices at the paragraph level will have implications for those that follow.

In explaining thematization, what it is and why it's important, we draw on the work of the British/Australian linguist Michael Halliday who in his many years as professor of linguistics at the University of Sydney and elsewhere had a profound effect on language teaching, learning, and use around the world. Halliday was a functional grammarian, and the approach we have taken to language in this book has been profoundly influenced by his work. The approach he pioneered is called systemic-functional linguistics. As we discussed in Chapter 1, this school sees language in communicative terms. It seeks to explain the link between grammatical form and communicative function and demonstrate how grammatical forms exist to enable us to make meanings. In the rest of this discussion, when we refer to 'the sentence', we are talking about simple sentences which as we saw in Chapter 1, are the same as a clause, having a subject, a finite verb, and expressing a single idea about the subject.

In explaining thematization, Halliday looks at the sentence in terms of message structure. All sentences have a message. As such, they are communicative events and are made up of two parts: an entity or event, called the theme, and a message about the theme, called the rheme. In making a word/word group the theme of the sentence, the writer is telling the reader "this is the thing I want to tell you something about". The rest of the sentence, the rheme, is the message. He says:

> We may assume that in all languages the clause [simple sentence] has the character of a message: it has some form of organization giving it the status of a communicative event. … In English, as in many other languages, the clause is organized as a message by having a special status assigned to one part of it. One element in the clause is enumerated [designated] as the Theme: this Theme combines with the remainder so that the two parts together constitute a message. … The Theme is the element which serves as the point of departure of the message; it is that with which the clause is concerned. The remainder of the message, the part in which the Theme is developed, is called … the Rheme. As a message structure, therefore, a clause consists of a Theme accompanied by a Rheme: and the structure is expressed in that order.
>
> (Halliday, 1985, p. 38)

Why does this matter? It matters because it gives writers a choice about which entity/phenomenon in a communicative event they want the reader to attend to and what they want the reader to learn about the entity/phenomenon. Halliday illustrates this issue of choice with the following rather quaint (and presumably invented) sentences (Table 2.1).

In the first, 'the duke' is the theme, and he is the focal point of the clause. The rheme tells the reader what happened to him. Halliday wants us to know about the act of gift giving, not that the duke has a wooden leg, that he marched his men to the top of the hill, or that he picks his nose in public.

Table 2.1 Examples of theme and rheme

Theme	Rheme
The duke	has given my aunt that teapot
My aunt	has been given that teapot by the duke
That teapot	the duke has given to my aunt

In the second, 'my aunt' is the theme, she is the focus, and the rheme tells us what happened to her. Notice that he can only achieve that end by using a grammatical resource – the passive voice. In the third, 'that teapot' is the point of the departure and the focus is on what happened to it. So, the writer has a choice. Does he/she want the story (or this part of the story) to be about 'the duke', 'my aunt', or the 'teapot'?

Beyond the sentence, the rheme of an initial sentence becomes the theme of the next sentence. The rheme of that becomes the theme of the next and so on. Here is an example explaining how milk gets from the cow to the consumer which shows graphically the way the given new patterning works. (It's a bit like a ping-pong game!) (Figure 2.1)

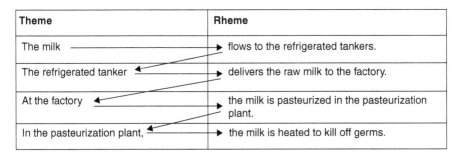

Theme	Rheme
The milk	flows to the refrigerated tankers.
The refrigerated tanker	delivers the raw milk to the factory.
At the factory	the milk is pasteurized in the pasteurization plant.
In the pasteurization plant,	the milk is heated to kill off germs.

Figure 2.1 A zig-zag pattern of theme/rheme as adapted from Polias and Dare (2006, p. 130).

We have just introduced you to the very simplest theme/rheme structure in which the theme is a noun or noun/nominal group. This is all the background you will need for the purposes of the following discussion. We won't venture into themes with multiple constituents or clauses in which the theme is *not* the point of departure for the clause.

It's now time to demonstrate ways in which thematization can improve the clarity and coherence of your writing. We will do so by examining the opening paragraph from a student essay. The paragraph consists of five simple sentences/clauses, each containing a single piece of information.

> Some educational systems have a large number of immigrants. Many immigrant students possess multilingual repertoires. Educational systems have policies. Policies favour traditional monolingual practices. Language and cultural uniformity are the norm.

Making connections

In Chapter 1, we said that English possesses a limited number of basic clause types. Each clause type is constructed of combinations of two, three, or four of the following grammatical building blocks: subject, verb, object, complement, and adverbial.

1. As a form of review, can you identify the clause types in the above paragraph in terms of the grammatical building blocks? (The first one has been done for you.)

   - S1 = S+V+O
   - S2 =
   - S3 =
   - S4 =
   - S5=

2. Underline the theme of each sentence.

   (1) <u>Some educational systems</u> have a large number of immigrants; (2) Many immigrant students possess multilingual repertoires; (3) Educational systems have policies; (4) Policies favor traditional monolingual practices; (5) Language and cultural uniformity are the norm.

3. How coherent is the paragraph? That is, to what extent does it seem to 'hang together'?

Here is the theme/rheme breakdown for each sentence (Table 2.2).

We asked several of our students to complete this exercise. All agreed that the content of each sentence is clear, there are no grammatical errors, and the pieces of information seem to be about the same general topic. However,

Table 2.2 A breakdown of theme/rheme from the Making Connections task

Theme	Rheme
Some educational systems	have a large number of immigrants
Many immigrant students	possess multilingual repertoires
Educational systems	have policies
Policies	favor traditional monolingual practices
Language and cultural uniformity	are the norm

there is something wrong with the paragraph. "It's a bit jarring", said one student. "It's not really coherent", reported another. A third astutely observed that there was a problem with sentence three. "The theme jumps back to the theme of sentence one, but there's nothing to connect it to sentence two. And what it tells us is that educational systems have policies which hasn't been mentioned before".

Doing a theme/rheme analysis of the student's paragraph can help us see where the lack of integration lies. One solution to the integration problem is to draw on a range of grammatical resources such as the creation of phrases and coordinating/subordinating clauses to link and integrate multiple pieces of information into one or two complex sentences. This requires care. Overburden the sentence, and it will collapse under its own weight, leaving the reader confused, if not downright irritated. So why bother going beyond the simple sentence? Grammatical resources such as different clause types enable us to describe and make explicit complex interrelationships between the entities, actions, and state-of-affairs that remain implicit in simple sentences. As we have already mentioned, one of the, if not *the*, major challenges in representing (**re**-presenting) the experiential world in written or spoken form is that language is linear. When we seek to re-present the experiential world in written form, we can only do so one word, clause, and paragraph at a time.

Here is an option for integrating the separate pieces of information in the five-sentence student paragraph into a single sentence. We would not recommend that you try to produce such complex sentences. We have included it here simply to illustrate some of the grammatical resources that can be used to integrate information from simple sentences into more complex ones. (If you're unsure about complex sentences, you can find an explanation and examples in the glossary.)

> Educational systems with a large number of immigrant students who possess complex multilingual repertoires disadvantage these students when they implement institutional policies that favour traditional monolingual practices in which language and cultural uniformity are the norm.

In creating this sentence, our first challenge was to decide what to thematize. We opted for "educational systems with a large number of immigrants". When you select a theme, you are saying to the reader, "What I'm going to tell you about, is …" (in our case, educational systems with a large number of immigrants). The next challenge was to integrate some of the grammatical resources noted above to integrate the rest of the information into our sentence.

Choosing which piece of information to thematize will be largely dictated by the audience for and purpose of the piece. (In Chapter 4, we go into greater detail on purpose and audience.) If we are writing a submission to a government inquiry into language policies in the school system, it would make sense to thematize 'institutional policies'. But what kind of institutional policies do we want to tell the inquiry about? The answer is those of educational systems favoring traditional monolingual practices in which language and cultural uniformity are the norm. This gives us a long and complex theme that is difficult to process: "Institutional policies of educational systems favouring traditional monolingual practices in which the language and cultural uniformity are the norm…". What do we want to tell the committee about these policies? That they "devalue the multilingual repertoires of large numbers of immigrants".

But what if we want the focus on the plight of multilingual students? A third option presents itself.

> Large numbers of immigrant students possessing complex multilingual repertoires are disadvantaged in educational systems based on traditional monolingual practices in which language and cultural uniformity are the norm.

Here is a theme/rheme analysis of the three options (Table 2.3):

Table 2.3 Theme/rheme analysis of the three options

Theme	Rheme
Option 1	
Educational systems with a large number of immigrant students who possess complex multilingual repertoires	disadvantage these students when they implement institutional policies that favor traditional monolingual practices in which language and cultural uniformity are the norm.
Option 2	
Institutional policies of educational systems favoring traditional monolingual practices in which the language and cultural uniformity are the norm	devalue the multilingual repertoires of large numbers of immigrants.
Option 3	
Large numbers of immigrant students possessing complex multilingual repertoires	are disadvantaged in educational systems based on traditional monolingual practices in which language and cultural uniformity are the norm.

Which is the 'best' option? The answer is, it depends. It is up to you, the author, to decide on the focus, or theme, of the sentence in the light of your purpose and audience. It also depends on how much information is in the form of pre-and post-modification of the head noun. A useful exercise is to identify the clause type (similar to what we asked you to do in the 'Making Connection' exercise above).

Type 2: S+V+O: Systems disadvantage students.

Type 2: S+V+O: Policies devalue immigrants.

Type 3: S+V+C: Students are disadvantaged.

You can then determine how much ballast you can add to the head word before it sinks. Let us reiterate a point we made above: we are not advocating overstuffing sentences with content. The point of this exercise is to demonstrate the options and choices available to you as a writer when distributing large amounts of content in a paragraph according to audience and purpose. Awareness of theme/rheme distribution in your writing can help in this regard. Hedge (2005) suggests beginning by breaking ideas into simple propositions which can then be built into more complex sentences (p. 84).

Making decisions about theme and rheme has implications for the rest of the paragraph. Ideally, one of the elements in the rheme of the first sentence in the paragraph becomes the theme of the next sentence. This theme/rheme patterning helps knit the paragraph together and (hopefully) makes it more coherent for the reader. This knitting together can be seen in the student assignment we have been working with in this section.

> Educational systems [theme] with a large number of immigrant students who possess complex multilingual repertoires disadvantage these students when they implement institutional policies that favour traditional monolingual practices in which language and cultural uniformity are the norm. These monolingual practices [theme] do not facilitate the acquisition of content and literacy for multilingual students. Such students [theme], who possess myriad linguistic resources, are educated as if they were monolinguals, which inhibits them from using their linguistic (and non-linguistic) resources to make meaning.

Making connections

Carry out a theme/rheme analysis of the sentences in a paragraph from your own writing.

Try out different themes. What effect does this have on the meaning you are trying to convey?

Cohesion and coherence

In the preceding section, we stressed the importance for a writer to assist the reader by making the text as clear and coherent as possible. We introduced the concepts of theme and rheme and demonstrated how selecting the appropriate theme for each sentence within a paragraph should strengthen the coherence of the paragraph. In this section, we want to take a closer look at coherence and introduce the concept of cohesion. Our first concern is to address two questions: What do we mean by coherence? And what role does cohesion play in establishing coherence? In dealing with these questions, we have to confront a paradox.

Coherence (and incoherence) are words that turn up constantly in everyday conversation. *The first speaker was incoherent. I couldn't make sense of what he had to say. The second speaker, on the other hand, was most coherent. His argument was well-organized, logical, clear, relevant and comprehensible.* These adjectives capture the concept of coherence. The phrase 'make sense of' is also telling. It is up to us to make sense of what we see, hear, smell, taste, and touch. Sense is not an inherent quality of entities in the external world, entities which includes spoken and written language. Herein lies the paradox. We can't create coherence for the reader because it's an "inside-the-head" phenomenon, not an "on-the-page" phenomenon.

What are the on-the-page phenomena that enable readers to perceive a particular text as coherent rather than a random collection of sentences? Further, what is it that makes one version of a paragraph more coherent than another? Familiarity with the subject matter helps. The degree of coherence will vary from reader to reader depending on how much they already know of the subject. Linguistic knowledge also helps. "While readers need to know the meaning of individual words and sentences in order to comprehend written texts, they also need to know how the sentences relate to one another" (Nunan, 2013, p. 113).

It is here that the writer can help. As we saw in the last section, distribution of information in a paragraph is most important. Does the writer use thematization and given/new structuring effectively so that successive sentences follow one another in a way that helps the reader make sense of the text or not? However, thematization and given/new information structure are insufficient. As Halliday (1985) notes:

> Theme and information constitute the internal resources for structuring the clause as a message. But in order that a sequence of clauses ... should constitute a text, it is necessary to do more than give an appropriate

internal structure to each. It is necessary, also, to make explicit the external relationship between one clause … and another, and to do so in a way that is not dependent on grammatical structure.

(p. 287)

He goes on to say that the non-structural resources that allow us to make explicit relationships between entities, actions, and states-of-affairs across clauses/sentences are known as cohesion. He illustrates the way that cohesion works by analyzing a children's nursery rhyme.

Little Boy Blue, come blow your horn!

The sheep's in the meadow, the cow's in the corn.

Where is the boy that looks after the sheep?

He's under the haycock, fast asleep.

Will you go wake him? No, not I!

For if I do, he'll be sure to cry.

The use of *he … him … he* to refer back to 'the boy that looks after the sheep' is an instance of reference. The forms *no, not I* and *if I do* exemplify ellipsis; they have to be interpreted as *no I (will) not wake him)* and *if I (wake him)*. The word *for* expresses a conjunctive relationship between 'I will not' and 'if I do, he will cry'. The word *sheep* in line three reiterates *sheep* in line two; *cow* related to *sheep*, *corn*, *meadow*, and *wake* and *asleep*; these are all examples of lexical cohesion.

(Halliday, 1985, p. 288)

The first comprehensive instruction to cohesion was published in 1976 by Halliday and Hasan. In it they describe linguistic devices which differentiate coherent texts from random sentences. For this reason, they were referred to as 'text-forming' devices. Writers employ these to 'pull sentences together into texts' and assist the reader to achieve coherence. In their book, Halliday and Hasan describe five cohesive devices. These devices signal relationships between entities, events, and states-of-affairs that occur in different sentences within a text. A sentence containing one of these devices cannot be understood if it stands alone outside the text. The five devices are reference, substitution, ellipsis, conjunction, and lexical cohesion. Halliday later collapsed substitution and ellipsis into a single category. However, here, we will retain the original five. At the risk of oversimplifying, we will give a brief description along with examples of these cohesive devices.

Reference: The use of various pro-forms (e.g., pronouns or demonstratives: *he, she, it, they, this, that*) to represent information provided elsewhere in the text. Encountered outside the text from which it has been taken, a sentence containing one of these items is uninterpretable. For example:

> Sentence out of context: *This necessitated the collection of additional data.*

> From the sentence presented out of context, it is not possible to answer the question *What required the collection of additional data?*

> Sentence in context: *Two studies were conducted, both of which were inconclusive. This necessitated the collection of additional data.*

Conjunction (also called logical connectives): These signal relationships such as causality, time, and concession that exist across and sometimes within sentences in the text. Examples include for example, however, therefore, in addition, although, and firstly.

> Sentence out of context: *However, the research team was encouraged to reapply.*

> Out of context, the sentence is uninterpretable.

> Given a textual context, however, it makes perfect sense. *After considerable discussion, ethics approval for the research was withheld. However, the research team was encouraged to reapply.*

> Without the conjunction, the two sentences would still make sense. As a writer, you have to decide whether the addition of the conjunction is helpful to the reader. Given the larger context of the entire paragraph, you might even decide to blend the two sentences using the conjunction 'but'. *After considerable discussion, ethics approval for the research was withheld, but the research team was encouraged to reapply.*

Ellipsis: Ellipsis is a noun formed from the verb 'to elide' or to leave out. The second sentence in the example above also serves to illustrate this cohesive device.

> Sentence out of context: *However, the research team was encouraged to reapply.*

> From the sentence presented out of context, it is not possible to answer the question *What was the research team encouraged to apply for?* (Or, if you want to avoid ending the question with a preposition, *For what was the research team encouraged to apply?*)

> However, given the context, the answer is (or should) be perfectly obvious. In the second sentence, the words 'ethics approval' are redundant and, in the interests of economy, have been elided, or left out. Again, as a writer, you are perfectly within your rights to restate them, but you would then be violating the principle of economy.

Substitution: Substitution and ellipsis are closely related. In fact, in a later version of their model of cohesion, Halliday and Hasan collapsed them into a single category. In the case of ellipsis, information assumed to be obvious to the reader is omitted. In the case of substitution, a noun, verb, or clause is replaced with a 'stand in' word such as do/does, one/ones, and so. While substitution occurs most commonly in spoken discourse, it can also be found in written texts.

> *Nominal substitution:* Effective use of cohesive devices enables you to highlight certain pieces of information. It also allows you to downplay <u>others</u> (others = certain pieces of information).

> *Verbal substitution:* The experimental group didn't follow the instructions. The control group <u>did</u> (did = followed the rules).

> *Clausal substitution:* I consulted my advisor on whether I should try to replicate the experiment. He said he thought <u>so</u> (so = try to replicate the experiment).

Lexical cohesion: As the label implies, lexical cohesion analyzes the way that networks of words that are related in some way contribute to the coherence of a text. The simplest is lexical repetition. Other types are synonym (similar in meaning), antonym (opposite in meaning), or a hyponym (where one word is an example of a more general word such as 'animal and 'dog') can be used. Collocational relationships are also part of lexical cohesion. Collocation exists when two words are related because they belong to the same semantic field, for example, 'student' and 'teacher'. This type of lexical cohesion can be problematic when searching for lexical patterns or chains, in texts. 'Table' and 'chair' clearly belong to the semantic field of 'furniture'; in fact, they are both hyponyms of furniture, but what about 'table' and 'leg'. Despite the headaches it can cause, exploring collocational patterns in texts can be fascinating. The most comprehensive treatment of this aspect of cohesion is provided by Michael Hoey (1983, 1991). Here are some examples of these types of lexical cohesion.

> Repetition: Clive James' first <u>memoir</u> was considered a classic. His second <u>memoir</u> was less favourably received.

> Synonym: Clive James' <u>autobiography</u> was well-received. Not so, his second <u>life-account</u>.

> Antonym: Clive James should have <u>stopped</u> with his first memoir. However, he <u>continued</u> with three more.

> Hyponym: The first <u>memoir</u> by Clive James is still in print today. The <u>book</u> was one of his favourites.

Collocation: To be counted as empirical <u>research</u>, any scholarly activity needs a number of essentials elements. It the first place, it requires a <u>question</u>. Next it has to have <u>data</u> that have relevant bearing on the question. <u>Analysis</u> and <u>interpretation</u> are fundamental. The researcher needs to deal with threats to <u>reliability</u> and <u>validity</u>. Finally, the <u>results</u> must be <u>published</u>.

Although cohesion doesn't 'create' coherence, as critics were quick to point out (Carrell, 1982), the ability to manipulate these devices can help you strengthen the coherence of your writing. As we have already pointed out, cohesion exists in the text. Coherence resides in the head. That said, while cohesive devices don't 'create' coherence, without them our writing would be clumsy and disjointed. (For a detailed discussion of the contribution of cohesion to the perception of coherence in texts, see Connor and Johns (1990).) Consider the following versions of a simple text.

Version 1

The research team could not agree on a site for their research. The research team argued about the site for their research for several days. Some members of the research team wanted the site for their research to be in a simulated setting. Some members of the research team want the site for their research to be in a naturalistic setting.

Version 2

The research team could not agree on a site for their research. They argued about it for several days. Some wanted it to be in a simulated setting. Others argued for a naturalistic setting.

In version 2, the use of cohesive devices (reference, ellipsis, and substitution) results in a text that is more readable and coherent than version 1. The identical content is expressed half the number of words.

In order to consolidate our students' understanding of the way cohesive devices function within written texts, we have them identify their cohesive chains in a text by tracking them with different colored highlighting pens. (A chain exists when a text entity is linked by a cohesive device across two or more sentences.) We then get them to do the same with one or two of their own paragraphs. An example of cohesive chaining is illustrated in the following box.

David's example of lexical chains

Here is an example of lexical chains in a passage from a semi-fictionalized memoir I wrote some years ago in which I described, among other things, meetings with famous writers (Nunan, 2012). In one chapter, I recount meeting Anthony Burgess who wrote many best-selling novels, including *A Clockwork Orange*, which was made into a film. At a writers' festival where I first met Burgess, I was deputed to chauffer him to a winery where a lunch was to be held in honor of the keynote speakers at the festival.

> Getting **Burgess** to the winery wasn't difficult. The town only had one main street and Hardy's winery was the largest enterprise in town. We were met by numerous members of the Hardy family. These including Frank – later to be dubbed Sir Frank Hardy for his services to yachting. (What would **Burgess** have made of that?). Also in the party was an elderly member of the family whom everyone called 'Uncle Tom'. We were taken to a massive barn where hundreds of wine barrels were stacked from floor to ceiling. Inside the barn, it was cool. A sweet, rotting smell came from the barrels. Through the gloom, I could see that at the rear of the barn trestle tables had been set with food and wine. 'This looks promising,' said **Burgess** eyeing the victuals, and rubbing his hands. **He** moved towards the spread like a hunter advancing on his prey. And then, **the celebrated author** pounced.

In this chain, there are five cohesive ties: three of lexical repetition, one of reference, and one synonym. Can you find any other examples of simple cohesion (one instance of a cohesive tie) and cohesive chaining (two or more cohesive ties)?

If you completed this activity, you may have found that there is one conjunction ('also', and a couple of instances of referential cohesion, but the vast majority of the items are lexical). Carrying out this type of cohesive analysis demonstrates the intricate interweaving that occurs in even a simple descriptive paragraph. There is not a single sentence that doesn't contain at least one cohesive link to one or more of the other sentences in the paragraph.

Making connections

Select a paragraph of your own writing. Ideally, it should be around 150–200 words. Go through the paragraph and identify the instances of cohesion. You can do this by underlining the items or changing the font or color of the words. Create a matrix showing the cohesive chains in the paragraph, using the one above as a model.

What did you learn about the way cohesion works to bind a text together?

Connections at the text level: signposting and summarizing

When writing, you should tell readers what you're going to write, write it, and then remind the readers of the journey on which you've have taken them. Signposting, or alerting readers of what's to come, and then summarizing the terrain that has been covered, are not only a courtesy to the reader, but an invaluable aid in helping them navigate their way through your text. You should do this regardless of whether you are writing a book or a short article of 1,000 words or less. If your text has sub-sections, as is usually the case with journal articles, each subsection should be signposted and summarized. (If you return to earlier paragraphs of this chapter, you will see how we signposted the content to come.)

Aitchison (2014), following Feak and Swales (2009), refers to the language used by writers to signpost as 'metadiscourse', i.e., talk about talk or discourse about discourse which, generally speaking, is empty of content. She says that at the beginning or ending of a chapter/article, or the beginning of a new section within a piece, the signposting can provide for the reader one of three orientation: a current, a backward, or a future orientation. Here are some of the phrases that can orient the reader in one of these three directions:

Current orientation:

The focus of this chapter is on …

This chapter reviews the literature on …

Backwards orientation:

This chapter follows from a detailed report of the finding that …

The previous chapter provided an historical review of the evolution of these models. To recap the main ...

Future orientation:

Having established the central argument, the next chapter ...

... and thus, the next chapter explores the key themes ...

She also points out that orientations can be combined:

Following from the discussion of key findings in Chapter 5, this chapter lays the ground for the resultant recommendations presented in the final chapter.

Making connections

Most academic journals require an abstract at the beginning of articles accepted for publication. An abstract is a formal type of signposting. In the following abstract, the authors begin by providing a context. They describe the problem to be addressed, make reference to several relevant studies, state the premises on which the study rests, describe the research method, and summarize the argument to be presented in the article.

1. Read the following abstract. Underline instances of metadiscoursal signposting and note the tense choices made.

In contemporary educational contexts, technology, globalization, and mobility have brought about a blurring of the boundary between language learning and activation in and beyond the classroom. (We prefer the term "activation" to "use" as it has a more dynamic connotation.) This contrasts with the pre-globalized, pre-Internet world when, in many EFL (and even ESL) settings, opportunities for language use outside the classroom were either limited or non-existent. These days, regardless of the physical context in which learners are living, there are many opportunities for language activation outside the classroom (see Benson & Reinders, 2011; Nunan & Richards, 2015, for over 40 case studies of such opportunities). Additionally, there is a problematic distinction between classrooms, as places where language is learned, and the world beyond the classroom, as spaces where classroom-acquired language and skills are activated. Inside the classroom, experiences can be created in which learning and activation can co-occur (Swain, 2000). Beyond the classroom, learners are not only activating their language in authentic contexts, they are also developing their communicative repertoires and acquiring language skills that are not readily acquired in the classroom (Choi, 2017). This paper thus rests on the following premises: learning and activation can co-occur inside and outside the classroom; and, language learning/activation outside the classroom offers challenges and opportunities that are not available inside the classroom. In the body of the paper, we will expand on, exemplify, and attempt to justify these premises. We will also argue that a blended, project-based approach, incorporating both in class and out of class learning/activation opportunities provides optimal environments for language development. In the body of the paper, we showcase the rich learning affordances in blended project designs drawing on four case studies from a range of contexts. Finally, we discuss the need to rethink the roles of teachers, learners and pedagogy within the blended model. (Choi & Nunan, 2018, p. 49)

This abstract consists of two principal moves, a summary of literature relevant to the article to come and a statement of the premises (claims) to be argued in the article and the justification for it. Signposting is signaled by the phrases *This paper thus rests on … In the body of the paper … We will also argue … we showcase … Finally* …. In Chapter 5, we introduce you to the concept of moves and how to carry out a move analysis.

Making connections

Select a picture or short video (5–10 seconds) taken in any social setting such as a park, a shopping mall, or a dinner party. Describe what is going on in about 20 short simple sentences. (Ensure that there is only one main verb per sentence.)

Here is an example from David based on his morning run around a harborside park on Hong Kong Island.

> It's mid-morning in Cyberport Park.
>
> The park is rapidly filling up with people.
>
> Kids of various ages belt around the path that circumnavigates the park.
>
> Some kids are on skateboards.
>
> Some kids are on bike.
>
> Adults scatter onto the grass to avoid injury.

A dad kicks a soccer ball to his small sons.

A pack of dogs of various sizes chase each other across the grass.

The harbourside is in full sun.

The sun bites into my back.

A stand of trees shades the landside of the park.

The shade and a breeze cool the sweat on my back.

Shall birds swoop and whirl.

The birds are brunching on insects.

Effortlessly, they take their prey on the wing.

A Hakka lady in a rattan hat clear the path of twigs and leaves with a broom made of brush.

On the harbour, a massive container ship makes slow progress towards the container port.

A diminutive fishing boat bobs dangerously in the wake of the ship.

Use the sentences to produce a short narrative. Draw on what you learned from this chapter. Now reflect on the contrast between the existential world as represented by the photo and the word world you have created.

Question from readers

Q: I'm still confused about the relationship between cohesion and coherence. Does cohesion create coherence or doesn't it?

A: This is an excellent question, and one that has caused quite a lot of controversy. In the 1970s, when Halliday and Hasan described their system of cohesion, it caused quite a lot of excitement. Halliday pointed out that the difference between random sentences and a text that was perceived as coherent was the existence of cohesion: linguistic devices that made explicit connections between sentences in a text. As we point out in the chapter, these became known as 'text-forming' devices. Some linguists hypothesized that the number of cohesive devices in a text divided by the number of clauses could give us an "index to coherence". However, the notion that a direct causal relationship could be established between cohesion and coherence turned out to be naïve. There were several problems. First of all, not all cohesive links have the same text-forming power within a given text. Second, it is perfectly possible to have texts that contain no cohesion, but are readily perceived as coherent: readers or listeners can make sense of them. (Although, we should point out that these are almost invariably short texts concocted by linguists to challenge the link between cohesion and coherence.) Conversely, it is possible to concoct texts containing cohesive devices that are incoherent. Here's an example:

> I bought a new car last **week**. On **Thursday**, the circus came to **town. It** used to be a medieval **village**. Daily life is very different **there** since the new expressway was built.

One of the most trenchant criticisms of the notion that cohesion could provide an index of textual coherence was made by Carrell (1982) in a widely cited *TESOL Quarterly* article entitled 'Cohesion is not coherence'. Her central argument was that Halliday and Hasan's cohesion concept assumes that "coherence is located in the text and … fails to take the contribution of the text's reader into account" (p. 479).

We believe that Carrell is correct in viewing coherence as an 'inside the head' factor. However, we disagree that Halliday and Hasan assume that coherence is a text factor. We also agree with Carrell that reading comprehension is an interactive process between the reader and the text. There is also evidence to support the view that the effective and appropriate use of cohesive devices on the part of the writer can assist the reader to make sense of the text (Nunan, 1983). Finally, research indicates that cohesive chains in texts do contribute to coherence (Hoey, 1983, 1991) although the relationship is much more intricate and complex than was assumed by those linguists who first sought to establish a relationship between the two concepts.

Summary

In this chapter, we introduce a number of complex concepts which are fundamental to clarity and coherence in academic writing. They include thematization, cohesion, coherence, and signposting. Understanding these concepts and being able to exploit them will provide you with tools to reflect on and rework your writing. (We will look in greater detail at the revision process in Chapter 8.) We called the chapter *Making Connections* because the function of these devices is to enable you to transform a multifaceted, multisensory world into a world of a very different kind: a linear world, constructed by you, one word at a time. If you succeed, you will be making the only connection that matters, the one between you and your reader. In the next chapter, we dig deeper into this extraordinary process of writing for ourselves to figure out the world as we see it to produce lines of print that someone else will, at the very least, recognize, and, at the very best, be enlightened if not transformed. In the words of E.M. Forster: "Only connect! ... That was the whole of her sermon. Live [and write] in fragments no longer".

Further readings

Burns, A., & Coffin, C. (Eds.). (2000). *Analysing English in a global context*. Routledge. This collection contains a number of seminal articles that speak to the issues and concepts presented in this chapter. We would particularly recommend papers in parts three and four of the collection: Analysing English: a text perspective, and Analysing English: a clause perspective.

de Oliveira, L., & Schleppegrell, M. (2015). *Focus on grammar and meaning*. Oxford University Press. For readers interested in how to teach grammar and meaning, this book will provide insights teachers can experiment with in their classrooms.

Hoey, M. (1991). *Patterns of lexis in text*. Oxford University Press. A comprehensive and authoritative treatment of many of the concepts and issues covered in this chapter, including the cohesion/coherence controversy and given/new structures in text.

Whittaker, R., O'Donnell, M., & McCabe, A. (Eds.). (2006). *Language and literacy: Functional approaches*. Continuum. This edited collection of essays examines the relationship between language and literacy from a systemic-functional perspective. Part three may be most relevant to readers interested in understanding literacy involved in specific disciplines and in examples of students' writings.

References

Aitchison, C. (2014, November 15). *Where's this going!?: Metadiscourse for readers and writers*. https://doctoralwriting.wordpress.com/2014/11/15/wheres-this-going-metadiscourse-for-readers-and-writers/

Benson, P., & Reinders, H. (2011). *Beyond the language classroom*. Springer.

Carrell, P. (1982). Cohesion is not coherence. *TESOL Quarterly, 16*(4), 479–488. https://doi.org/10.2307/3586466

Choi, J. (2017). *Creating a multivocal self: Autoethnography as method*. Routledge.

Choi, J., & Nunan, D. (2018). Language learning and activation in and beyond the classroom. *Australian Journal of Applied Linguistics*, *1*(2), 49–63. https://dx.doi.org/10.29140/ajal.v1n2.34

Connor, U., & Johns, A. (Eds.). (1990). *Coherence: Research and pedagogical perspectives*. TESOL.

Feak, C. B., & Swales, J. M. (2009). *Telling a research story: Writing a literature review* (vol. 2). University of Michigan Press.

Forster, E. M. (1910). *Howards end*. Edward Arnold.

Halliday, M., & Hasan, R. (1976). *Cohesion in English*. Longman.

Halliday, M. A. K. (1985). *An introduction to functional grammar*. Edward Arnold.

Hedge, T. (2005). *Writing* (2nd ed.). Oxford University Press.

Hoey, M. (1983). *On the surface of discourse*. Allen and Unwin.

Hoey, M. (1991). *Patterns of lexis in text*. Oxford University Press.

Nunan, D. (1983). *Discourse processing by first language, second phases, and second language learners*. [Unpublished doctoral dissertation]. Flinders University.

Nunan, D. (2012). *When Rupert Murdoch came to tea*. Wayzgoose Press.

Nunan, D. (2013). *What is this thing called language?* (2nd ed.). Palgrave Macmillan.

Nunan, D., & Richards, J. (2015). *Language learning beyond the classroom*. Routledge.

Polias, J., & Dare, B. (2006). Towards a pedagogical grammar. In R. Whittaker, M. O'Donnell & A. McCabe (Eds.), *Language and literacy: Functional approaches* (pp. 123–143). Continuum.

Swain, M. (2000). The output hypothesis and beyond: Mediating acquisition through collaborative dialogue. In J.P. Lantolf (Ed.), *Sociocultural theory and second language learning* (pp. 97–114). Oxford University Press.

3
Product and process approaches to writing

In this chapter, we look at product and process approaches to writing. Although we have divided the chapter into two major sections, the first focusing on product-oriented and the second on process-oriented approaches, we have done so partly for organizational convenience. The process/product labels refer to differences in emphasis and orientation, not categorial distinctions. Approaches to writing exist on a continuum from more product-oriented at one end to more process-orientated at the other. Writing is both a process and a product, and any of the approaches we examine in this and other chapters will have elements of both. Assigning an approach to one orientation rather than another is a matter of relative emphasis. If the approach is based on a predetermined template to which the writer is required to conform, we will assign it to the product-oriented category. An example from the world of accounting would be an audit report, which has a format that must be adhered to by the auditor. In the legal profession, the same holds for tort cases. If there is no pre-determined framework, and writing/rewriting is a process of exploration and discovery out of which a structure emerges for a final product that satisfies the writer, then we will deem the approach to be process-oriented. Personal letters to family and friends usually emerge in this way. We may have a mental or written list of what we want to say but only the vaguest idea of how we want to say it. The final product emerges through the process of writing. In scholarly writing, the process/product distinction is clearly visible. Some academic disciplines have predetermined, often rigid, and sometimes unspoken, templates for presenting the results of an empirical study. Other disciplines have principles of procedure which give the writer greater freedom.

Maggie Sokolik argues that writing is a process which results in a product. She provides the following description of the relationship between the two.

DOI: 10.4324/9781003179092-4

> The writer imagines, organizes, drafts, edits, reads, and rereads. This *process* of writing is often cyclical, and sometimes disorderly. Ultimately, what the audience sees, whether it is an instructor or a wider audience, is a *product* – an essay, letter, story, or research report.
>
> (Sokolik, 2021, p. 88)

We begin the chapter by looking at product-oriented approaches. In this section, two important concepts, register and genre, are defined and illustrated. These concepts were developed within systemic-functional linguistics and have had an important influence on writing pedagogy. We then turn to process-oriented approaches where we explore the relationship between thinking and writing and introduce the notion of writing as a thinking process.

Product-oriented approaches to writing

A product orientation has, and arguably still is, the dominant approach to the teaching of academic and other forms of non-fiction writing. Students are taught rules and principles underlying 'good academic writing' and are often provided with a template or model to follow. Accuracy of spelling, grammar, and punctuation is given a high priority when it comes to assessing a piece of written work. The focus is on the outcome such as an environmental science report, a journalistic essay on the causes of the war in the Middle East, or a procedural text on how to operate a piece of machinery. The process through which the end product was arrived at is largely overlooked.

In our Introduction, we referred to Strunk and White's widely read and cited book *The Elements of Style*, which provides advice on how to write clearly and succinctly. In the book, the authors argue for a product orientation, with a nod to process.

> A basic structural design underlies every kind of writing. The writer will in part follow this design, in part deviate from it, according to his skill, his needs, and the unexpected events that accompany the act of composition. Writing, to be effective, must follow closely the thoughts of the writer, but not necessarily the order in which the thoughts occur. This calls for a scheme of procedure … [I]n most cases planning must be a deliberate prelude to writing. The first principle of composition, therefore, is to foresee or determine the shape of what is to come and pursue that shape.
>
> (Strunk & White, 1959, p. 10)

We now return to systemic-functional linguistics and elaborate on the description presented in Chapter 2. The model originated from several strands of European linguistics and has evolved from there into one of the most important branches of contemporary linguistics. (Some would say the most important branch of contemporary linguistics.) In recent years, it has become increasingly influential in the teaching of writing. Two concepts developed within systemic-functional linguistics are relevant to our discussion: register and genre. While they are relevant to both speaking and writing, given the purpose of this book, we will focus on the latter.

Register

Register analysis was developed to study the relationship between language and the situational contexts in which it is used. Linguists identified three register variables as being particularly important:

- What is the topic or content of a spoken or written text? (This variable refers to what people are 'on about' when they communicate. The options here are vast ranging from intercultural communication to childbirth, from business ethics to fly fishing.)
- What is the relationship between those involved in a particular communicative act? (Again, the options here are considerable: parent to child, neighbor to neighbor, shop assistant to customer, teacher to student, most particularly in our case, author to reader).
- What is the medium of communication? (Spoken versus written is an obvious distinction, but modern communication demands finer distinctions. Variables include phone, face-to-face, email, text messages, Zoom/Skype, and other technological affordances.) The technical terms for these variables are field, tenor, and mode, respectively. Holding one of these variables constant and ringing the changes on the other two will result in considerably different discourses marked by distinctly different linguistic features.

Making connections

Read the following vignette.

Val, a graduate student, is doing an ethnographic study into intercultural communication in a high a school where students, teachers, and support staff come from many different linguistic and cultural backgrounds. Last week was a busy one. She had numerous academic, professional, and personal commitments. She is so excited about and focused on her research, it's all that she wants to talk about. On Monday morning, she had an informal meeting in the faculty coffee lounge with her supervisor to discuss the draft of a paper she had worked on over the weekend. Later that afternoon she had drinks at a wine bar with two recently graduated fellow students to get advice on a data analysis problem she was having. On Tuesday, she had a formal meeting with her supervisor in his office. Wednesday was busy. In the morning, she had a Zoom meeting with one of her lecturers to go over a presentation she had to give to a research foundation to which she had applied for research funding. That afternoon, she gave the presentation, which was followed by a round-table discussion. On Thursday, she had a long Face Time chat with a friend and fellow student who was on a field trip in Thailand. That evening she attended a family dinner party at her parents' place where she described the nature of her research to an uncle and aunt who were visiting from interstate. Friday was important. In the afternoon, she gave a confirmation seminar to an audience of faculty and fellow students. She spent the weekend revising a journal article in the light of feedback from an anonymous reviewer. She submitted the revised article on Sunday evening along with a cover letter to the editor documenting and justifying the changes she had made. In good ethnographic fashion, Val kept audio recording and journal notes of all these events. These would become part of the database for her dissertation.

Carry out a register analysis of the events in Val's week. The field, Intercultural Communication, is the constant. Tenor and mode vary. The first one has been done for you.

Event/context	Tenor	Mode
Monday: Coffee with supervisor	Student – Supervisor	Face-to-face; informal
Tuesday:		
Wednesday:		
Thursday:		
Friday:		
Saturday:		
Sunday:		

Varying just one register variable will change the nature of the communica-tive event. So, in Val's case, holding the field (intercultural communication) and the mode (face-to-face) constant and varying the tenor (student-to-supervisor/student-to-student) will change the nature of the event. An audio recording of the two conversations will reveal that the different tenor rela-tionship is reflected in the discourse. In the vignette, to illustrate this point, we held field constant and introduced changes to both tenor and mode.

On Wednesday morning, Val had a Zoom meeting with one of her lecturers. If, on a subsequent occasion, she had a follow-up conversation on the same subject with the same lecturer, but this time on the phone, the conversa-tion would be different in several respects. If, for example, the topic of both conversations concerned a diagrammatic model she was developing, in the phone conversation, she couldn't talk about "this part of the model" or "the relationship between these two factors". She would have to be more explicit and detailed in describing the features and factors she was referring to than in a face-to-face meeting when she could point to the feature of interest and use cohesive 'pointing' devices such as 'this' and 'these'.

The tenor relationships in the vignette include student to teacher/supervisor, stranger to stranger, friend to friend, student to student, and family member to family member. Of course, the relationships can overlap. Some of Val's colleagues could be both fellow student and friend (or fellow student and rival). Mode variables included face-to-face in a variety of setting (coffee shop, meeting room, office, home, wine bar) as well as remote (Zoom, Face Time, written).

The spoken versus written distinction is a fundamental one. Writing is an unnatural act. This is underlined by the fact that many languages don't have a written form. In the case of languages that do have a written form, there are millions of speakers who never master that.

Val drew on a wide range of spoken and written source texts in writing her dissertation. She found it particularly challenging to transform recordings of informal coffee shop conversations into formal academic English. She no-ticed that not even well-educated, articulate people spoke in full sentences. The conversations were fragmentary. In the coffee shop or wine bar with fel-low students, topics shifted about, changed, and then returned to the original topic. She found it extremely challenging to organize messy conversations into coherent, linear arguments.

In the next section, we'll see that there are many different forms (genres) in a given language. Academic writing in its various guises differs in fundamental ways from informal genres such as letters to family and friends or personal diary entries. (Later in the book, we'll discuss the assertion that academic language is no-one's mother tongue.)

Initially, it was assumed that spoken language was a corrupted version of written English. With its hesitations and false starts, it was equated to the first draft of a piece of writing. However, McCarthy (1998) has argued that spoken language is not a 'corrupted' version of writing but has its own grammar and discourse features. Phenomena in the real world occur simultaneously, but writing is linear. In the last chapter, we introduced some of the linguistic resources such as thematization and cohesion for dealing with the limits of linearity.

Another feature differentiating written from spoken language is that it has a greater ratio of content words to grammar words. This is known as lexical density. Halliday (2001) explains lexical density in the following way:

> If we compare written with spoken English, we find that English typically shows a much denser pattern of lexical content. Lexical density has sometimes been measured as the ratio of content words to function words: higher in writing, lower in speech ... Lexical density is the number of lexical elements [content words] in the clause. Here is a sentence taken from a newspaper with the lexical elements in bold.
>
> Obviously the **government** is **frightened** of **union reaction** to its **move** to **impose proper behaviour** on **unions**.
>
> There are nine lexemes [content words] all in the one clause – lexical density 9. If we reword this in a rather more spoken form we might get the following.
>
> Obviously the **government** is **frightened** | | how the **union** will **react** | | if it tries to make them **behave properly** | |
>
> There are now three clauses, and the number of lexemes has gone down to six – lexical density 6 / 3 = 2.
>
> (Halliday, 2001, pp. 182–183)

The lower the lexical density, the easier it is for the reader or listener to process a sentence. The higher the lexical density, a register variable of academic writing, is a result of nominalization, that is, turning verbs such as 'react' into nouns: in this case 'reaction'. This enables the writer to pack more information into the sentence, and to make generalizations, and through the use of passive voice, to shift the focus from the performer of an action to the action and its consequences. A noun formed from a verb is what Halliday refers to as a grammatical metaphor. We'll have more to say about this phenomenon in Chapter 6. Being familiar with this process can help you make decisions about how much information to pack into a given sentence.

According to Martin (2001) register was developed in an applied, educational context for studying the development of children's writing abilities from infant through secondary school.

As the study progressed, however, it became clear that register was not an appropriate tool for the purposes of the research. For example:

> … it fails to give a satisfactory account of the goal-oriented beginning-middle-end structure of most texts (for example, the Orientation, Complication, Evaluation, Resolution, Coda structure for narratives). We felt a need to give a more explicit account of the beginning-middle-end (or schematic) structures which characterise children's writing in different genres. So we took the step of recognising a third semiotic system, which we called genre, underlying both register and language.
>
> (pp. 154–155)

We now turn to genre, defining the concept and providing examples so you have a clearer idea of what it is.

Genre

A genre is a purposeful, socially constructed oral or written text such as a narrative, a casual conversation, a poem, a recipe, or a description. The starting point for genre analysts is the overall purpose or function of a text. The purpose will determine the internal generic structure of the text as well as its key grammatical features. Three key questions form the point of departure for analyzing a given text: 'What is the purpose of this instruction booklet, narrative account, or argumentative text?', 'How is the purpose reflected in the overall structure of the text?', and 'What linguistic (grammatical/lexical) features characterize this genre?'

Common genres include recounts, narratives, procedures, reports, explanations, expositions, and discussions. The purpose of each of these texts is as follows:

- *Recount*: to tell what happened, to document a sequence of events and evaluate their significance in some way
- *Narrative*: to create a sequence of events culminating in a problem or crisis and a solution or resolution
- *Procedure*: to instruct the reader on how to make or do something
- *Report*: to present information on an event or circumstance
- *Explanation*: to explain how and why something occurs

- *Exposition*: to present an argument in favor of a proposition
- *Discussion*: to look at an issue from a number of different perspectives before reaching a conclusion (Nunan, 2013, pp. 120–121)

Genres can be clustered together into 'families' according to the general functions they perform. For example, narratives, recounts, and (auto)biographies form what we might call the 'story' family, expositions, discussions, and debate fall into the 'argument' family, and reviews, interpretations, and expository responses belong to the 'text response' family.

Here is an example of a familiar genre, the narrative. The narrative describes the death of Neil Davis, a celebrated war correspondent and cameraman, who covered regional wars and conflicts in the Asia-Pacific region, most notably the Vietnam War and the civil war in Cambodia. Davis was based in Bangkok. From here, he travelled around the region covering topical stories for an international news service based in Tokyo. Unfortunately for Davis, he happened to be in Bangkok one September morning when a series of events occurred that resulted in his death. The account below follows the generic structure of a narrative as described by systemic-functional linguists.

> Early on the morning of Monday 9 September, Davis's soundman Bill Latch was taking his daughter to school when he noticed tanks on the streets. Thailand was about to experience another coup d'état – something that veteran correspondents regarded as part of the cycle of life in Bangkok, like the wet and dry seasons **(Orientation)**. Latch called the head of their news service, Bruce MacDonnell, in Tokyo **(Event)**. MacDonnell, an experienced newsman, was not overly excited by the news, but he appreciated the early tip-off on what could develop into a major story **(Event)**. He called Davis and, with some apologies, put paid to his plans for a relaxing day **(Event)**. In Bangkok, Davis and Latch filmed military activity in the street and made arrangements to have the early footage shipped out to Hong Kong to be sent to New York by satellite **(Event)**. Suddenly they came under direct tank and machine gun fire, and took cover behind a telephone junction box. The ground shuddered beneath them and shrapnel sprayed indiscriminately. The noise was stunning **(Complication)**. A withering burst of fire was directed into the wall directly behind them, spewing out thousands of steel fragments **(Crisis)**. There was just time for Davis's brain to register that he had been mortally struck. He turned the camera on himself and filmed his own death **(Resolution)**. Through the crash of explosions could be heard his last words. There was not exclamation and expletive, but monumental irritation as he registered the futility of it all 'Oh...shit!' **(Coda)**.

This passage is adapted from Tim Bowden's dramatic account of the incident in his biography of Davis entitled *One Crowded Hour*. It displays the essential stages of a narrative: orientation, event, event, event, complication, crisis, resolution, and coda. Narratives are closely related to another genre – the recount. Both tell the story of a past event or series of events. Grammatically, both make extensive use of the simple past tense. The key difference between the two genres is that at the heart of the narrative is a crisis or problem followed by a resolution or solution. These two steps are absent from recounts.

We have included genre in the product-oriented section of the chapter because the goal is focused firmly creating a product: a set of instructions on how to make or do something, to explain how and why something occurs, to present an argument in favor of a proposition, and so on. However, as we pointed out at the beginning of the chapter, and as Sokolik (2021) has argued, when it comes to writing, or the teaching of writing, product-oriented approaches will also contain processes, and process-oriented approaches will ultimately result in a product of one sort or another.

Making connections

Study the following vignette. What aspects of the instruction are process-oriented, and which product-oriented?

Jake teaches English to science majors in an English medium university in Hong Kong. He uses a genre-based approach. The theme for his current semester with a group of first-year science majors is environmental studies and the project for the students is to write a report on waste disposal in the local city area. At the beginning of the semester, Jake introduces the topic, which is a major problem in Hong Kong. This leads into a discussion of the sociocultural context underlying the problem. Jake then introduces the genre of report writing. He provides examples of reports and guides students, working in small groups, to identify the generic structure and typical grammatical and lexical features of reports. The groups are then broken into pairs. The pairs are directed to collaboratively construct a draft report. As the pairs work on their reports, the teacher circulates and provides assistance when needed. The following week, when the class reconvenes, the teacher analyzes three of the draft reports and provides corrective feedback, indicating where the reports have deviated from the generic structure of the models they had studied the previous week as well as pointing out grammatical errors and problems of vocabulary. The students then revise their reports in light of the feedback from the teacher.

The genre approach has been criticized for being mechanistic, rigid, and lacking in opportunities for the writer to display any creativity or imagination. We have observed writing classes in elementary and secondary schools in which these criticisms are justified. We have also observed classes in which students are given little if any explicit instruction on the structure and linguistic features of the academic texts they will need to master to succeed academically. While some develop academic writing skills intuitively, many flounder.

We like Jake's approach because it illustrates the point we made at the beginning of the section. His goal is product-oriented, that is, to have the students produce a report which follows the generic structure and grammatical/lexical features of a report as stipulated by the genre approach. However, numerous elements in his classroom are process-oriented. These include class discussion, group and pair work, teacher feedback, and student revision.

In academic writing, there is a range of genres. The student essay/assignment and thesis/dissertation are probably the ones of most interest to you. Others include refereed journal articles, chapters in edited collections, scholarship applications, examiner's reports, and monographs. Each of these can be further divided into a sub-genre according to purpose and audience. For example, assignments can be divided into those requiring the student to collect and analyze original data (primary research) and those requiring a survey of the literature related to a particular topic or problem (secondary research).

The conventional genre in disciplines dominated by the positivist paradigm is the scientific report. While there are minor variations, the typical generic structure is: abstract, introduction/overview, problem statement, questions/hypotheses, method, data, analysis, discussion, conclusion, and references. While academic writing in naturalistic inquiry can follow this structure, greater flexibility and innovation are allowed and even encouraged. Julie explores these tensions in the next section through her own writing experience.

The argument that the genre-approach to writing, by definition, lacks opportunities for creativity and innovation is challenged by Christine Tardy (2016). In her book, *Beyond Convention: Genre Innovation in Academic Writing*, she argues that genres aren't fixed, and that creativity and innovation are possible. This does not mean that breaking or even bending conventional rules is not likely to go unchallenged, a point we make in Chapter 5. She points out that conventions are necessary. Without them, neither creativity nor innovation would be possible. Also, if the innovation strays too far from the conventions, it will no longer be an innovation but a new genre. She cites a number of studies that change the conventions of the written academic journal article. For example, a chapter in an edited collection by Matsuda and Atkinson (2008) is based on a conversation between the authors on the subject of contrastive rhetoric. Rather than repackaging the substance of the discussion into one of the sub-genres of a scholarly article, they present it as a conversation. They justify this stance "because contrastive rhetoric (CR) may be at a critical point in its history ... we decided to match this exploratory moment with an equally exploratory genre: the academic conversation" (p. 277).

The academic conversation comes in numerous forms: face-to-face and on-line interactions between members of a community of practice (CoP), blog post, conference symposia and panels, etc. Unlike other genres, such as a formal academic debate, which has a conventional generic structure and rules of the game, the academic conversation has a much looser structure. Its aim is not to win an argument or develop a theory, but to explore an issue, problem, or puzzle.

At the beginning, the Matsuda and Atkinson article looks like a conventional piece of academic writing, with an abstract and an introduction. These describe the physical context in which the conversation takes place and articulate the problem statement: Given that it is at a crucial point in its history, what are the future possibilities for contrastive rhetoric for the 21st century, and how they plan to address the problem.

The rest of the piece consists of the conversation. For readers unfamiliar with the notion of an academic conversation, a cursory look might lead them to believe that it has the generic characteristics of an everyday conversation. It includes listener clarification requests, confirmation checks, feedback, elaboration, listener completing the speaker's utterance, and so on. However, it quickly becomes apparent that the discourse reads more like academic written language than spoken conversation. Topic shifts are signposted by subheadings (*First experience with CR...*, *The relationship between research and pedagogy in CR...*, *Renaming and reconceptualizing CR...*, *Contrastive rhetoric as a field?...*, *Future directions for CR...*). The turn-taking is atypical: each speaker taking lengthy turns, many running to several hundred words. There are no run on or incomplete sentences, no pauses, repetitions, false starts, and hesitations. The discourse incorporates numerous in-text citations and concludes with a list of references.

We have discussed the Matsuda and Atkinson chapter at some length because it supports Tardy's claim that genres aren't set in stone. Whether the academic conversation as exemplified by this piece is an innovation or a genre in its own right is a matter for conjecture. We believe that it is. It also sits comfortably with a trend by some qualitative researchers to make their writing more engaging by appropriating techniques from the domains of fiction and creative non-fiction.

In this section, we introduced the concept of genre. The concept has been influential in the teaching of academic writing in a range of in secondary and tertiary contexts. We discussed it in this section because of its emphasis on the outcome or final product of the writing process. In some contexts, this results in a narrow, prescriptivist approach in which writers are required to adhere a template setting out the steps for the genre in question. "It's a bit like painting by numbers", as one jaded writer observed.

The section concludes with a discussion of Tardy's thesis that creativity and innovation are possible, and that genres are more fluid than the prescriptivists maintain. Unfortunately, limited space precludes our dealing with Tardy's approach and its practical implications in greater detail; however, it provides a segue into the next section on process-oriented approaches to academic writing.

Throughout the section, we have been at pains to point out that *all* writing has both process and product dimensions. This is true of the most narrowly prescribed reports produced within the positivist paradigm with its emphasis on objectivity and authorial invisibility. While references to the processes are downplayed, they do make cameo appearances, often at the end of the report under headings such as 'limitations of the study' and 'suggestions for further research'.

While we discuss writing products and include many samples of different kinds of writing in this book, our main focus is on the writing process. In the next section, we turn our attention to the processes involved in crafting a product. We begin by describing process writing, a method that grew out of the whole language movement.

Process-oriented approaches to writing

The name most associated with the whole language movement is Kenneth Goodman. Goodman was a vigorous proponent of the process writing method, based on his theories of language development. His academic output was prodigious. In addition to his many articles, book chapters, and presentations, he wrote over single or co-authored 80 books. His book *What is Whole in Whole Language?* was an international best-seller for an academic text with sales exceeding 250,000 copies.

While the writing process is not synonymous with process writing, we think it is useful to provide an overview of the method because some of its principles influenced the development of process-oriented writing. The method developed as an antidote to the traditional mechanistic, product-oriented approach to the teaching of writing that had dominated educational systems for many years. Based on a behaviorist notion, in this approach, learners were given models to reproduce. Beginning writers were not to be given the freedom to write as they liked because they would make mistakes. These mistakes would then have to be "unlearned" – a lengthy and tedious process. Proponents of process writing rejected this premise, arguing that it was mechanistic, and behaviorism was a discredited theory of human learning. Creativity was fundamental to the education of the child. The process writing method led the writer through five stages: pre-writing, drafting, revising, editing, and publishing. At the pre-writing stage, the teacher would engage learners in discussing a topic of interest. They would be encouraged to explore the topic, to pose questions, and seek answers to the questions through library research, making notes as they did so. Using the notes, they would develop a first draft. This reflective and recursive process is fundamental to current process-oriented approaches and one we endorse. In producing their first draft, writers were to write freely, to use their creativity and imagination. At this developmental stage, they are not to worry about grammar, spelling, and punctuation. Our attitude is that at the first draft stage they shouldn't be overly concerned about these conventions but should not ignore them entirely. We'll have more to say on this issue in Chapter 8 where we spell out our approach to the stages in the revision process.

At the next stage, students discuss their draft with the teacher. In the jargon of the process writing method, this stage was called 'conferencing'. They then revise their initial draft in the light of feedback and suggestions from the conferencing session. At the third draft stage, the writers edit their work for errors of grammar, spelling, and punctuation. The final stage, publication, involves sharing their work with others. (For an updated account of Goodman's work, see Goodman, 2014.)

Proponents of the genre approach criticized process writing on the grounds that, while encouraging creativity and imagination were important, process writing over-emphasized narrative. Students became adept at writing recounts and stories, but many struggled to produce procedural texts on science experiments, laboratory reports, historical explanation, expositions on environmental issues, and so on. The genre school argued that to navigate one's way through secondary school successfully, it was necessary to master these academic text types. Middle-class students were able to develop writing skills in relation to these genres implicitly, if not explicitly, by virtue of their privileged social and economic position, access to literary resources in the home, membership of local libraries, and so on. Many working class and non-English speaking background students were not.

Ironically, the genre approach to teaching writing, initially developed in Australia in reaction to the shortcomings of process writing, has been criticized on the grounds that it represents a return to the traditional practice of copying model texts. In the initial, we don't see this as a bad thing. Imitating models is a legitimate strategy for developing academic writing skills.

In addition, as we showed in the previous section, the pedagogical model developed for teaching genres can incorporate elements from process writing such as establishing the field through teacher led discussion, collaborative peer group drafting, revising, and polishing initial efforts, and so on.

In academic writing at the university level, process-oriented writing is having an impact among scholars engaged in naturalistic inquiry. These scholars challenge the positivism paradigm which has a well-developed and articulated procedure in which question formation, data collection, and analysis precede the writing up and publication stages. They reject the procedure initially proposed by Strunk and later elaborated by Strunk and White (1959) that a fully developed plan must precede the writing phase and that it's only when your ideas have been fully developed that you can start writing.

The alternative view is that writing and thinking are bound together that it's through writing that we develop and clarify our ideas. Writing as a thinking process has been described by Laurel Richardson, one of its most prominent advocates, as a messy, fluid process in which writing and thinking co-occur.

> I write because I want to find something out. I write in order to learn something that I did not know before I wrote it. I was taught, though, as perhaps you were, too, not to write until I knew what I wanted to say, until my points were organized and outlined. No surprise, this static writing model coheres with mechanistic scientism, quantitative research, and entombed scholarship.
>
> (Richardson, 2001, p. 35)

This quote is taken from an article in which Richardson challenges the notion that thinking and writing are two separate processes and that thinking precedes writing. Rather, writing is a method of self-discovery. Through it, we find out about ourselves and the knowledge we are building.

Richardson also questions the notion that the sole purpose of writing is to inform others of ideas, states-of-affairs, and so on. This could well be the *product* of writing. But the product is preceded by a *process*, a process of writing to find out something we didn't know. This is not a new idea. Many years ago, Mary Lawrence wrote an influential little book called *Writing as a Thinking Process* (Lawrence, 1972). The book went through many editions before finally going out of print. Although written specifically for the second-language learner, the book contained an important insight for all writers: one does not formulate ideas which are committed to print resulting in a product – an essay, a report, or a thesis. It is through the process of writing, and rewriting, that one develops one's ideas. Producing good writing is like producing good bread. You won't get good bread without giving the dough a good pummeling. Without pummeling your words, you won't get good texts. This complex nexus between the process of writing and the final product was captured by the novelist E.M. Forster (1974) when he said, "How do I know what I think until I see what I say?"

In an article, *Getting Personal: Writing-Stories*, Richardson (2001) gives a graphic account of how writing recused her career and, in a sense, saved her life. In a car accident, she sustained multiple injuries including serious brain damage. Through the accident, she says, "I had lost access to my brain. I had lost language: my sword and my shield. My habitual routines for naming things were torn up, blocked off: paths to words and formulae were gone" (p. 33). It was through writing that she slowly and painfully regained access to her brain and developed a new perspective on the relationship between thinking and writing. If she couldn't retrieve a word, she left a blank space to be filled in later. Writing gave her a feeling over time and space, and a faith that she would recover.

> Writing was the method through which I constituted the world and reconstituted myself. Writing became my principal tool through which I learned about myself and the world. I wrote so I could have a life. Writing was and is *how* I come to know.
>
> (p. 33)

Of course, it isn't necessary to have a near-death experience to benefit from Richardson's insights into the relationship between writing and thinking. Other writers have made a similar point. William Zinsser frames his perspective rather differently, but the essence is the same.

Julie's process and product writing experience

As a child, I have always enjoyed writing – mostly diaries and letters to friends. Writing allowed me to put my thoughts and feelings down on paper and escape into an imaginary world where I could be the sole author of the stories I wanted to create. At the time, writing was probably more of a therapeutic process than a thinking process. Not until writing my doctoral thesis, did I come to understand writing as a thinking and discovery process. My thesis project involved autoethnographic writing where I, as researcher and participant of my research, used my own multilingual experiences and research writing to understand processes of multilingual identity development. My stories, which turned out to be a combination of analysis of various artifacts from my history, memories of personal encounters with others, and interpretations of these experiences drawing on academic and non-academic literature, felt stilted, disconnected, and unrelatable when I separated the content and practices into traditional doctoral thesis sections (i.e., Introduction, Literature Review, Methodology, Data Analysis, Discussion, and Conclusion). The stories needed to be scholarly, but I also wanted them to connect and resonate with readers. I began looking into storytelling writing techniques from genres such as creative non-fiction, which enabled me to engage in a creative process of melding academic and non-academic writing processes. I experimented (often with great frustration and uncertainty) with many different narrative structures and writing advice from different books but as soon as I brought my experiences to the writing, I found myself abandoning the models. I realized there was no existing structure I could follow and none of the advice made sense to my own ways of thinking and making meaning. Coming across Richardson's article on 'writing as a method of discovery' was a revelation; I instantly stopped trying to fit into other people's templates and started to discover what my story was about using writing/thinking processes that made sense to me.

Meaning started emerging in ways I understood to be meaningful. But this creative process also made me realize how vague my understandings of the expectations in each of the sections were, and how important it was to learn them *explicitly* in order to make sure I was producing a text that would be recognized as 'legitimate' by a community of scholars. This sounds terrible, but up until my doctorate, I don't think I gave much thought to the need for an explicit understanding of what I was expected to produce. Like many others, I learned to write academically through imitation, and one could 'get away with' a bit of vagueness in their writing.

I became obsessed with learning about the expectations of each section carefully and when I had a crystal-clear understanding, the 'rules' no longer felt like requirements or constraints. They became valuable thinking tools that helped me to produce a particular kind of knowledge that would not have been possible otherwise. The tools provided me with structure. The product of my thesis (also, now turned into a book, see Choi, 2017), what my research story turned out to be, are products of trusting in my own creative process and using the 'rules', the expectations, as tools to not only figure out what I wanted to say but also to make an original contribution to knowledge in my field. Done purposefully and strategically, one might say in this context, "the act of playing the game has a way of changing the rules" (Gleick, 1987, p. 24). But one has to know the rules before anything can be changed.

I learned the structures, rules, and expectations at a time when it was meaningful to learn them and had a context to plug in the information. Without freedom to explore, some sense of power that my ways of thinking are legitimate, a purpose, and resources to learn the rules of the game, I don't think I would be able to appreciate what both processes and product approaches offer in providing the kind of 'transformative' experience that writing can provide. My own transformative experience has now helped me to see writing in the way Foucault once described his way of understanding writing:

> An experience is something that one comes out of transformed. If I had to write a book to communicate what I'm already thinking before I begin to write, I would never have the courage to begin. I write a book only because I still don't exactly know what to think about this thing I want so much to think about, so that the book transforms me and what I think.
>
> (Foucault, 2001, pp. 239–240)

Making connections

Think about your own writing process.

Do you make lists and notes, brainstorm with peers or fellow students, write drafts, etc.? What is the most effective and least effective aspect of your writing technique?

How do your techniques change depending on the subject/topic and goal of the writing task – to produce an assignment, to write a letter to the editor, to produce a blog, etc.?

Where would you place yourself on – the product-oriented/process-oriented continuum?

Think of a topic or subject that is of interest to you but about which you know comparatively little. Without consulting the Internet or other resources, brainstorm a list of everything you know or think you know about the topic. Now begin writing. Don't try to polish your text as you go or worry too much about grammar, spelling, or pronunciation. The aim is for you to experience the method of writing as a thinking process. Try to write about 500 words. Revise and polish your initial effort.

Evaluate your experience. Was it challenging? Did you learn something you didn't know, or didn't think you knew about the topic? Did you learn something new about yourself?

> … we write to find out what we know and what we want to say. I thought of how often as a writer I had made clear to myself some subject I had previously known nothing about just by putting one sequence after another – by reasoning my way in sequential steps to its meaning. I thought of how often the act of writing even the simplest document – a letter for instance – had clarified my half-formed ideas. Writing and thinking and learning were the same process.
>
> (Zinsser, 2013, pp. viii–ix)

Questions from readers

Q: You mention the use of fiction techniques in writing up qualitative research. When I was in high school, I wanted to be a creative writer. I wrote tons of short stories and even got one published in a local newspaper completion, but that's as far as I got. Can you say a bit more about the use of fiction techniques in academic writing? I don't know if I'd have the courage to try out fiction techniques in one of my term papers. What do you think?

A: Let's deal with your second question first. Christine Tardy isn't opposed to creativity and innovation, of course, or she wouldn't have written *Beyond Convention*. But she warns of the dangers of pushing innovation too far, particularly if you are a younger, inexperienced writer. Established writers have a better chance of pushing academic boundaries because they've demonstrated mastery of conventional genres. Regarding term papers, we would say, 'proceed with caution'. You're writing for a known audience – your teachers. How are they likely to react?

Let's return to your first question. Fiction techniques have been used for many years by creative non-fiction writers. That's no surprise. Fundamental to both forms are narrative and storytelling. In academic circles, not all qualitative researchers are keen on the idea. In fact, some hold views that are as conservative as their quantitative counterparts, although they're in the minority, and it's a minority that continues to dwindle. Many leading proponents of adapting techniques from the world of fiction argue that the distinction between fiction and non-fiction has always been fuzzy. With the passage of time, it grows fuzzier. Norman Denzin (2018) goes so far as to argue that everything written is fiction, pointing out that the Latin derivation, *ficto*, means 'something constructed'. This echoes Richardson's assertion that when we write, we are constructing a representation of the experiential world with words. However, she warns, the word-world is not the same as the experiential world. Ethnographers and autoethnographers draw on a wide variety of sources to tell their lived stories. In her own autoethnography, Julie lists "short stories, poetry, fiction, novels, photographic essays, personal essays, journals, fragmented and layered writing, and social science prose" (Choi, 2017, p. 28). Norman Denzin (2018) goes so far as to suggest that ethnographic and autoethnographic writing is a performance.

Q: How does process writing deal with writing texts such as writing scientific reports? Do they have specific strategies?

A: As we've said, the scientific report has a rather rigid generic structures and conventions when it comes to the final product. If you're studying or working in one of these areas, it's advisable to stick to the demands of the discipline. However, there is nothing to stop you borrowing techniques from process approaches as you produce an initial draft, and then revise, push, pull, and polish successive drafts until you have a product that is acceptable to your audience, whether this is a member of the academic, business, or some other community.

Q: Julie talks about the moment she had a 'crystal-clear understanding' that helped her to go beyond seeing rules as requirements or constraints. What did this understanding involve? What exactly does one have to learn to begin to see rules like this?

Julie: It involves learning about genres. Having a clear understanding of the purpose of the text, a structure to work with, and common language features helped me to organize my thoughts and made me feel more confident because I knew I was producing what was expected. However, I don't think I was just carrying out 'the expected'. I thought a lot about how to create scholarly first-person narratives and what the best form of representation would be for the message I wanted to get across. My writing decisions weren't dictated by templates or rules; they were helpful tools to ensure I was creating appropriate texts, but they had to be thought about creatively and strategically in relation to other elements of writing such as voice, purpose, audience, and so on. I sometimes wonder whether it would have been good for me to have a 'crystal clear understanding' of the thesis writing genre when I started. It could have constrained me. In some ways, not being so clear forced me to experiment, explore, and exercise my creativity.

Q: I teach adult learners who have never learned to write. What approach (process, product, writing as a method of discovery) should I be taking with such learners to start their writing journey?

David: Writers who have low levels of literacy need clear frameworks and models to follow in the initial stages of learning to write. For example, copying a model email to a friend, but inserting into a gap-fill email template content that is relevant to them such as their name and where they are living. As they develop a basic mastery over genres such as personal emails to family and friends, aspects of process writing can be introduced. Years ago, when I was teaching low-literacy immigrants and refugees, as my students began to develop their writing skills, I encouraged them to begin keeping simple diaries. Then, through a dialogue journal approach, I helped them revise and polish their initial efforts. (For a description and discussion of dialogue journals, see Chiesa & Bailey, 2015.)

Summary

In this chapter, we have looked at product- and process-oriented approaches to writing. Throughout the chapter, we argue that all writing is a process that results in a product. Although the rest of this book focuses mainly on writing as process, we don't want to imply that the product is unimportant. The destination of most thinking/writing journeys is a product: a term paper, a journal article, a report on the state of the economy, a newspaper account of a battle in a war zone, an autobiography, or some other form of personal narrative. However, as Richardson reminds us, not all writing will be destined to land on the desktop of an external (and usually unknown) reader. If we employ writing as a tool to facilitate our thinking and as an aid to untangle jumbled vaguely held notions, the product may be a journal or diary entry which has an audience of one – ourselves. We will pursue this notion further the next chapter where we address the issues of purpose and audience.

Further readings

Hyland, K. (2009). *Teaching and researching writing* (2nd ed.). Pearson Education.
    Written by one of the major authorities in the field, this book is a guide to current theoretical, empirical and practical approaches to the teaching and learning of writing. It presents complex concepts in a manner which will prove useful for the experienced teacher/researcher, while being accessible to less experienced students.

Martin, J., & Rose, D. (2012). *Learning to write/reading to learn: Scaffolding democracy in literacy classrooms*. Equinox Publishing.
    This book provides insights into genre-based pedagogy informed by research of the 'Sydney School' in language and literacy pedagogy. It is written by two experts on the subject.

Nunan, D., & Choi, J. (Eds.). (2010). *Language and culture: Reflective narratives and the emergence of identity*. Routledge.
    In this edited collection, we invited key authors in the field to write a narrative based on a critical incident involving language learning, teaching, or communicating. They were then to analyze the narrative, drawing on relevant literature. Contributions to this collection provide models of how critical incident analysis can be carried out and exemplify the creative potential of academic writing.

References

Bowden, T. (1987). *One crowded hour: Neil Davis combat cameraman 1934–1985*. William Collins.

Chiesa, D., & Bailey, K. (2015). Dialogue journals: Learning for a lifetime. In D. Nunan & J. C. Richards (Eds.), *Language learning beyond the classroom* (pp. 53–62). Routledge.

Choi, J. (2017). *Towards a multivocal self: Autoethnography as method*. Routledge.

Denzin, N. (2018). *Performance autoethnography: Critical pedagogy and the politics of culture*. Routledge.

Forster, E. M. (1974). *Aspects of the novel and related writing*. Edward Arnold.

Foucault, M. (2001). *Power*. The New Press.

Gleick, J. (1987). *Chaos: Making of a new science*. Penguin Books.

Goodman, K. (2014). *What's whole about whole language in the 21st century?* Heinemann Educational Books.

Halliday, M. A. K. (2001). Literacy and linguistics: Relationships between spoken and written language. In A. Burns & C. Coffin (Eds.), *Analysing English in a global context* (pp. 181–193). Routledge.

Lawrence, M. (1972). *Writing as a thinking process*. University of Michigan Press.

Martin, J. R. (2001). Language, register and genre. In A. Burns & C. Coffin (Eds.), *Analysing English in a global context* (pp. 149–166). Routledge.

Matsuda, P., & Atkinson, D. (2008). A conversation on contrastive rhetoric. In U. Connor, N. Nagelhout, & W. Rozycki (Eds.), *Contrastive rhetoric: Reaching to intercultural rhetoric* (pp. 227–298). John Benjamins.

McCarthy, M. (1998). *Spoken language and applied linguistics*. Cambridge University Press.

Nunan, D. (2013). *What is this thing called language?* (2nd ed.). Palgrave Macmillan.

Richardson, L. (2001). Getting personal: Writing stories. *Qualitative Studies in Education, 14*(1), 33–38.

Sokolik, M. (2021). Writing. In D. Nunan (Ed.), *Practical English language teaching* (2nd ed.). Anaheim University Press.

Strunk, W., & White, E. B. (1959). *The elements of style*. Macmillan.

Tardy, C. (2016). *Beyond convention: Genre innovation in academic writing*. University of Michigan Press.

Zinsser, W. (2013). *Writing to learn: How to write and think clearly about any subject at all*. HarperCollins.

4
Audience and purpose

The celebrated actor, Sir Ian McKellen, best known these days for his role as Gandalf in the film version of Tolkien's novel *The Lord of the Rings*, tells of setting aside the better part of a year to write his autobiography. However, he never completed the project because he couldn't get a clear sense of his audience. As a stage actor, he would be acutely sensitive to the importance of audience. Being physically present, he was able to connect with audience members and engage them in the performance. For McKellen, changing roles from actor to author and redefining his notion of audience proved insurmountable.

In this chapter, we focus on purpose (why we write) and audience (for whom we write). While the two differ conceptually, when it comes to the act of writing, they're inseparable. This can, and does, cause problems for the writer when a piece intended for a particular purpose and audience ends up being used for a different purpose by someone for whom it was never intended.

Who gets to define purpose and audience? The answer to this question will depend on the type of writing and the genre. In the world of fiction, there are certain genres such as crime, thriller, science-fiction, historical novel, and so on. The purpose of such genres is reasonably circumscribed (to entertain, to inform), and the audience is self-selecting. As a student, when it comes to academic writing, your primary audience will be your teachers. A secondary audience could be your peers. There may also be times when you are writing for yourself, keeping a diary or journal, or, as we saw in the last chapter, writing as a form of self-discovery. Your primary reason for writing will be to fulfil course requirements, and the rationale for writing will be determined by the teacher or course director. In their book on writing, Coffin et al. (2003) list, as examples, the following purposes:

- as an aid to critical thinking, understanding, and memory
- to extend students' learning beyond lectures and other formal meetings

DOI: 10.4324/9781003179092-5

- to extend students' communication skills
- to train students as future professionals in particular disciplines

The importance of audience has long been acknowledged. Over 30 years ago, Kroll wrote that, "From Aristotle's *Rhetoric* to the latest composition textbook, we can find broad agreement that the writer's consideration of his (or her) audience exerts considerable influence on written communication" (Kroll, 1984, p. 172). Kroll goes on to point out that despite its centrality to effective communication, views on the nature of audience differ considerably. While it is not our purpose to spend time discussing theoretical arguments for or against these different views, we do want you to note that the notion of audience is complex and can be problematic.

As a writer, some audiences will be familiar to you, and some will not. If you are a student, the audience for most of what you write will be your teacher. It's reasonable to assume that writing for an audience you know, such as your teacher, will cause fewer problems than writing for an audience you don't know well, although this is not always the case, as we show later in the chapter.

The next section is given over to a conversation between David and Kailin Liu, an early career secondary school teacher and recently graduated university student. In the conversation, they discuss the challenges of audience and voice in academic writing.

Audience matters: a conversation with an emergent academic writer

The conversation began as an email exchange between David in Hong Kong, and Kailin in Melbourne. It was initiated when Kailin asked for feedback on a piece of writing. David was working on an early draft of this book, and Kailin was in her second year as a secondary school teacher. Later, when David was in Melbourne for an extended period during the second Covid outbreak, the conversation continued face-to-face. Originally from China, Kailin holds masters' degrees in applied linguistics and TESOL. In her applied linguistics thesis, she looked at how graduate students responded to different kinds of written feedback. Neomy, her supervisor, was so impressed with the research that she encouraged Kailin to revise and submit her thesis to a peer-reviewed journal. Neomy mentored her throughout the revision process and co-published the article with her when it was accepted for publication. Julie also played an important mentoring role in Kailin's development as a writer.

Much of what Kailin said in various email exchanges gave us insights into the dimension of 'audience', so we decided to turn the interview into an academic conversation presenting the information in three sections corresponding to different academic writing domains. Our purpose was to learn more about what is involved in thinking about 'audience' in academic writing. At three pivotal points, Julie enters the conversation and provides a reflective commentary on what she, as a university lecturer, is learning from Kailin's comments. The introduction of a 'third voice' is an innovative feature that you won't find in other academic conversations. (For example, see Heath & Kramsch, 2004; Matsuda & Atkinson, 2008.) You may want to make similar notes before reading Julie's thoughts and then compare the two.

Audience in coursework assignment writing

DN: When you wrote your university assignments, did you think about your audience: in your case, your lecturers and what you knew about their attitudes and interests?

KL: I think it depends. For some lecturers I know well and who demonstrate to me their particular position or interest toward certain issues, topics, or theories, I would be more inclined to try thinking, writing, and exploring from their perspective. I think this could be a rewarding experience as I may genuinely find their interests, concerns, or points of view resonant with my own life experiences and it helps extend my thinking. Yet, there are times where I find few connections with the theories they put forward. On these occasions, I found myself writing simply for the sake of gaining acknowledgment.

DN: And better marks, perhaps?

KL: Oh, better marks, for sure. At other times I don't know my lecturers well. I don't know what they value and how they evaluate my assignments (e.g., the rubrics may be too general to offer me any guidance, the lecturers may not provide feedback, or their feedback is too formulaic for me to learn anything from it). At these times, I may look at their previous research articles – if I can find any – to see what kind of person they are, what they care about, and what their stances are on certain issues. By getting to know them better through their writing or the way they teach in class, I can sense whether they'll like my assignments and how many marks they'll give me. Yet I think this process is just for me to get to know them. When I'm doing my writing, I'm still doing my own thing without thinking that I'm writing for them. I'm just trying to make the writing make sense to me and using writing as a way for me to organize my ideas. I think I don't tailor everything toward them not only because I don't know what they like but also that I feel some lecturers don't really care about my assignments. Maybe to avoid the disappointment of getting nothing from the lecturers on my writing, I downplay my expectations that they'll read my assignments carefully or to give me any meaningful feedback on drafts of my assignment. Writing assignments then becomes my own thing; it's a way to talk to myself and to work through the issues through writing and thinking.

DN: So you were basically writing for yourself – writing was part of the thinking process.

KL: Yes. Julie passed me various articles that got me thinking in that way.

DN: Such as?

KL: Such as Richardson's (2001) article about getting personal. And that gave me the idea for my thesis.

DN: Which was …?

KL: I wanted to explore the question of how L2 graduate students engage with and learn from different kinds of feedback. That question grew out of my own experience of the kind of feedback I got from my own lectures, as I already mentioned.

DN: This is interesting. I find reactions to my feedback varies enormously. Some students want to challenge me, some want more detailed feedback than I have time to give. Others don't seem to care about the comments – all they cared about is the grade. At the end of semester, I leave the assignments, with feedback attached, to be picked up at the faculty office. Some are never retrieved. The students get their grades online and just don't care about the feedback. Why do you think this is? What did you learn from the feedback you got on your thesis?

KL: My purpose was to explore the question of how graduate students from L2 backgrounds like me engage with and learn from different kinds of feedback. I wanted to get insights that I could apply to improve the quality of the feedback I give my own high school students – the kind of quality feedback that Julie gave me on my own assignments when I studied with her. Most existing studies didn't give the insights I was looking for. They were too limiting, only discussing written corrective feedback. Probably the best article I came across was by Dr. Ellis (2010) which was scholarly and thorough, but it didn't give me much to go on in terms of the questions I wanted answers to.

DN: That may not have been his purpose!

KL: Probably not. Anyway, during the process of researching, talking with my participants, and writing the thesis, another purpose came up – I wanted my participants' voices to be heard. I *really* did. I understood where they were coming from because their experiences were just like mine. I understand that in class, lecturers may not have a chance to get to know these students, so I hoped my little study could help them understand a bit more about these learners and how they engage with and learn (or don't learn) from the feedback.

Julie's commentary: meaning-full self-strategies to sense 'the audience'

In this increasingly 'de-humanized', mechanistic educational economy of pushing out content with fewer instruction hours and opportunities to connect with students in increasingly large classroom sizes, I find it amazing that there are still highly thoughtful students like Kailin who do just the opposite, enacting all the rich humanly ways in which we learn, i.e., thinking, writing, exploring from others' perspectives, getting to know the lecturers better by reading their articles, and gaining a sense not only of a lecturer through the ways in which he/she teaches but also relating that sense back to whether the lecturer will like what she produces. These are not simple tricks and tips in thinking about 'audience' but ways of learning full of meaning-making ('meaning-full' strategies?) that require time, cognitive energy, and thoughtful relational work. Unsurprisingly, discourses of "how many marks" also commonly feature in these assemblages of thinking about audience and writing assignments as part of one's coursework.

It is a shame that students have come to accept and adopt a position of low expectations in receiving "any meaningful feedback" on their assignments. That perception about the audience also shapes students' writing. But interestingly, this negative understanding doesn't seem to deter Kailin. She uses this phenomenon to investigate the issue further which not only extends her own literacy repertoire into the domain of research but also creates knowledge that contributes to the field (i.e., providing knowledge for busy lecturers, helping marginalized voices to be heard, and gaining insights to improve her own feedback to her current students).

I spend an inordinately crazy amount of time trying to give what I think of as meaningful feedback in my students' assignments (and this is not easy to do when you have a 150 papers to mark each semester with only three weeks turnaround time!), but if "the kind of quality feedback that [I] gave" has played some role in motivating Kailin to improve on her own feedback responses, that feels really rewarding. It just goes to show that students need to experience and see what 'quality' and 'meaningfulness' look like if we want them to enact these in the future, which also begs the question, 'have teachers ever written for an audience that gave them meaningful feedback?' And if so, what did that meaningful feedback look like? This is a question we take up in the chapter on feedback.

From thesis to journal article

DN: So now you've had your article published for publication in a respectable referred journal. Let's talk about how this came about and the challenges and stumbling blocks you encountered along the way.

KL: When I was doing the study, it never occurred to me that it might be considered for publication. The suggestion first came from two anonymous examiners in the faculty. One of them said reading the thesis helped her understand more about her learners. This was the first time I realized that my research question had some value and could be shared with many others. That's the moment I thought my findings, and the message that learners engage with feedback in complex ways, could be shared with a wider audience. And of course, on a practical or strategic level, I knew that if this paper was published, it could be very helpful for a PhD application in the future. So, I think all these made me want to grab this chance and revise my thesis in whatever ways to get it published.

DN: How about when you were working on your thesis? What were your thoughts about your audience?

KL: I don't think I had a particular audience in mind when I was working on my thesis. I knew Neomy, my supervisor, would be reading my thesis and giving me feedback, but I don't think I was particularly writing for her. Rather than considering Neomy as 'the audience', I thought of her more as a mentor, someone who was actively involved in the process of my creation, offering me ideas and ways of organization. As I mentioned before, the process of writing this thesis was mainly about me trying to get the ideas straight for myself – to use writing as a way to help me explore and understand the question that I was asking and to describe my understandings in a way that was coherent and made sense to me. My writing needs to make sense to me first so that I can then hand it over to other people, such as Neomy, to see if it makes sense to them. But problems did come up with purpose and audience.

DN: In relation to the thesis or the journal article?

KL: Both. As I mentioned earlier, in my thesis, I wanted my participants' voices to be heard. When I was writing the findings and discussion sections in particular, I had strong hope that some university lecturers could read this and develop a greater understanding of graduate L2 learners. While I'm not entirely sure how this desire impacted my ways of writing, I think maybe it encouraged me to try to write in a way that clearly reflected my participants' ideas. I wanted to present my research in a way that didn't accuse certain people or turn people off, but would attract both university lecturers and my participants to read the paper.

DN: You mean that you didn't want university lecturers to be offended by your conclusion that they didn't listen to or want to know how their L2 learners dealt with feedback on assignments?

KL: Exactly. Then when I was revising the paper for publication, the audience was even more blurry to me. I knew the paper would be critically examined by many experienced researchers, but I wasn't quite sure what they would be looking for. I went back to my principle that I wanted my writing to make sense to me. I then wholeheartedly followed Neomy's advice for revision.

DN: Journal reviewers always have recommendations for revisions. How many reviews did you receive? Did the reviewers agree and/or diverge on the changes that would need to be made for the article to be accepted? Did you accept all recommended changes? How did you respond to the journal editor regarding recommended changes you disagreed with?

KL: We received feedback from four reviewers. The suggestions didn't diverge too much. The main issue was to incorporate a conceptual/theoretic framework and refer to it throughout the article. Although I strongly agreed with the advice, I was a bit reluctant to begin with because it meant refocusing and rewriting the entire article. But in the end, I did it.

DN: Did you think that you had to incorporate all their suggestions into your revised article?

KL: Yes. But Neomy said that wasn't necessary. She advised me on which to follow and which to disregard, also how we could address certain issues.

DN: She is right, but it's a good idea to let the editor know why you're not incorporating certain recommendations.

KL: In this process of getting the paper published, I just became a humble little person, listening to and accepting all the suggestions and ideas coming from Neomy and the reviewers. I just wanted to get this paper acknowledged in the field. Some of their criticisms I didn't quite understand. For example, one reviewer said that our statistical analyses weren't well developed. I worried about how I could make this better, but Neomy said that we could ignore this comment because we were only using descriptive stats, not inferential ones. In any case, Neomy and I were in the process of writing and revising together. My writing had been reviewed and revised hundreds of times by her, which made me feel like I have an ally and together we can cope with whatever comes at us from the public.

Julie's commentary: supervisors/mentors/experts as mediators to 'the audience'

Just as there are practical considerations such as 'marks' involved in thinking about 'audience', here we also see personal strategic dimensions (PhD application possibilities) and negotiations of how much actual work is involved (time, energy, etc.) in taking on feedback from the audience.

Unlike coursework where students generally submit a piece of writing and put it aside, in this domain of thesis writing and publishing, students take on the role of an apprentice. Supervisors may or may not be experts in students' actual research focus, but they have the knowledge that can guide students to the other side of the fence. This knowledge involves subject content knowledge as well as their understanding of the field, the scholarly practices, and cultural discourses they have accumulated over many years of experience to develop a sense for what the audience (the reviewers) want. In this regard, they are not only supervisors/mentors but also mediators that can help students gain a sense for what the audience expects. Thesis writing and publishing are generally high-stakes activities so the seriousness of it all I think can bring students to realize themselves as a "humble little person" which I think can also be a conducive disposition to have when one is an emerging academic writer. Humility also doesn't mean that the apprentice isn't thinking for herself. A recurring strategy in Kailin's way of learning to write in her ever-expanding academic environments is her need to make sense of the writing for herself first. And that's really where the bulk of the thinking and creative work happens. The supervisors can then provide their own input on whether the ideas work or not, which they often do in many rounds of discussion, and we can see in Kailin's case, all that collaborative revising work create a sense of confidence in putting forth her work.

So, unlike the first part of the conversation where there is a lot of personal guesswork that students need to do to gain a sense for one's audience (with little meaningful feedback), in research-related practices we see how supervisors can play an explicit role in helping students to gain a clearer understanding of what examiners/reviewers are looking for. Importantly, what I am learning is what makes 'audience' matter for students. We see in Kailin's comments, receiving feedback from experts saying something she wrote mattered to them and the possibilities for sharing her work on a public platform where her work could have the potential to do something in the world, also played a role in wanting to write better (i.e., learning to represent the participants' thoughts as accurately as possible and at the same time working on the tone so that the work will be inclusive and engaging).

Going public

DN: How did you feel when the article finally appeared?

KL: I was thrilled, seeing my name and my article in print. I'm very happy that it was accepted for publication. I still can't quite believe it!

DN: Overall, then, the experience was a positive one. Do you plan to continue offering articles for publication? Would you consider writing for a journal or magazine that isn't peer-reviewed?

KL: Overall, yes, I think it was positive, although I felt that during the process the focus became directed more toward publication than my original purpose which was to get my participants' voices heard and my desire to build connections between students and lecturers. Publishing became the overriding purpose, and writing was about how I could weave my data nicely together under the new theoretical framework. While this was also an interesting experience as it enabled me to see something new in my data, at the same time I might have lost the kind of human touch or care that I had while writing my thesis. This paper was created more for the sake of publication than a genuine exploration as was the case with my thesis. Having said that, I've learned a lot through this experience. Writing for publication has altered my ways of thinking about and doing research.

I would like to continue exploring the questions that I'm interested in for language education, and if I can write well and am fortunate enough, I would love to see my work reach a wider audience through publication. I'm not quite sure about writing for non-peer-reviewed journals or magazines. I don't know the audience for these journals or magazines and don't yet have the confidence to think about publishing by myself. By sending my work to a peer-reviewed journal, hopefully I'll receive some experienced reviewers' feedback or acknowledgment before showing my writing to the public.

Julie's commentary: audience matters

While a public platform can stimulate our writing (as pointed out in the previous commentary), getting caught up in publication goals can also sideline intentions and passions that originally drove our work. However, as in all the comments Kailin made throughout this process, it is clear that she is thinking carefully about where she can continue to contribute her work, according to her knowledge about the audience and places where she can continue to grow. By continuing to send in her work to peer-reviewed journals, she is developing her own 'feel' for the context, audience, and purpose. This kind of learning by doing begins to move young academic writers away from their reliance on their supervisors and into more agentic roles as independent writers and thinkers. If they have opportunities to become journal article reviewers themselves, this new role will strengthen their "feel" for the audience.

I particularly like what Kailin says, "writing for publication has altered [her] ways of thinking about and doing research". Thinking about all that I have learned from Kailin's experience, I now understand matters of 'audience' and purpose in particular domains of academic writing (in this case, research writing) is never just about who our audience is and what the purpose is, but a concept that involves negotiations between strategies, meaningfulness and meaninglessness, power, knowledge, networks, as well as grades, future possibilities, and other logistical considerations such as time and energy. For students interested in writing, good mentors can open incredibly powerful academic pathways for thinking, writing, and becoming.

The art and craft of writing

'How to' books on writing often begin with the cliché that writing is both an art and a craft. (Google '*the art and craft of creative/academic/business writing*' and you'll see what we mean.) While accepting the claim, in this book we have focused on writing as a craft. The word is most commonly defined as the skilled creation by hand of an object such as a piece of furniture, pottery, or tapestry. In a sense, the definition fits. Essays, dissertations, journal articles, and other written genres are 'objects' you produce by hand. The degree of skill evident in the final product will be determined by your audience.

If you want to develop the skills to make furniture you need to find someone who has already develop these skills and learn them from observation, imitation, feedback, guidance, and direct instruction. In other words, you have to apprentice yourself to a master furniture-maker. This can take years, which brings us back to the academic conversation. In it, Kailin details the apprenticeship she received through Neomy's supervision.

David made a more modest contribution to her development through an extended conversation that began when she asked for feedback on a piece she had written. The parts of the conversation that are relevant to audience and purpose were shaped into the academic conversation you have just read.

Rather than taking a red pen to the piece, David revised it and asked Kailin to read the revised version and note the modifications that he made. They then discussed the nature of the changes and why these were made. Some were motivated by factors outside the text such as audience and purpose. Others were determined by factors inside the text. David sought to strengthen paragraph level coherence by adjusting theme/rheme structuring sentence-by-sentence, so the link from one sentence to the next was made explicit for the audience. Text-level coherence was improved by switching a number of paragraphs around within the piece.

David pointed out to Kailin that constructing a paragraph that is clear and coherent to the reader is a form of problem-solving. Here's where the art comes in. Knowledge of theme/rheme, coordinate, and subordinate clauses and other grammatical devices are the tools, the hammer, and chisel, you use to sculpt a paragraph that will convey your intended meaning clearly to the reader. You start with the purpose you have for your paragraph in relation to the purpose of the text as a whole as well as the audience you're writing for – insofar as you know who your audience is. In most cases, if your audience is a teacher, you'll be writing a 'display' piece. The purpose is not to tell your teacher something she doesn't already know, but to display to her what *you* know. So, you include everything that is pertinent to the topic. If your purpose is to convey content to a 'real' audience, you have to make decisions about what information to include and what to leave out. You won't want to include everything. If you do, the audience may assume you're either patronizing or simple-minded.

Let us give you a concrete example by describing how we began to fashion the first paragraph of this section. To start with, all we had was the section title and a general idea of what we wanted to tell you. Just as the first paragraph is key to the success or otherwise of the rest of the section, the first sentence is key to the success or otherwise of the rest of the paragraph. It sets the direction for the rest of the paragraph. How it's structured, limit the options available to you when it comes to the second sentence. As such, it will present the problem of how the second sentence should be structured. Solving that problem will present you with the problem of how to structure sentence number 3 and so on throughout the construction of the rest of the paragraph.

Our first attempt at the sentence began as follows:

As we said at the beginning of the previous section, including a conversation … We didn't even complete the sentence because it was pointing us in a direction we didn't want to go. Also, the lengthy, somewhat clumsy, and redundant clause at the beginning, threatened the sentence with collapse before it had been completed.

We tried again:

The previous section explores challenges confronting, and opportunities presented to …

Better, but not much. We needed to take our marching orders from the section heading. We wrote:

It's a cliché to suggest that writing is an art and a craft…

The paragraph was heading where we wanted it to go, but not as precisely as we wanted. Already, we were considering sentence 2. Finally, at the fourth attempt, we arrived at a sentence that we were happy with. Although not absolutely sure of how the theme would evolve, the direction had been set. Sentence 2 was an aside, and we signaled this by enclosing it in brackets. The succeeding sentences were knitted together thematically. (You might like to return to the paragraph and examine how we did this in terms of thematization and given/new structuring.)

In the rest of the section, we revisit the register variables of field, tenor, and mode, show how they relate to audience and voice, and demonstrate how they are fundamental to achieving clarity and coherence in your writing. Confused and confusing paragraphs (ours as well as yours) are a result of failing to keep in mind our audience and our relationship to that audience (tenor), our purpose, that is, what we want to tell our audience about the subject at hand (field), and the mode (how we are going to inform our audience). As we craft each sentence, we should ask ourselves:

- Is what I've just written appropriate to my audience in terms of my use of language?
- Is it appropriate in terms of what I want to say?
- Is the mode I have selected appropriate for the audience and purpose?

While field, tenor, and mode are interrelated, particular attention needs to be paid to the second question, relating to field, the *what* of we want we want to say. At the level of paragraph construction, this does not relate to the overall topic and purpose of our piece of writing. This should be covered in the introduction to the text, regardless of whether it is as limited as an assignment on climate change or as extensive as book or academic writing. It has to do with that aspect of the subject we want to address in any given paragraph. Herein lies the problem. It stems from the non-linearity of the experiential world we are trying to represent in print. There will always be many things we want to tell our audience – far more than our paragraph can encompass. Our brain fizzes with ideas that are not connected in a clear, coherent, linear sequence. (Brains don't work like that!) To produce a clear, coherent paragraph, the ideas have to be presented in a linear sequence, the logic of which is made clear to our audience through theme/rheme structuring. Failure to obey this injunction is one factor that leads to confused and confusing writing.

And so, as you've seen from our example, the struggle begins with the initial sentence. This will, or should, determine the direction of the entire paragraph. We showed you the struggle we had to set the direction for the first sentence of the paragraph that initiated this section. We did so, not because we wanted sympathy, but to show you that the challenge never goes away, regardless of how experienced of a writer you are.

After much massaging, you have an initial sentence for your paragraph. You work hard to craft the next sentence, so it flows in a clear, linear fashion from the first. Then what happens? You have another brain fizz. An idea pops into your head that demands your attention. Rather than parking it aside for a future paragraph or abandoning it altogether, you write it down. When your piece finally goes public, the effect on your audience, in this case your lecturer, is jarring. Your paragraph has lost its way, and you have lost your reader. She scratches her head, wonders what on earth your paragraph is on about, and reaches for her red pen.

We conclude the section with an example of how a writer's confusion of audience, purpose, and mode leads to a failure on the part of the writer to achieve her purpose.

Making connections

Below is an email to Julie from a prospective student. What is the purpose of the email and why does it fail to achieve its effect?

> *Dear Prof. Choi,*
>
> *For a research project I do need to get my hand on your thesis 'narrative analysis of second language acquisition and identity formation'. I'd highly appreciate it if you could possibly mail it to me.*
>
> *By the way, I am currently reading your invaluable and innovative book 'Language and Culture: Reflective narratives and the emergence of identity' co-edited by Prof. Nunan. The narratives are hilarious. Nice job. Looking forward to reading more from you.*
>
> *My best wishes*

Retrieve from your sent mailbox an email related to work/study and a recent piece of academic writing. Compare the two in terms of subject (field) and relationship of you to the audience (tenor). Keeping the field constant, rewrite each piece swapping the tenor and mode (i.e., rewrite the email as an academic piece and vice-versa).

- What changes to the language did you make to each piece?
- What insights did the exercise reveal about the relationship between the register variables and language?

Tailoring your writing to different audiences

Before you begin writing, you should ask yourself three questions:

* What do I want to say?
* What do I want to achieve?
* Who am I writing for?

Answering these questions will help you deal with a fourth: How will I craft my text to achieve the desired effect on the intended audience? This question takes us to issues of style, tone, and voice as well as the stance you take toward the content you are dealing with. These issues are the subject of the next chapter. Obviously, your work will be more positively received if your views match those of your audience. Politicians are well-versed in tailoring their message to their audience, which can result in charges of hypocrisy when they take one position on a controversial issue with one audience and a different position with another. As we saw in the conversation with Kailin, these questions aren't always easy to answer. Like Kailin, you are probably a student, and your primary audience will be your teachers, and, like Kailin, some teachers you will know well, and some you won't. Although your primary purpose will be to get a good grade, you won't always want to do so by matching your views to those of your teacher – assuming you know what they are.

In the rest of this section, we illustrate how David took a text intended to achieve a particular purpose with one audience and tailored it to a different one.

Making connections

What do you think David's purpose was for each text? Who was his intended audience? How are these reflected in the language choices he makes?

Text 1

There is some contention in the literature over the distinction between the verbs 'to educate' and 'to teach' and the corresponding nouns 'educator' and 'teacher'. Some argue that there is no difference, others that the difference is palpable. A parent teaches her son to tie his shoes. It would be unremarkable to hear the parent performing such action referred to as a teacher, but never as an educator. Teachers of non-academic subjects impart knowledge and teach skills, that are often intricate and take considerable time and effort to master, such as how to wire a house, drive a car, or make a sponge cake. The implication is that when it comes to these skills, the learner is a *tabula rasa*, a blank slate. Educators, rather than pushing information in, have a more sophisticated conceptualization of the learning process. Learners are not blank slates. Even young children possess considerable and rapidly expanding bodies of knowledge (Gopnik, Meltziff, & Kuhl, 1999). The educator's task is to draw upon this nascent knowledge and use it as a scaffold on which to construct new knowledge. 'Education', they point out, is derived from the Latin 'educere' or to 'draw out'. Craft (1984) argues that this is an oversimplification, that the English word 'education' is based on two Latin roots with quite different meanings: 'educare', to train or mold, and 'educere' to lead out. Philosophers of education argue that there is a basic distinction between education, which is devoted to the acquisition of abstract knowledge and higher order thinking skills, and vocational teaching which focuses on practical skills such as knowing how to drive a truck or plumb a house (Dearden, Hirst, & Peters, 1972).

Bass and Good (2004) argue that both meanings can be integrated in educational systems such as public schools and universities which have a responsibility to both educate and teach.

Text 2

For most people, the terms 'teacher', 'instructor', and 'educator' are synonymous. Educator is a fancier, and more pretentious, term for the classroom practitioner. Certainly, most dictionaries see the terms as synonymous. I just consulted the online Oxford Dictionary of English and checked the meaning of *educator*. The dictionary stated that an educator is a person who provides instruction or education; a teacher. Let's put aside the circularity of the definition – "*an educator is someone who provides education*" – and examine the concepts more closely.

If you ask a person on the street what it means to teach, he or she is like to reply.

> It means to show or to explain to someone how to do something, you know, to pass on information that the other person doesn't have, or to teach them a skill such as how to read or how to drive a car.

(I know this is the likely reaction, because over the years I've asked plenty of non-teachers what it means 'to teach'.)

This view of teaching is known as 'transmission' teaching because one person (the 'knower') is transmitting information into the heads of other people, known as learners, students, or pupils. In schools, there are people who are masters of certain content knowledge – mathematics, science, and the like – who are paid to pass this content on to those who don't possess it. They are known as teachers or instructors.

I would argue that this is a very limited view of that art and craft of teaching. In the first place, the 'transmission' view is a poverty-stricken one. The mind of the child is not an empty vessel waiting to have information poured into it. In fact, research has demonstrated that for learners of any age, the lecture is one of the least effective means of bringing about learning. Educators, who take a broader view, have always known this. Over 2,000 years ago, the philosopher Socrates, possibly the first of the great educators, said that "Education is not the filling of a vessel, but the lighting of a flame". In fact, the English word *education* is derived from the Latin word *educere*, "to draw out", to work with what learners already know, and to shape, refine, and develop that knowledge to build bridges between what they already know and what they need to learn.

Here is David's commentary on the texts.

The audience for the first text was aimed at graduate students and teachers. Its purpose was to tease out differences between educating and teaching/ instructing in the context of a discussion on the purpose of education. In the second text, I wanted to discuss the same issue for an educated but non-specialist audience. It's extracted from a column I write on educational issues for lifestyle and culture magazine. The purpose of the column is to entertain, inform, and provoke thought in generally well-educated readers. There are no in-text citations or references to the work of other authors. I elaborate on terms that may be unfamiliar. For example, 'transmission teaching', is defined as "passing on, or transmitting, information to someone else who doesn't know". The colloquial expression, 'person on the street' which may be unfamiliar to some audiences, is glossed as a 'layperson' or "someone without specialist knowledge". Finally, the Latin derivation of 'education' is provided to stimulate deeper understanding of the central point of the article.

Making connections

Take a paragraph or two from a text that has been written for an academic audience. It could be a text you have written or a published piece written by someone else. Rewrite it so that it accessible for a non-specialist (lay) audience. What changes did you make?

Writing for yourself

As we've already mentioned, if you are a student, most of the writing you do will be for a known audience – your teachers. We also noted that this isn't always straightforward. Some teachers will be more approachable and sympathetic to your ideas and feelings than others. If you write for public consumption, for example, writing a newsletter piece, producing an article for a journal, or posting your writing on the Internet, your audience could be anyone who happens to open the journal or stumbles across your blog. In addition to the audience, you know and the audience you don't, there is one other individual you need to consider – you!

But why would we write for ourselves? Purposes vary. A hastily scribbled shopping list reminds us not to forget the washing powder and eggs. Keeping a diary can provide us with a reflective record of our everyday life as well as a note of appointments and commitments. In the last chapter, we wrote about how Richardson described personal writing as a thinking process, the idea being that through writing we can discover things we didn't know. You may have wondered how this is possible, that the notion is counterintuitive, paradoxical even. In our own work, we have found that the process of writing our way into a topic we know little about or trying to find our way toward an unknown destination (as we illustrated earlier in the chapter) can open up all sorts of possibilities. It can peel back layers of memory, making explicit facts and phenomena that have been locked away in our subconsciousness. It can help us see connections between things that we had previously thought to be unrelated. It can restructure and bring into sharp focus vaguely formed ideas and shards of information. Writing as a means of discovery can work in these and other ways. In the conversation between Kailin and David, Kailin touches on Richardson's article. It was so influential it set her on a path that led to her to the thesis topic that had, to that point, proved elusive. While you may later share with others the discoveries you made and insights you generated, in the first instance, you are your own primary audience. Writing for yourself, in the first instance, can help you address the first of the key questions we posed above: What do I want to say? This will be crucial when it comes to writing for others.

A journal, like a diary, is another example of writing that, initially at least, is intended for the self. An academic or professional journal provides an opportunity to reflect and record, not on everyday life, but on concerns and issues to do with your student or professional life. As authors, we keep track of our various writing projects along with problems, frustrations, and occasional successes. Here's a suggestion for graduate students on keeping a research journal from two highly experienced writers and researchers.

> Each time you think of a question for which there seems to be no ready answer, write the question down. Someone may write or talk about something that is fascinating, and you may wonder if the same results would obtain with your students, or bilingual children, or with a different genre of text. Write this in your journal. Perhaps you take notes as you read articles, observe classes, or listen to lectures. Place a star or other symbol at places where you have questions. These ideas will then be easy to find and transfer to the journal. Of course, not all of these ideas will evolve into research topics. Like a writer's notebook, these bits and pieces of research ideas will reformulate themselves almost like magic. Ways to redefine, elaborate or reorganize the questions will occur as you as you read the entries.
>
> (Hatch & Lazaraton, 1991, pp. 11–12)

Making connections

Using the suggestions of Hatch and Lazaraton as a point of departure, keep a journal relating to your studies or professional life. It could have a specific focus such as research, or it could be a reading journal in which you note your reflections and reactions to the set readings for your course. However, it could be more general, relating to one or more of the courses you are taking. If possible, keep it over the course of a semester. If that proves difficult, keep it for at least a month. Write something every day and try to write a minimum of 200 words. During this period, resist the temptation to look back over what you've written. (Kathi Bailey suggests that you tape or staple the pages together to help you resist temptation.) Be as candid as you can. Remember, you're writing for an audience of one! At the end of the period, reread what you've written. What themes or issues emerge? What do you learn about yourself as a student, reader, or writer?

For an authoritative and comprehensive overview of journal writing and audience, see Casanave (2014). Although the book is aimed at the field of second-language education, it contains helpful information and background for anyone interested in keeping a journal.

Questions from readers

Q: One of my biggest challenges is getting stuck. It can happen before I even put finger to keyboard or at any point during the process. When I read your draft chapter, I thought it might have something to do with the fact that I'm often unsure of the audience I'm writing for or have doubts about what it is that I'm trying to say. Can you give me some advice?

A: There's a technical term for your condition – writer's block. Every writer suffers from it at some time or other. And, yes, being unsure of who you're writing for and your purpose in writing, other than fulfilling program requirements and getting a passing grade are two causes of writer's block. One way to get 'unblocked' is to follow the advice of a famous American writer who said that your audience should be a single reader. Rather than trying to write for an unknown audience, pick out a person, real or imagined, and write for them. Our friend and colleague, the late Ruth Wajnryb, said that's what got her through the writing of her doctoral dissertation. When she suffered a crippling bout of writer's block, she obtained a photo of a writer she really admired, taped it to the wall above her desk, and wrote the thesis for him. She got outstanding reports from her examiners.

Another cause of writer's block is that we run out of steam. We think we have nothing more to say on the topic. One solution here is to stop writing for the day, or evening, while you still have something to say on the subject, or when you know what you're going to say next. You'll then have a head start the next time you boot up your computer. If that doesn't work, try 'speed writing'. Turn off your phone and iPad so you won't be tempted to check your bank account or send a congratulatory birthday text to your favorite niece. Open a blank word document and write 300 words relevant to the assignment you're working on. Don't worry about spelling, punctuation, or grammar – you can deal with those later. Don't stop writing until you're the word counter on your computer tells you that you've reached you target.

Q: The writing I have to do for my course is completely artificial. The only person who reads the stuff is my teacher and you can hardly call her an 'audience', can you? I'm a business studies major, and at the moment I'm writing an essay on marketing. She knows way more about the subject than I do. I won't be telling her anything I don't already know, and I'll in any case, I'll probably get it wrong. Her role is to test me, not to learn something, right?

A: Up to a point, this is true. But audiences play different roles. Don't expect your teacher to be cognizant of what you know. What she wants to learn is what you know about the topic and how clearly you can express what you know. Yes, she will be critically evaluating you, but that will be the case with most, if not all, audiences. If you leave out certain facts on the grounds that your teacher already knows them, she's free to assume you don't know them and may mark you down accordingly.

Summary

Purpose and audience go hand in hand. A mismatch between what you wanted to say, why you want to say it, and who you want to tell will lead to problems. Clarity of purpose and audience will go a long way to achieving clarity in your writing. However, as a writer, you will not always have control over who reads your work. While knowing your audience can reduce the chances of your work being misinterpreted or misunderstood, this is not guaranteed. As a student, you may think you know your teachers. Some you will know better than others. Knowing your teachers well, knowing their biases, pet theories, and attitudes toward the topic you have chosen or been asked to write on will go some way toward getting you the grade you desire, but this is not always the case. In her interview, Kailin also described the tension between the need to gain a good grade by writing what the lecturers wanted to hear and the desire to pursue themes and perspectives that were important to her. At the heart of her dilemma was her desire to satisfy two audiences: herself and lecturers who were not particularly interested in reading what she had to say. In the end, she remained true to herself. Writing was a thinking process, and what she wrote had to make sense to her before she could produce a text that would make sense to others.

Writing for an unknown, or even partially unknown, audience brings its on challenges. The audience might be anonymous faculty member, external thesis examiners, or reviewers of referred journals. Having your writing evaluated by an unknown critic can result in writer's block, a malady feared by professional writers. It can be crippling, particularly if the deadline for submitting your writing is looming. Writing for an unknown audience is not the only cause of writer's block of course. Uncertainty about what you want to say and the direction your writing needs to take, are other causes and probably reflect lack of confidence about your audience.

In this chapter, we argued that producing a clear, coherent text involves problem-solving. Every sentence you write places constraints on the one that follows in terms of what you can say and how you can say it. Fortunately, linguistic tools such as thematization and cohesion can help you create a smooth pathway for your readers, not one where they have excessive inductive work to do to establish a logical progression from one sentence to the next.

In the next chapter, we turn to the related issues of identity and voice in academic writing. You will see that the concepts are not only closed related to each other but also to the concerns of this chapter as well.

Further readings

The Writing Center. (2022). *Audience.* https://writingcenter.unc.edu/tips-and-tools/audience/
This guide to addressing your audience in academic writing is clear, and practical. It provides a useful checklist of questions to guide you in identifying your audience and addressing their needs.

Coffin, C., Curry, M. J., Goodman, S., Hewings, A., Lillis, T., & Swann, J. (2003). *Teaching academic writing: A toolkit for higher education.* Routledge.
As the title suggests, this is a book containing practical suggestions and tasks for helping students develop their writing skills.

References

Bass, R. V., & Good, J. W. (2004). Educare and educere: Is a balance possible in the educational system? *The Educational Forum,* 68(2), 161–168.

Casanave, C. P. (2014). *Journal writing in second language education.* University of Michigan Press.

Coffin, C., Curry, M. J., Goodman, S., Hewings, A., Lillis, T., & Swann, J. (2003). *Teaching academic writing: A toolkit for higher education.* Routledge.

Craft, M. (Ed.). (1984). *Education and cultural pluralism.* Routledge.

Dearden, R. F., Hirst, P. H., & Peters, R. S. (Eds.). (1972). *Education and the development of reason.* Routledge.

Ellis, R. (2010). A framework for investigating oral and written corrective feedback. *Studies in Second Language Acquisition, 32*(2), 335–349.

Gopnik, A., Meltziff, A. N., & Kuhl, P. K. (1999). *The scientist in the crib: Minds, brain and how children learn.* William Morrow & Co.

Hatch, E., & Lazaraton, A. (1991). *The research manual: Design and statistics for applied linguistics.* Newbury House.

Heath, S. B., & Kramsch, C. (2004). Individuals, institutions and the uses of literacy. *Journal of Applied Linguistics, 1*(1), 75–91. https://doi.org/10.1558/japl.v1.i1.75

Kroll, B. (1984). Writing for readers: Three perspectives on audience. *Composition and Communication, 35*(2), 172–185. https://doi.org/10.2307/358094

Matsuda, P., & Atkinson, D. (2008). A conversation on contrastive rhetoric. In U. Connor, N. Nagelhout, & W. Rozycki (Eds.), *Contrastive rhetoric: Reaching to intercultural rhetoric.* (pp. 227–298). John Benjamins.

Oxford Union. (2017, December 7). *Sir Ian McKellen | Full Address and Q & A* [Video]. YouTube. https://www.youtube.com/watch?v=oVH0nM4_IaU&ab_channel=OxfordUnion

Richardson, L. (2001). Getting personal: Writing stories. *Qualitative Studies in Education, 14*(1), 33–38.

5
Toward active voice

As we indicated in our introduction to the book, this is not a "how to" guide. Our aim is to introduce you to concepts that will help you be an effective writer. Two such concepts are voice and identity, the central concerns of this chapter. As you embark on the chapter, we need to warn you that it won't be an easy read. (If it's any consolation, it wasn't easy to write, either.) The concept of voice, and its relationship to identity is complex and elusive. And if Martin Amis, a master craftsman if ever there was, spends most of his time trying to find his voice, you can look forward to doing the same.

Voice matters in the sort of writing we are advocating in this book. It challenges one of the central principles of traditional academic writing, that of objectivity. The purpose of the linguistic conventions of traditional style – avoid first-person singular, privilege the passive voice, etc. – are to render the author invisible, to silence his/her voice. Richardson (2001) says that this 'objective', scholarly writing puts her to sleep. She objects to it because it

> …requires writers to silence their own voices, to view themselves as contaminants. Homogenization occurs through the suppression of individual voices and the acceptance of the omniscient voice of science or scholarship or the social-script as if it were our own. Writing as a method of inquiry is a way of nurturing our own individuality and giving us authority over our understanding of our own lives.
>
> (p. 35)

Early in our careers as academic writers, we were instructed to keep our writing objective and impersonal. "There is no place for subjectivity in academic writing", we were warned. "Avoid the first person 'I'". As graduate students, and then entry-level academics, we dutifully obeyed. Although we began our careers in different decades, we soon grew tired of the anemic

DOI: 10.4324/9781003179092-6

prose we felt we had to produce. It was inconsistent with the type of work we were doing: the medium failed to match the message. Although we were uncomfortable at being rendered invisible, we felt bound by the conventions of traditional academic writing. Things changed when, in our own separate ways, we came across writers with whom we could identify, who showed us that there was another way. For David, Shirley Brice Heath's monumental *Ways with Words* was an inspiration. When Richardson derided the static, voiceless writing model for its 'mechanistic scientism' which put her to sleep, Julie knew exactly what she was talking about. It was these, and other authors like them, who opened up ways of representing our work in print that we had never considered, certainly not for young, untested writers.

In this book, we have attempted to add color and life to the prose by injecting it with anecdotes, stories, and narratives – our own as well as the occasional contribution from our students, colleagues, and other authors. These have a purpose other than adding entertainment value. They elaborate on or illuminate the content under discussion or the argument being made. We have set these off in boxes so they don't interrupt the flow of the chapter.

The purpose of this chapter is to unpack key concepts and perspectives on voice and identity. We review what prominent qualitative researchers and writers have to say about the concept: how they make the "I" visible in their own writing, and the challenges this sometimes presents when it comes to publication. By the end of the chapter, you should have an idea of what is meant by voice in academic writing and how you can develop your own authorial voice and the payoffs and pitfalls in doing so. For a more detailed treatment of identity and voice, we recommend Ivanič (1998) who describes three 'selves' that capture the identity of a writer. These are the 'autobiographical self', the 'discoursal self', and the 'self as author'. Later in the chapter, we will say more about the autobiographical self.

Before we get into substantive issues to do with voice and identity in academic writing, we should point out these concepts will not be relevant for all genres: institutional reports, meeting minutes, grant submissions, or documents produced by a committee for other bodies who will, in all likelihood, have a 'house style' and house rules. With such genres, you need to be aware of required format and the rules of the game. These usually include depersonalized, mechanistic, product-oriented writing. Although, as Tardy (2016) reminds us, no genre is 'set in stone', and there are many opportunities for innovation and creativity in most genres.

The evolving story of voice in academic writing

Some years ago, we wrote a paper in which we traced the historical evolution of 'voice' in qualitative research. We thought that sharing a precis of the terrain covered in that piece would be useful background for you in understanding the evolution of voice as a key ingredient in academic writing. In the paper, we argued for the centrality of the author's personal voice to research in terms of *what* the story is and *how* the story is told, in particular, making our role a central element in the research story.

> 'Traditional' research admitted a limited number of voices. Typically, the researcher was an invisible "I". In this piece we shall explore some of the ways in which making the "I" visible, that is, part of the research story, challenged and transformed not only the nature of the research report, but the ways in which research can be defined.
>
> (Nunan & Choi, 2011, p. 222)

Our purpose was not to claim ownership over the personal stance in qualitative research. That honor belongs to others. Our aim was to tell the evolutionary story of the emergence of voice and to argue that use, for example, of the first person "I" was not a superficial case of surface style, as some have argued. Rather, it was central to what we mean when we talk about research. It places the writer within the text and makes explicit the active role he/she lays in the research process. It allows researchers to pose challenging questions such as: Who gets to define a given activity as research? Who gets to lay out the ground rules in terms of how the story should be told? On what authority?

We began the story in the 1960s, although the battle lines had been drawn long before then. In that decade, and into the next, qualitative researchers accepted the ground rules of the positivists. They sought legitimacy by attempting to show how their writing could meet the rules. For example, in a major contribution to the debate, LeCompte and Goetz (1982) articulated a set of steps that qualitative researchers could take to strengthen the internal and external reliability and validity of their research. Hard-line positivists remained unconvinced.

By the 2000s, qualitative researchers had not so much given up, but simply turned their back on positivists within the academy and began developing their own ground rules. Reliability and validity were waived in favor of 'transparency', 'believability', 'experiential resonance', and similar criteria.

Research genres and boundaries began to blur. While deference was paid to longstanding methods such as ethnography, case study and narrative inquiry, concepts, practices and perspectives crept in from cultural, media, gender studies, and a range of other perspectives and disciplines. Autoethnographies appeared more frequently. Writing techniques were appropriated from fiction. Traditional academia was appalled when research output appeared as playscripts and poems.

With this new assertiveness in which qualitative researchers unashamedly inserted themselves into their research story, voice and identity came increasingly under the spotlight by both proponents and critics. In the next section, we look at how several key scholars have defined and characterized voice and identity in academic writing.

What is 'voice'?

Voice and identity are elusive concepts. So is the way that writers reveal their writerly selves through the texts they construct. Academics who write about voice define the concept in different ways. Here's the definition we came up with in paper we summarized in the preceding section.

> By 'voice' we are referring to the centrality of the human story to qualitative research in terms of *what* the story is and *how* the story is told. Stories touch the human heart as well as the mind. From time immemorial they have provided a vehicle for entertainment, but, more importantly in pre- and non-literature societies, for passing cultural knowledge from one generation to the next. In taking this stance, we believe that research methodology has to do with not just how the research is conceptualized and conducted, but how it is represented. We are aware of the ambiguity in the term 'represent'; that it can be taken two ways – 'to stand for' and 'to re-present'.
>
> (Nunan & Choi, 2011, p. 222)

In this definition, we argue that qualitative researchers reveal themselves in what they choose to write about and how they choose to report their research. The best way to make concrete the elusive concepts at the heart of this chapter is to show you some examples.

We take the first example from Jerome Bruner, a world-renowned psychologist and educator. Bruner begins an article entitled *Life as Narrative* as follows.

Jerome Bruner's voice

I would like to try out an idea that may not be quite ready, indeed it may not be quite possible. But I have no doubt that it is worth a try. It has to do with the nature of thought and with one of its uses. It has been traditional to treat thought, so to speak, as an instrument of reason. Good thought is right reason, and its efficacy is measured against the laws of logic or induction. Indeed, in its most recent computational form it is a view of thought that that has sped some of its enthusiasts to the belief that all thought is reducible to machine computability.

But logical thought is not the only or even the most ubiquitous mode of thought. For the last several years, I have been looking at another kind of thought, one that is quite different in form from reasoning: the form of thought that goes into the constructing not of logical, or inductive arguments but of stories or narratives. What I want to do now is to extend these ideas about narrative to the analysis of the stories we tell about our lives: our "autobiographies" (Bruner, 1987, p. 11).

In a chapter with the intriguing title of *Coat hangers, Cowboys and Communicative Strategies: Seeking Identity as a Proficient Foreign Language Learner*, Kathi Bailey describes growing up on a flower range in southern California and attempted to acquire Spanish by interacting with the Mexican farm workers. Here is part of her story.

Kathi Bailey's voice

Under those circumstances, I should have learned Spanish easily from the workers and my neighbors. But there were invisible social barriers more powerful than our physical proximity, and like other Anglo children in our school district, I started to learn Spanish as a foreign language in junior high school. After two years of grammar exercises and vocabulary lists, I was bored with Spanish and switched to Latin in high school because it would surely be helpful if I decided to become a doctor or a nun. (No, I'm not Catholic, and yes, you may laugh.) Studying Latin consisted of textbook exercises, translating texts into English, learning the cases, and taking vocabulary quizzes. There was never an expectation that we would speak the language. At best, the Latin classes gave me word-attack skills and a certain amount of meta-language that would be useful in the future for taking standardized tests (Bailey, 2010, p. 14).

We hope you agree that the author's voice is clear. How does she do this? First of all, she has an arresting title which draws on figurative language. She contextualizes the research by telling a personal story. She reveals her feelings and emotions ("invisible social barriers", "was bored", "would be useful in future"). She brings in irony and humor and speaks directly to the reader ("No, I'm not Catholic, and, yes, you may laugh"). These devices work together to convey a sense of who she is, that is, they reveal her identity as a writer.

Storytelling

The most transparent way of inserting yourself into your writing is to tell a story in which you are one of the characters. Your role in the story may be central, as is the case with Jerome Bruner and Kathi Bailey, or peripheral, an observer and commentator of an incident in which the action is performed by others. The story can be a complete narrative or a snippet – a vignette. It could recount a series of physical actions with some editorializing along the way, as is the case with Kathi's story, or be an interior narrative, as is the case with Bruner's. Essentially, Bruner is taking us into his confidence, telling us the story of how he came up with an idea. He isn't sure if the idea is plausible but wants to try it out on us. As Adrian Holliday (2002) says, he's "showing us the workings". The proposition he proposes is that there are two ways of making sense of the world/existence. The first is through a process of deductive or inductive reasoning. The second is through the stories we tell about our lives. His speculations conclude with the observation that "we seem to have no way of thinking about 'lived time' save in the form of a narrative" (p. 11).

The following vignette by Stacy Holman Jones is called "Am I that name?", a title just as intriguing as Bailey's. We've selected this piece because Holman Jones has a strong, clear voice, and because the piece makes an important statement about identity.

The Holman Jones piece is presented in two parts. In the very first sentence of part 1, she tells us that as an undergraduate, she had an identity problem: she didn't know who she wanted to become. In the rest of the paragraph, rather than tackling the problem head on, she circles it. She is in limbo, waiting for something to happen. Why doesn't she come right out and proclaim her identity as a writer? She's too good a writer for that. She doesn't tell us, she *shows* us. She gives us hints – "waiting takes place in language … possibility is made in writing … waiting in language" (p. 111). There's another hint at

Stacy Holman Jones' voice

As an undergraduate, I didn't know who I wanted to be, who I wanted to become. True to form (or was it content?), I was an Interdisciplinary Studies major. This designation – this name – was a placeholder for the undecided, the emergent, the *possible* (and not, as I assured my parents, a flimsy legitimizing discourse that covered over underachievement, failure, and lack of choice). This name was a space of waiting – for something to come together, for something to happen. My scholarly interests were spaces where waiting takes place in language – in politics, in journalistic portraits, in story and verse. These were spaces where possibility is made in writing, though not in some utopian, fixed sense of an inscription that makes something tangible or something *real*; object and objectified. They were spaces of possibility where "actual lines of potential that a something coming together calls to mind and sets in motion" (Stewart, 2007, p. 3). Mine was a waiting in language as "becoming, difference, encounter, motion, creativity" (LeVan, 2007, p. 50). Process, rather than product, to use the cliché, though I didn't know it then. I was waiting.

I see the invitation, written in red: *Please see me*. Never mind his comments on my short story. Never mind his encouragement, his gentle prodding, his attention to my work in words. I was being summoned to his office. I was in *trouble*, though at the time I didn't think of trouble as something positive, something affectively *good* in the sense of subversion of whatever norms I might have violated. And, indeed, I know I have violated … something. I just don't know what.

I arrive early and lean against the cinderblock wall outside his office. I have never been upstairs to the faculty offices. I spend many of my days in the basement of this building, reading the poetry and short stories of others and offering up my own. Until now, there was no invitation, no reason to go upstairs. The door opens and his head emerges, swiveling around until his gaze lands on me, on my body pushed up against the wall.

"Hi. I didn't know you were here. Come in".

I follow him into the office, which is no bigger than a closet and crammed full of books and a massive desk piled high with paper. He inches around the desk and sits behind the stacks of paper, which rise high on either side of him. I take the chair opposite him, pulling my backpack around my body and hugging it to my chest. "You wrote on my paper that I should come and see you".

"Yes. I wanted to talk to you about something."

"I know my story wasn't finished. I didn't quite get where I wanted to go, but I didn't want to hand it in late."

"Your paper is fine. Quite inventive, really. I've made what I think are some good suggestions for revision. That's not what I wanted to see you about, though."

"Oh?"

"No. I want to talk to you about graduate school. Have you thought about it?"

"Graduate school? Um, no. I haven't thought about it."

"Well, you should. You're a wonderful writer, very smart."

"I am?"

"Yes. Didn't you know that?"

"No."

"Well, you are. And you should know."

He said more that day, about graduate programs he thought would be a good fit with my interests and my work, about how to prepare for the GRE and request letters of recommendation, about ordering transcripts and meeting deadlines, though I don't recall any of these details. What struck me then, what strikes me now, was what *happened* in our conversation. In a moment, in the movement of his pen on the page and in our brief conversation, he waltzed me an imaginative *what if*. What if I was a writer? What if that is my name? (Holman Jones, 2010, pp. 111–112).

the end of the paragraph. Although she didn't know it at the time, writing is a process of becoming not of being.

Another reason is provided in the second part of the piece which takes the form of a narrative. Proclaiming herself as a writer was beyond the limits of her imagination. It required an audacity she didn't possess. It required an authoritative figure, an unnamed professor to proclaim it for her. "You're a wonderful writer, very smart". Only then could she entertain the possibility. Textual devices she uses include the simple present, which brings an immediacy to the narrative, direct rather than indirect speech, and italics which brings her voice into sharp focus. We can *hear* her emotional state at different points in the narrative: trepidation, bemusement, incredulity.

If you decide to include a story of one sort or another in your work, you need to have a justification for doing so besides adding color to the piece. If necessary, you should make the purpose explicit to the reader, as we have done in this book. Another consideration is where to position the story within the piece. Beginning with a story can draw the reader in, create interest, or even a sense of mystery. Julie does this in a piece entitled *"Living on the hyphen"*. She begins with the following conversation.

> "How do you get the glass table so clean?" I ask Sophia, my Korean cleaner in Sydney who has been coming every two weeks for the last three months.
>
> "You need to use … some kind of … sponge. Mmm … no, like some cleaning material … No …"
>
> "You mean like a cloth?" I interrupt.
>
> "Yes, yes, like cross [cloth]. Mmm … bery [very] soft cross."
>
> "Some kind of special fabric?"
>
> "Special? Mmm … yes … sha … sham … Mmm … I don't know what you say English … I show you…" and she goes to get it.
>
> (Choi, 2010, p. 66)

She goes on to say that her Anglo partner, who has overheard this rather tortured conversation, asks her with a touch of irritation why she hadn't simply asked Sophia in Korean, why she has hidden from the cleaner the fact that she is Korean-American and that they share a common language. Julie's response opens up complex intergenerational cultural issues. While Stacy Holman Jones could have initiated her article with the story of her encounter with her professor, she begins with a framing paragraph that creates intrigue and provides a segue into the action narrative.

The personal in academic writing

Various devices are used by the authors of the three vignettes we have presented so far to reveal their voice. All three are present in the text. All three tell a story. Bruner's is the story of how he came to the view that there are two ways of making sense of the world, through logical thought and by analyzing the stories we tell about our lives. Bailey relates early encounters with language other than her first. Holman Jones talks about a meeting with one of her professors during which the notion that she could legitimately consider herself a writer becomes a possibility. All three reveal personal feelings, attitudes, and insecurities. We have a sense that all three are speaking directly to us, although Bailey addresses us directly ("yes, you may laugh"). Tone of voice (humor, irony, etc.) also gives us a sense of the author's identity as does the use of figurative language which is the topic of the next chapter.

As we have noted at several points on the book, the practice of researchers inserting themselves into their writing is becoming increasingly common. This practice reflects a growing assertiveness on the part of qualitative researchers not to play by the rules of positivism. However, not all writers agree that voice matters in academic writing. Stapleton (2002) is one critic who is skeptical of the practice, suggesting that it's substance (i.e., content) that matters, not style and that voice is irrelevant to academic writing. He argues that the extended (i.e., excessive) focus in journals and monographs implied that voice is far more important than it deserves to be, and that "… if passed down to students, may result in learners who are more concerned with identity than with ideas" (Stapleton, 2002, p. 187).

Cynthia Nelson, an exceptional writer by any measure, disagrees. She acknowledges that authorial subjectivity has been perceived as "irrelevant, self-indulgent, or insufficiently critical", but defends the practice of inserting one's "subjective experiences, thoughts, and impressions" into one's writing (Nelson, 2005, p. 315). However, she adds a caveat. The personal stance must contribute to knowledge-making and be relevant to the subject at hand. In negotiating the delicate balance between underacknowledging and overacknowledging your presence in your writing, you should ask yourself what's the point and what's the effect likely to be on the reader?

Textual features and voice

In the preceding section, we discussed the most transparent way of inserting ourselves into our text: weaving into the text personal texts in which we feature as protagonist or onlooker. Voice and identity are closely entwined, voice being a key concept in capturing a writer's identity (Matsuda & Tardy, 2007). As we said in the previous section, what we choose to write about, and how we choose to write it reveals the identity we want to present to the reader. Actually, we should use the plural because we have multiple voices and identities. In everyday life, we identify/affiliate with, or desire to affiliate with, different cultural groups – football fan clubs, wine appreciation societies, mah-jong groups, expectant parent gatherings, and so on. These intersect, overlap, and sometimes conflict. The different subgroups within a particular culture will have their own rituals, discourse conventions, vocabulary, and patterns of interaction.

When speaking, we have resources that are not available to our writerly self. We can shout, whisper, cajole, pause for dramatic effect, and use body language (gesture, wink, scowl, and smile). Through linguistic and non-linguistic resources, we convey our thoughts and emotions and reveal aspects of our identity and personality. When we use the word 'voice', as in "Don't use that tone of voice with me", or "Ellie's voice sank to a whisper as she terminated her relationship with Jack", we are using the word 'voice' literally.

When we use 'voice' in writing, it takes on a metaphorical meaning. We can be ironic, humorous, or somber. We can hedge an assertion by adding caveats and conditions, but in doing so, we rely entirely on the written word. In writing, then, voice refers to the personal tone or style you adopt in crafting a piece of work. Because vocal resources and body language are unavailable, we have to use textual resources of a very different kind. These resources are many and varied. Here is a sample: sentence length (long or short), sentence structure, word choice, tense choice, thematization, active vs passive voice, direct vs indirect speech, tone of voice, pronoun choice, writer stance toward the reader, use of figures of speech, and the way the text is presented on the page (choice of font type and size, paragraphing, use of bold or italic type, punctuation, e.g., choice of colon, semi-colon, or dash, bracket, quotation marks, exclamation marks, etc.). Non-discoursal elements such as tables, chart, figures, diagrams, photographs, and many other forms of realia are also important and becoming more so in a multimedia world. Some of these were used by the authors of the vignettes we shared with you earlier. For example, Stacy Holman Jones used italics to very good effect in expressing attitudes and emotion. For a more detailed and nuanced discussion of these features of voice, see Matsuda (2001).

Matsuda and Tardy (2007) argue that it is a reader's interpretation and re-action to these features that assist them to construct their own sense of the writer's voice, and from that to larger identity issues: Is this writer male or female? A first or second-language speaker? A student or an academic? In a study reported in their article, they show how two readers can arrive at answers to questions such as these but do so by focusing on different features. Two reviewers of an article submitted for journal publication, for example, identified the author as male. Reader 1 did so "primarily because of the ways in which he positioned and framed other works within the manuscript" while Reviewer 2 did so because the author "ignored the issue of gender" even though gender and race were central to the topic of the article (p. 246). Because of the number of features and the fact that the effect on the reader is the key to their definition of voice, Matsuda and Tardy say it would be inappropriate to determine a set of features a priori. "Instead, we sought to identify the overall impression of the manuscript first and then to identify discursive and non-discursive features that contributed to that impression" (p. 239).

Making connections

How much can you deduce about the identity of the authors of the following texts in terms of gender, age, occupation, level of education, first-language background, etc.? What is it about what they said and how they have said it that helped you make these deductions? What do you think was the source from which the texts were extracted – e.g., a magazine article, a student essay, and a tourist guide?

Text 1

Every journalist who is not too stupid or too full of himself to notice what is going on knows that what he does is morally indefensible. He is a kind of confidence man, preying on people's vanity, ignorance, or loneliness, gaining their trust and betraying them without remorse. Like the credulous widow who wakes up one day to find the charming young man and all her savings gone, so the consenting subject of a piece of non-fiction writing learns – when the article or book appears – his hard lesson. Journalists justify their treachery in various ways according to their temperaments. The more pompous talk about freedom of speech and "the public right to know"; the least talented talk about Art; the seemliest murmur about earning a living.

Text 2

It's dusk by the time I get to Soho. I shoulder my way into Staunton's Bar and Grill between the knots of suited wage slaves. Different bars tend to be patronized by different professions and people from different walks of life. Sporting types gravitate toward The Globe. The Makumba Bar attracts musicians, designers, and artists. Lawyers, airline pilots, dentists, and investment advisors form the core of Staunton's clientele. Not really my types. However, the bar has a number of advantages. Being situated next to the escalator makes it a perfect people-watching spot if you're drinking alone. Because of its location, visitors and others unfamiliar with the jumble of narrow streets and alleyways that constitute Soho have little trouble finding it. For some years, I lived in a cramped little studio apartment just opposite, so it was also convenient from that point of view. The bar girls, mostly Nepalese, all know me.

Developing your own voice

Your identity as a writer will be strongly conditioned by your purpose and the audience you are writing for. If you are a graduate student, your audience will most likely be one of your teachers. Your overriding purpose will not be to inform the teacher of certain facts relating to the topic of your piece that he/she doesn't know. You will have several interrelated purposes: to demonstrate the extensive reading you have done to inform yourself of the topic, your mastery of the genre, be it a report, a procedure, or an analytical text, your creativity and so on. The extent to which you inject your personality into the piece through irony, humor, and hedging will depend on the relationship you have with the teacher you are writing for. (Unless you know your teacher well, we'd advise you to think carefully before trying humor. The last thing you want is to become the butt of the teacher's joke.) When you write, you are putting on a performance through the written word. The 'act of writing' is more than a metaphorical phrase. As Denzin (2014) reminds us, writing is a performance.

In our introduction, we mentioned the struggle we had to develop our own voices. Our diffidence stemmed from several sources. Like Stacy Holman Jones, we were unpublished students. Our authorial identities were not only unformed, they were non-existent. We had no authority to proclaim ourselves as writers. Our response to Stacy Holman Jones' "Am I that name?" was a ringing "No!" Whenever the "I" crept into drafts of David's academic writing, including his doctoral thesis, it was struck through with a red pen and replaced with "one". It was only with time and the vicarious encouragement we received from reading the work of writers we wanted to emulate that our voices began to emerge.

We encourage our students to develop their voices and identities as writers, beginning with their 'autobiographical self', described by Ivanič as "a writer's

Making connections

How do you feel about calling yourself a writer? Do you think that only those who have published successfully have the right to identify themselves as writers? When David's early attempts at 'performing the personal' were struck through with a red pen, he felt his emerging writer's voice was being dismissed. Have you ever had a similar reaction to corrections of your own work?

sense of their roots, or where they are coming from…" (Ivanič, 1998, p. 24). When you sit down to write, you bring with the task your past history, which is constantly changing as your life history evolves. You also bring with you the beliefs, attitudes, and dispositions which are shaped by your past history as you have constructed it for yourself. Ivanič says that a writer's autobiographical self may be difficult to get at because the writers themselves may not be consciously aware of the way their writing is shaped by their life histories. She suggests that the relationship might be revealed by addressing questions such as: "What aspects of people's lives might have led them to write in the way they do?" and, more generally, "How does autobiographical identity shape writing?" (p. 25). In other words, how do your experiences and perceptions shape the writing itself? Another important point stressed by Ivanič is the notion that your 'writerly' identity is only one of your numerous identities, as we have discussed earlier. The notion reflects another point we made, that writing is a performance, and the persona you present through your writing will be shaped by your purpose and your (real or imagined) audience.

The following vignette captures Ivanič's sentiment. In it, Julie's master's student, Cat, describes her distaste for academic writing. This distaste stemmed from the denial by her teachers of her embryonic autobiographical voice. Only by producing pale imitations of her teachers' prose could she escape censure.

Cat's journey in academic writing

At dinner one night with Julie and David, I made a comment about how much I 'hated' academic writing. Having recently completed a research degree with Julie (who was my academic supervisor at the time), I ranted about how mentally gruelling it was to write such long stretches of prose, so many times over. There was no such thing as a 'perfect' first attempt. Every time I sent my writing to Julie, I secretly hoped that she would skim through my writing, find no errors, and let me move onto the next section. It was foolish of me to ever think that. Every time I opened up my feedback, I was confronted by a thousand comments from Julie questioning what on earth I was saying. How does one not get frustrated?

A few days later, Julie tells me what David said to her about my comment.

"It's such a shame that she doesn't enjoy writing. It's through writing and rewriting that she'll discover what she really wants to say".As I reflect on David's comment whilst writing this piece, my feelings toward academic writing and the frustrating journey to find my own writer's voice draws me back into my own life history and socialization. In high school, teachers would drill into us that there was no 'I' in an academic essay, the passive voice was a big 'no-no' and one needs to 'stick' to the sample. I was so wedded to reproducing these structures that I never really wrestled with what I wanted to say. In my mind, there simply wasn't a place for it. I just had to follow the structure.

In university, I continued to rely upon models and sample texts found in the work of my professors – it was like an academic form of training wheels. I could not make my own linguistic choices. I was so afraid of trusting myself to the point that I hid. I hid behind the work of my professors and slightly edited their sentence structures. I hid behind endless citations to try and shield my writing from attacks of plagiarism. If you were to look at my in-text referencing alone, you would assume that I had read the literature widely. However, beneath the surface of every single essay was a messy patchwork of text that screamed deep insecurities.

Cat's journey in academic writing continued

When I enrolled in a research degree, Julie saw straight through it.

"The way you cite the work of others, it's like you don't know what you want to say".

She suggested that I pick three articles and carefully analyze the 'moves' that each author makes. I was initially skeptical of such a simple task since I had always written looking very closely at the work of others. But the way in which Julie made me interrogate the text allowed me to see how writers were strategic with their linguistic choices. After multiple rounds of highlighting, annotating, and making notes, she brought to my attention how writers hedged, used reporting verbs and transition words to make their voice cut through the pages. Such a task helped me see how I could add nuance to my own claims and assertions rather than unthinkingly copy another person's voice or rely on generic phrase banks. In some ways, it felt like the training wheels had come off. Although, I still fall sometimes and get stuck in the voice of others, I know now that there is no academic prose I can copy to try and say what I want to say. Only I can say what I want to say by writing it. Yes, it is exhausting; but in many ways, it has become rewarding.

At the moment, I am experimenting with more evocative forms of narrative writing for reflection. I could never have imagined myself writing in such literary ways especially in the genre of research writing. Here's a small snippet of a piece I recently wrote about an incident that happened to me as a beginning teacher:

> *With two loud clicks, my attendance on a spreadsheet is marked off. She begins to run a red pen along the boxes in my form, reading out numbers under her breath. 1.1… tick…2.3…tick… 3.4…tick…. The form is flipped over. In the silence, her pen passes over paper and 'buzz' words are written down. Evidence, strategies, ZPD, confirmation, endorsement. As her red pen struggles to tick one of the boxes, a question emerges. My fast reply allows her to continue being engrossed in the act of marking each standard off. Nearing the end of the form, the next person announces their arrival. My supervisor stands up and shows me out of her office, quickly signing off a key form for my probation.*

The opportunity to write in more creative and compelling ways has paved another uncertain yet exciting road for me. It has made me look forward to discovering a bit more about who I am and the world around me through text.

We have shared Cat's story in full because it illustrates some of the key themes of the chapter. The training wheels metaphor is a familiar, but particularly apt one. She describes how, with Julie's guidance, she shed her training wheels and realizes that no one else's voice can enable her to say what she wants to say. Only through her own voice, can she discover what she wants to say. In the next section we describe the value of apprenticing yourself to a writer you admire, but that, like Cat, you will only discover what you want to say by discarding your training wheels. At the end of the vignette, she gives a glimpse of her emerging voice in describing how her progress in the complex art of teaching is reduced to atomistic items on a checklist.

Here's an example of how Cat used Julie's 'move analysis' technique (Figure 5.1).

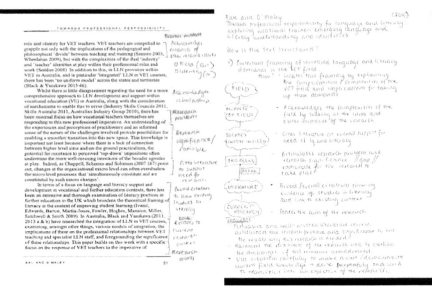

Figure 5.1 Deconstructed text showing move analysis technique.

Making connections

Using Cat's example as a model, review an assignment you have recently completed or are currently completing. Identify the different moves in the piece. Ask yourself, what am I doing here? Is my voice appropriate to the move? If not, how can I strengthen it?

Possible moves might be:

- Giving background to your topic
- Signposting to the reader the terrain to be covered
- Providing a personal narrative
- Summarizing what others have discovered or claimed
- Including data such as journal entries, interview transcripts, and observation notes
- Analyzing data
- Interpreting data
- Discussing your personal feelings and attitudes (e.g., to your data, toward what others have asserted)
- Summarizing and making concluding remarks
- Admitting to limitations and shortcomings of your work

Injecting yourself into your academic writing takes courage because you may be criticized by readers who subscribe to conventional notions of what constitutes acceptable academic style. If you are a graduate student, this could include an unsympathetic thesis examiner. If you offer a piece for publication, you may be criticized by gatekeepers such as editors and reviewers whose rules of the academic publishing game include objectivity and authorial invisibility. Regardless of the audience, you should keep in mind Nelson's (2005) point that admitting a subjective voice into your writing has to have a point, that is, it has to add something to the piece you are writing.

Adrian Holliday tells a cautionary tale about a student who as a graduate student, found it an affront to be forced to conform to traditional conventions which sanctioned creativity and the polemical voice he had developed as an undergraduate majoring in English literature.

> Mark had a first-class bachelor's degree in English literature from a well-known university in England. He then became a language teacher and after accruing a considerable amount of professional experience, he enrolled on a master's program in language education. As a master's student he displayed considerable ability as a critical thinker with a sophisticated awareness of the politics and ideology of education. However, he 'failed' as an academic writer. His assignments were articulate and elegantly written, and succeeded in communicating a profoundly critical argument; but they were in the wrong genre. Mark wrote competently in the polemic style of his undergraduate literature days, not in the technical genre of the social sciences. He found the latter impossible to work with and eventually left the programme.
> (Holliday, 2002, pp. 125–126)

Mark's experience is unfortunate. While it underlines the fact that institutions and disciplines vary when it comes to the conventions of academic writing, things are changing. This is true, not only in the human sciences but also in the so-called 'hard sciences' such as physics and engineering. As Canagarajah (2005) notes, "[t]he personal has become mainstream in research writing. Even quantitative studies make a nod towards acknowledging the personal in the article" (p. 309). Tardy (2016) has also written about an increasing interest in creativity and innovation in disciplines such as environmental science.

In this section, we have looked at the relationship between voice and identity in writing. We made the point that when it comes to writing, the word 'voice is used metaphorically. Although not wishing to overstate the case, we have also warned of the potential perils of speaking personally. Developing a personal voice is a tool for giving clarity and coherence to your writing as well as making your writing more interesting for the reader. In the next section, we will give you some suggestions and examples of how you can develop your voice by, paradoxically, imitating one or more writers who have influenced you.

The apprenticeship of writing

A key source of inspiration and guidance for the apprentice author who is struggling to find his/her voice is the work of others. In the preceding section, Zinsser (2013) says that "writing is learned mainly by imitation" (p. viii). The general reader focuses on content, reading a book or article for what the author has to say. They are generally unaware of the techniques or 'tricks of the trade' used by the author to pull them into the text and to keep them there. As a writer, you need to read other authors, particularly the ones you admire, not only for *what* they have to say but also *how* they say it. What is it that makes the voice of a Bill Bryson or a David Sedaris instantly recognizable?

It's not clear how many people read the American author Ernest Hemingway's work these days. He has been dead for years, and his machismo as well as lifestyle are no longer palatable. Despite this, there are plenty who seek him out in search of a writing style. Google *How to Write like Hemingway*, and you will find over a dozen sites. They are all directed at novice writers and offered a list of tips based on that author's analysis of Hemingway's style. Despite some variations, the lists are similar. 'Clarity' and 'simplicity' are the adjectives most frequently used words to capture his style and remain one of the most recommended models in 'how to' books, websites, and courses for budding writers.

Making connections

Identify a writer you admire. It can be a writer of fiction or non-fiction. What is it that attracts you to this writer? What three to four things about writing did you learn from them that you might try out in your own writing?

Write a short piece in the style of one of the writers you admire.

Then try rewriting it in your own voice.

David's voice: learning from a master – a cautionary tale

I was a voracious reader from an early age. I was a glutton for words and, while still in primary grade, was determined to become a writer. In junior high school, while my classmates honed their skills on the football field, I sat at my desk chewing he end off a BIC biro and staring at a blank sheet of foolscap paper. This was going to be a long, hard road. In secondary school, my English teacher thought I had 'promise'. She wasn't going to flatter me with 'talent', and I'd have despised her if she had. She bullied me into entering essay writing competitions. I came second in one, after a girl from the nearby convent school. This was a consolation. First prize would have convinced me that I was the only entrant.

I discovered Hemingway in senior high school and was immediately captivated by the power of this prose. His voice was instantly recognizable. He produced a prodigious body of work before running out of ideas and shot himself in 1960. I read every novel and short story I could get my hand on. I reread them, hungry for his secrets. His prose was a model of clarity, his voice strong and clear. Mine was anything but: clumsy rather than clear, awkward, not authoritative. I was never temped to put a gun to my head on re-reading my turgid, muddy prose. Nor was I tempted to give up. If writing is in your blood, you have no choice. With Hemingway at my elbow, I pressed on.

He preferred short, simple sentences, particularly for action scenes. If a descriptive piece called for it, he could use more complex constructions such as prepositional phrases and relative clauses as in the first sentence of A Farewell to Arms (1929): "In the late summer of that year, we lived in a house in a village that looked across the river and the plain to the mountains". In his lexical choices, he preferred single rather than multisyllabic words, high frequency, simple words rather than low frequency complex ones.

And so, I set out to renovate my prose on these principles. My sentences became skinnier. I privileged single syllable words of Anglo-Saxon or low German origin over those with Latinate or Norman roots. When it came to vocabulary, I chose clever over erudite, like as opposed to akin. When it came to adjectives and adverbs, out came the red pen. Interestingly, when used as an adjective, the word 'fine', one of the weakest in the English language, was so overused by Hemingway, that it became one of the defining features of his voice.

Over time, with Hemingway as a model, my prose grew closer to his in style. As more time passed, however, I realized that my writing was a weak parody of Hemingway's, a crippled imitation of his voice rather than my own. I was stuck with his voice and, if I didn't move on, would never develop one of my own. I extracted myself before imitation had hardened into a habit that would be impossible to break. But the year of living in Hemingway's skin wasn't wasted. Some of the lessons I learned during that period became part of the voice that I eventually developed.

As the vignette demonstrates, if you slavishly follow someone else's voice, you will never develop your own. It's important to remember that statements such as "keep your sentences short", "use high-frequency, simple words rather than low frequency difficult words", and "treat adverbs and adjective with cautions" are principles to bear in mind rather than rules to be obeyed. Used appropriately, they will increase the clarity of your writing. Applied unthinkingly will result in boring, repetitive prose. There are times when the meaning you really want to get across will only be achieved by using complex sentences and words with more than one syllable. Anne Lamott put it eloquently when she said there's nothing wrong with appropriating the voices of a writer we admire, but we need to realize that they're just props, temporary artifacts on the road to finding your own voice. They're just on loan and have to be returned. Here's the advice she gives to her students.

> [It's] natural to take on someone else's style ... it's a prop that you use for a while until you have to give it back. And it just might take you to the thing that is not on loan, the thing that is real and true: your own voice.
>
> (Lamott, 1995, p. 195)

In the rest of this section, we will elaborate on what we have said in this paragraph using examples related to the principles above. These are tips for you to think about as you revise your writing and work on uncovering your own voice: they are not rules to be slavishly followed.

Interrogating advice for aspiring authors

In this chapter, we have looked at numerous factors that will have an impact on your voice. These include the use of personal narratives, figurative language, and critical commentary on the subject matter of what you write, revealing beliefs and attitudes relevant to the subject at hand, use of hedging to indicate degree of certainty regarding your own claims and assertions and those of others. Voice, and its understudies, style and stance, will also be revealed by the words you choose, the way you arrange them into sentences and combine these into paragraphs. In this final section, we look in greater detail at how grammar and vocabulary choices can help or hinder you in your quest for voice. We'll do this by commenting on three pieces of advice that commonly appear in books for aspiring authors: 'Keep your sentences short', 'Privilege simpler words over harder ones', and 'Treat adverbs and adjectives with caution'.

Keep your sentences short

We dealt with sentence length earlier in the book. We return to the topic now looking at it through the lens of voice and identity. In general, we like shorter sentences because they are easier for readers to process as they generally only contain one idea. They can work well with narratives and critical incidents if you want to create a sense of suspense. However, they have to be appropriate to the text you are producing. If you overdo it, your prose will come across as staccato, and the last thing you want is for your reader to hyperventilate. Chopping what you want to say into a sequence of short sentences can also result in a text that is more difficult to process.

Here is how the above paragraph reads as a sequence of short sentences:

We dealt with sentence length earlier in the book. We return to the topic now. We look at through the lens of voice and identity. We like shorter sentence. They are easier for readers to process. They generally only contain one idea. They can work well with narrative and critical incidents. You might want to create a sense of suspense. They have to be appropriate to the text you are producing. Don't overdo it. Your prose will come across as staccato. The last thing you want is for your reader to hyperventilate. Don't always chop what you want to say into a sequence of short sentences. The text will be more difficult to process.

We're sure you agree that this version is more difficult to process. Presenting the same information as a sequence of shorter sentences and removing linking devices such as cohesive conjunctions increases the processing load on the reader because relationships that are made explicit in the original are implicit in the second. As a consequence, the reader has inferential work to do to establish the relationship.

Reading aloud what you have written will help you get a sense of how your text will come across to the reader. Hearing the text reveals overloaded sentences, clumsy expressions, and lack of connectivity between sentences. It can reveal which sentences are too long, but also sentence sequences that are too short. The technique enables you to hear your voice in a literal sense.

In much academic writing, complex concepts demand complex sentences. Grammatical devices such as cohesion, subordinate clauses, and non-finite constructions facilitate the process of making explicit the complex inter-relations between entities, events, and states-of-affairs in the text. To illustrate this point, consider the following sentence, written by one of our students. The student was asked to write a reflective piece based on a language portrait she had produced as part of her course assessment. Here we present the original sentence, our thoughts on the sentence, and our rewritten version.

Original sentence:

To begin with, I would like to admit from the start, that this assessment task was my very first experience with employing human artefacts and their respective analysis to extract meaning and shape an argument with regards to a topic.

Our concerns:

Although the writer states her position in relation to the writing assignment, the sentence is unnecessarily wordy. Beginning the sentence with *to begin with … from the start* is tautological. Removing the prepositional phrase and initial clause allows the writer to begin the sentence with the real topic of the paragraph - the assessment task. It does so, without removing her personal voice. Cutting the sentence in two makes it easier for the reader to process. *Experience* is replaced by the more precise *opportunity*. The largely puzzling phrase, *employing human artifacts* and the vague *a topic* are replaced by *language portraits* which makes explicit the nature of the human artifact. The result is much easier on the reader's eye.

Our revised version:

This assessment task gave me a first opportunity to use language portraits as a data collection tool. The data was subsequently analyzed as part of a small-scale investigation into language identity.

Privilege simpler words over harder ones

Leaving aside the complexities involved in deciding what makes one word simple and another hard, we agree with this injunction – up to a point. While we do our best to make our writing accessible, our main criterion is appropriateness rather than simplicity. We certainly don't pick difficult words to demonstrate our erudition or, to put it more simply, to show how clever we are! Appropriateness can be judged according to a number of criteria. Precision of meaning is one of these. In our critical appraisal of injunction 1, we gave an example of how we helped a student improve the readability of her text by presenting the information in two sentences rather than one and finding more precise vocabulary. Sometimes the distinction can be subtle: use of *opportunity to* rather than *experience with*, for example. There's nothing wrong with *experience with*, but *opportunity* is more precise.

The ability to select the word or phrase that most precisely expresses your meaning requires an extensive vocabulary. You can't select a word if you don't know it exists. It also requires developing an ear for the rhythms and music of language: the ways words and expressions cluster, collocate and please the ear, the way sentences are woven together into paragraphs. Developing a rich vocabulary, as well as an 'ear' for language, demands extensive reading. So, as we say, 'easy' words can add clarity and ease the task for the reader, but precision is just as important.

Treat adverbs and adjectives with caution

This is another piece of advice we agree with – up to a point. In the final stages of revising your writing, it's a good idea to scan the manuscript for adverbs and adjectives. This holds for everything intended for public consumption, regardless of whether it's an assignment with an audience of one, or a school newsletter/magazine article intended for a larger audience. Carefully chosen adverbs and adjectives can add a distinctive voice to your prose. Poorly chosen ones will weaken its impact. You should minimize the use of so-called 'flabby' modifiers such as 'nice', 'good', 'very', and delete those that add little or nothing to the meaning or impact of your message. (In an earlier draft of this chapter, we had written *ruthlessly expunge*. We ruthlessly expunged the phrase and replaced it with *delete* which, while it lacks the dramatic impact of the original, is less cliched.) You should also pay particular attention to what are known as weak 'ly' adverbs such as *sweetly* and *angrily*. These are often redundant, as in, *She smiled sweetly as the sleeping infant* and *The crowd shouted angrily at the referee*.

Read the following texts aloud. Which sounds better? Why have we left the adjective *insipid* in version 2?

Version 1

Adjectives and adverbs are very fundamental to the beautiful English language. They can add extreme subtlety and great power to what you are trying to say. Used inappropriately, they will honestly weaken your text and probably lead to insipid prose.

Version 2

Adjectives and adverbs are fundamental to the English language. They can add subtlety and power to what you are trying to say. Used inappropriately, they will weaken your text and lead to insipid prose.

We hope you agree that version 2 sounds better. All of the adverbs and adjectives in version 1 are unnecessary – all except *insipid* which is fundamental to meaning.

Making connections

Select a 300–500-word piece of your own writing. Make a copy of the piece. Carry out the following tasks on the copy.

- Underline any words that seem vague or imprecise. Can you find alternative words or phrases that more precisely express your ideas?
- Are there any words, phrases, or even sentences that are redundant? Delete them. (You should try to reduce the piece by 25–30%. If the word count of the original is 500 words, you should aim to reduce it to 375 or even 350 words.)
- Underline the adverbs and adjectives. Are any of these superfluous? Delete them.
- Are there any sentences that contain more than one clause (have more than one main verb)? Try rewriting them as two sentences, using cohesive devices to maintain coherence.
- Now, and this is the hard part, revise the piece so it reflects your own personal voice. Ask yourself, would a friend or family member recognize the piece as having been written by me?
- Now compare the revised version with the original. Which do you prefer? Ask a friend, or several friends to read both versions. Which do they prefer? Are they able to identify the changes you made?
- Finally, and most importantly, reread your piece. As you do, consider the following question, which we've adapted from Ivanič (1998): What aspects of your life have led you to write in the way you did? In other words, how has (and does) your autobiographical identity shape your writing and reveal your voice?

Questions from readers

Q: I was interested in what you had to say about modeling your writing on good authors you admired. When I was in high school, our English teacher groaned whenever a new Harry Potter book came out. "Now I'm going to get 30 essays that are imitations of J.K. Rowling – and not very good at that".

A: It's interesting you should say that. Anne Lamott is a great fan of Isabel Allende. She says that every time a new Allende book appears she's happy and unhappy. Happy because she'll get to read the latest offering of an author whose work she loves. Unhappy because half her students will attempt to write like Allende. That's not necessarily a bad thing. What Lamott is getting at is that you should always bear in mind when learning through imitation that you are 'borrowing' someone else's voice. Ultimately, you must return it if you're to discover your own.

Q: Cat's journey as a writer really resonated with me. I had the same experience. I ended up following the writing style of my teachers. But the style wasn't mine. I was bored, and my writing was boring. How can I kick off my training wheels and find my own voice?

A: First, stop copying writers who bore you. In the chapter, we invited you to identify several writers you admire and identify three to four principles in their writing you would like to try out. Write a piece in the style of one of these writers. Write about something that interests you that connects with your own passions and experiences. Then try rewriting it in your own voice. Write it as though you're addressing the person you admire. When you've finished, review each sentence in your piece, ask yourself, what move am I making here? What effect do I want to have on the reader? To inform? To convince? To summarize? How is my autobiographical self-reflected in the sentence?

Summary

In this chapter, we have made a case for voice as an important element in academic writing. After an introductory overview, the substantive part of the chapter introduces a brief history of the challenge mounted by qualitative researchers to the view that academic writing must be objective and that the author must remain anonymous. In the next section, we present and discuss three vignettes. Our purpose here was twofold:

first, to show you ways in which accomplished authors reveal themselves in their writing, and second, to illustrate the nexus between voice and identity.

The most transparent way of making your presence felt is through stories drawn from your own life. These stories can be related to an incident or incidences that illustrate or dramatize a theme you want to develop, a problem you hope to resolve, or a question you need to answer. You also reveal yourself in the reactions, beliefs, and feelings you have toward the ideas, events, or states-of-affairs that form the substance of your text. In writing ourselves into our work, Canagarajah says:

> [A]lthough we cannot speak outside discourses and institutions, we should not conform to them wholesale. We have to negotiate a position in the interstices of discourses and institutions to find our own niche that represents our values and interests favorably. This is how we construct a voice for ourselves.
>
> (Canagarajah, 2004, p. 268)

Central to the creation of voice are style, tone, and stance toward your subject, various linguistic devices such a sentence length, choice of vocabulary, and modifiers such as adjectives and adverbs as well as non-discoursal devices such as choice of font, subheadings, diagrams, photographs, and other realia.

Learning to write by apprenticing yourself to accomplished authors you admire is another strategy you can use to improve as a writer, but there are dangers. If you only shadow other writers, you will never develop your own.

Despite the advances that have been made in arguing for alternative rules such as transparency and subjectivity, risks remain in admitting the personal into our writing. One may have one's work tinkered with, manipulated, or rejected outright. Not even Harry Wolcott, an eminent American anthropologist and educator, could escape having his personal voice silenced by editors who thought they knew better. He tells of his indignation when a journal editor changed his text into impersonal third-person language without his permission or even informing him of the changes. He only discovered the alternations when the piece was published.

He goes on to state that:

> Because the researcher's role is ordinarily an integral part of reporting qualitative work, I write my descriptive accounts in the first person. I urge that others do (or in some cases be *allowed* to do) the same. …

Recognizing the critical nature of the observer role and the influence of his or her subjective assessments in qualitative work makes it all the more important to have readers remain aware of that role, that presence. Writing in the first person helps authors achieve that purpose.

(Wolcott, 2009, p. 17)

The quote illustrates the fact that choice of pronouns isn't a trivial matter when it comes to representing the writer's voice and positioning him/her in terms of the research enterprise. Critics of those who promote personal voice argue that it is self-indulgent, and that linguistic markers such as active voice and personal pronouns are essentially trivial. Harry Wolcott thinks otherwise, asserting that the "I" is anything but innocuous.

Further readings

Lamott, A. (1995). *Bird by bird: Some instructions on writing and life.* Doubleday.
This delightful book is a model of clarity. In it, not only does Lamott make the difficult concept of voice accessible, but her own voice rings clear on every page.

Nunan, D., & Choi, J. (Eds.). (2010). *Language and culture: Reflective narratives and the emergence of identity.* Routledge.
Several of the contributors to this volume are cited in this and other chapters in the book. We won't identify particular authors here. All have distinctive voices and any one of them could serve as models of excellence.

References

Bailey, K. B. (2010). Coat hangers, cowboys, and communication strategies: Seeking an identity as a proficient foreign language learner. In D. Nunan & J. Choi (Eds.), *Language and culture: Reflective narrative and the emergence of identity* (pp. 14–22). Routledge.

Bruner, J. (1987). Life as narrative. *Social Research, 54*(1), 11–32.

Canagarajah, S. (2004). Multilingual writers and the struggle for voice in academic discourse. In A. Pavlenko & A. Blackledge (Eds.), *Negotiation of identities in multilingual contexts* (pp. 266–289). Multilingual Matters.

Canagarajah, S. (2005). Rhetorizing reflexivity. *Journal of Language, Identity and Education, 4*(4), 309–315. https://doi.org/10.1207/s15327701jlie0404_7

Choi, J. (2010). Living on the hyphen. In D. Nunan & J. Choi (Eds.), *Language and culture: Reflective narrative and the emergence of identity* (pp. 66–73). Routledge.

Denzin, N. (2014). *Interpretive autoethnography*. Sage.

Hemingway, E. (1929). *A farewell to arms*. Penguin.

Holliday, A. (2002). *Doing and writing qualitative research* (2nd ed.). Sage.

Holman Jones, S. (2010). Am I that name? In D. Nunan & J. Choi (Eds.), *Language and culture: Reflective narrative and the emergence of identity* (pp. 111–117). Routledge.

Ivanič, R. (1998). *Writing and identity: The discoursal construction of identity in academic writing*. John Benjamins.

Lamott, A. (1995). *Bird by bird: Some instructions on writing and life*. Doubleday.

LeCompte, M., & Goetz, J. (1982). Problems of reliability and validity in educational research. *Review of Educational Research, 52*(2), 31–60. https://doi.org/10.3102%2F00346543052001031

LeVan, M. (2007). Aesthetics of encounter: Variations on translation in Deleuze. *International Journal of Translation, 19*(2), 51–66.

Matsuda, P. K. (2001). Voice in Japanese written discourse: Implications for second language writing. *Journal of Second Language Writing, 10*(1–2), 35–53. https://doi.org/10.1016/S1060-3743(00)00036-9

Matsuda, P., & Tardy, C. (2007). Voice in academic writing: The rhetorical construction of author identity in blind manuscript review. *English for Specific Purposes, 26*, 235–249.

Nelson, C. (2005). Crafting researcher subjectivity in ways that enact theory. *Journal of Language, Identity, and Education, 4*(4), 315–320. https://doi.org/10.1207/s15327701jlie0404_8

Nunan, D., & Choi, J. (2011). Shifting sands: The evolving story of "voice" in qualitative research. In E. Hinkel (Ed.), *Handbook of research in second language teaching and learning* (Vol. 3, pp. 222–236). Routledge.

Richardson, L. (2001). Getting personal: Writing-stories. *Qualitative Studies in Education, 14*(1), 33–38. https://doi.org/10.1080/09518390010007647

Stapleton, P. (2002). Critiquing voice as a viable pedagogical tool in L2 writing: Returning the spotlight to ideas. *Journal of Second Language Writing, 11*(3), 117–190.

Stewart, K. (2007). *Ordinary affects*. Duke University Press.

Tardy, C. (2016). *Beyond convention: Genre in academic writing*. University of Michigan Press.

Wolcott, H. (2009). *Writing up qualitative research* (3rd ed.). Sage.

Zinsser, W. (2013). *Writing to learn*. HarperCollins.

6
Using figurative language

In this chapter, we address the use of figurative language in academic writing. This phrase refers to the use of language in which words and phrases carry a meaning which differs from their literal or everyday meaning. They can be unexpected and creative, or, overused. For some figurative expressions, the meaning can be derived from their literal origins. In other instances, the relationship between the figurative and the literal is (metaphorically speaking) lost in time, and it takes an etymologist, a linguist who studies the origins of words and the way their meanings have been transformed through time to reveal the relationship.

Types of figurative language discussed in the chapter include similes, metaphors, idioms, colloquialisms, clichés, and slang. It isn't always easy to assign a phrase to a particular figurative 'label'. Through extended use and overuse, similes and metaphors, which begin life as fresh and creative, can become idioms which can, in turn, become cliches. We focus on similes and metaphors more than the other figures of speech because they are more common in academic writing. You'll also find idioms and colloquialisms and occasionally clichés and slang. In the hands of an experienced writer, these can give a chatty, humorous, or ironic tone to the text. Our advice is to treat idioms and colloquialisms with care and to avoid cliches and slang.

Literal and figurative meanings

There is considerable confusion over terminology in the literature. Some writers argue that *figurative language* and *figures of speech* are synonymous that both refer to the use of expressions whose meaning can't be derived from the literal or dictionary meaning of a word. Others argue that *figurative language* is a broader category that includes not only figures of speech but also literary concepts such as alliteration. We accept this distinction. However, for the

DOI: 10.4324/9781003179092-7

purposes of this chapter, we'll continue to use them interchangeably as literary devices such as the ones referred to above are not relevant.

Figures of speech are important because they are ubiquitous, that is, they occur in all types of spoken and written language. In fact, they are so common that native speakers are often unaware that they are using them. As children, they encounter whimsical language in nursery rhymes and poems. In the following rhyme, the prepositional phrase 'over the moon' is used literally, and in children's books the poem is accompanied by an illustration of a cow jumping over the moon.

> Hey Diddle Diddle!
>
> The cat and the fiddle
>
> The cow jumped over the moon;
>
> The little dog laughed to see such fun
>
> And the dish ran away with the spoon.

As they get older, they experience the phrase figuratively as in the following exchange:

> How did Kim respond to the examiners' reports on her thesis?
>
> Oh, she was over the moon.

Hearing it used dozens of times in a range of contexts, highly advanced users of the language develop an implicit understanding of the sense of the term. For many second-language speakers however, the situation is very different. Figurative language presents considerable challenges even to advanced users of a second language. In the statement, *She was over the moon*, knowing the preposition 'over' and the noun 'moon' is of no help in working out the meaning of the idiom. In some situations, the context might help (*Harry was over the moon when Sally accepted his proposal of marriage* could only mean one thing.). However, helpful contexts are not always available.

While it's true that most native speakers have an acquired 'common stock of (usually implicit) knowledge' when it comes to their home language, all speakers are challenged when it comes to academic writing. That said, the lack of implicit knowledge creates particular problems for speakers of other languages. We'll say no more on the subject at this point. Later in the book, we discuss the observation that no one is a native speaker of academic language.

Figures of speech deserve your attention because a well-chosen expression can enliven your writing and give your reader a clearer sense of your voice. (Can you identify the words in the preceding sentence that are used figuratively?) You also need to be aware of those expressions that weaken your prose or are inappropriate in academic writing.

As we said in the introduction, figurative language abounds in all forms of spoken and written language. Academic writing is no exception. In statements such as *Data suggest that the economy will shrink in the second quarter*, the word *suggest* is being used figuratively. Data don't suggest anything. Nor do they *imply*, *argue*, or *indicate* because data don't speak (or write)! The author of the statement is ascribing a quality or characteristic of human beings to a non-human entity. The technical term for this type of figurative language is personification.

The literal meaning of a word or expression is the definition of the word that is provided in a dictionary. If you look up the word *suggest*, the definition will be something like the following: *to advance an idea, usually about a course of action* as in, *I'm not happy with the results we got in the latest experiment. I suggest we replicate it.* In the example we provided in the previous paragraph,

---

David's students' struggles with figurative language

Some years ago, I developed and taught a thesis writing course to a group of doctoral students. The courses were compulsory and involved students from a range of faculties. Regardless of whether they were first or second-language speakers of English, the majority struggled when it came to mastering academic English, although the nature of their problems differed. Native speakers had few problems with figurative language. The second-language speakers did. In advance of a session on the topic, I asked students to bring expressions from their current reading that they didn't understand, and we would discuss them. In one seminar, Zena, a second-language student of environmental studies asked about *red herring*. "I came across a sentence in an article in which the author wrote, *Johnson's observation on climate change is a red herring*", she said.

> I know what *red* means, of course, but not *herring*. From my dictionary, I learned that it's a kind of fish. A red fish? It didn't make any sense. I asked a first language colleague if she knew what it

meant. She said it refers to a statement that is intended to mislead the reader. Whoever wrote the article is arguing that Johnson's observation on climate change is misleading. That's all very
well, but it still doesn't make any sense, so I asked her where
the expression came from – what the connection was between a
red fish and misleading. She didn't have a clue but knew what it
meant.

"That's the problem with all kinds of figurative expressions", I told
Zena.

There's no relationship between the literal meaning of the words
and, in this case the metaphorical meaning. In medieval times,
prison escapees drew smelly, dead fish across their escape path to
mislead police bloodhounds into chasing in the wrong direction.
So that's how the expression came to be generalised to any attempt to mislead or deceive.

"I like the history lesson, but I don't think I could ever use expressions
like this in my writing", said my student.

Well, the good news is that when it comes to writing up your thesis, these expressions are best avoided. In this case, a red herring
is a colloquialism – we'll discuss these another time. It probably
shouldn't have been used in an academic article.

"But if we're curious, what are we supposed to do?"

"Google it!" I replied. "There are plenty of free online dictionaries of
English idioms".

---

suggest is used figuratively not literally. It is unlikely that this instance of
figurative language will pose problems for second-language students. Others
will.

In discussing the metaphorical use of *suggest*, we said that the literal, meaning in spoken English is *to advance an idea, usually about a course of action*. In
the sentence, the word takes the form of a verb. However, like a great many
English content words, it can occupy other word classes. It can be a noun,
as in *The suggestion that climate change is a myth is simply ridiculous*, and as an
adjective: *She was offended by his suggestive offer*. Dictionaries usually present
these other literal meanings. Sometimes, if the figurative meaning is widely
used, it will also be included.

You can select any number of words that fill multiple roles. Here are just a few that we came up with at random: *blue, beat, stream, catch, hit. Blue* has the following literal meanings:

- adjective: (blue, bluer) *Blue shirts are mandatory at our school.*
- verb: (blue, blued) *Moisture rising from the ground blued the atmosphere.*
  Figurative meanings for blue in some dictionaries include:
- *I woke up feeling really blue this morning.* (depressed)
- *The money I received in my great-aunt's will came out of the blue.* (came unexpectedly)
- *I shouted at my kid to stop making a noise until I was blue in the face.* (make an effort to do something or change a situation with no success)
- *I made a real blue this morning when I asked the boss for a raise.* (mistake)

The meaning of *blue* in these statements is figurative because it is not possible to derive the sense in which the word is used from the literal meaning, which is an item on the color spectrum.

Notice that in the first exercise above, the statement, *I'll catch you later*, can be taken literally (*Later you will be captured by me.*) or figuratively (*I'll meet up with you later.*). Many figures of speech can be taken literally as well as figuratively. Second-language learners who are unfamiliar with figurative expressions will have a natural inclination to interpret these literally. This can lead to mutual confusion and misunderstanding, as in the following exchange.

> NS: I'll see you later.
>
> NNS: What time?
>
> NS: What do you mean?

Here the native speaker is using *I'll see you later* figuratively, meaning *Goodbye*. The non-native speaker, unaware that this is a common way of bidding farewell, interprets it literally.

Making connections

In which of the following statements is catch used figuratively? Rewrite the statements so that the meaning is expressed literally.

- He catches the ball.
- I'll catch you later.
- It was a spectacular catch.
- She was considered a great catch.

Consult a dictionary. Following the model, we provided above for the word blue, list the different word classes these words can occupy: *beat, stream, hit.*

Write a sentence to illustrate the literal use of the word as a noun, or verb and/or adjective, depending on the word classes that you have identified. (Don't simply appropriate examples from a dictionary. Make up your own.)

Now find at least one figurative meaning for the word and incorporate it into a sentence. (In brackets, indicate the literal meaning of the word.)

For example: I have a chemistry quiz tomorrow, so I'm going to have to hit the books tonight. (hit the books = study)

Come up with three words of your own and repeat the exercise.

A closer look at figures of speech

In this section, we will describe and illustrate the following figures of speech: simile, metaphor, idiom, colloquialism, cliché, and slang. We don't want you to be too concerned about definitional differences, which can be subtle. Our main concern is that you understand the degree of acceptability of different figurative expressions in academic writing.

Simile

A simile is a device for comparing one thing with another that it does not resemble, but which the author believes captures the essence or special feature of the entity or phenomenon in question. Not all statements involving "as … as" constructions are similes. "The Bentley is as stately as a Queen" is a simile. "The Bentley is as stately as a Rolls Royce", is not. "Buenos Aires is like a fading rose", is a simile. "Buenos Aires is like Rome", is not.

The simile is a popular device among creative writers, particularly poets of a romantic persuasion. William Wordsworth begins his celebrated poem *Daffodils* with the following lines:

> *I wandered lonely as a cloud*
> *That floats on high o'er dales and hills.*

They are also used to make a point in a humorous or dramatic way, as in, *A woman without a man is like a fish without a bicycle* is more striking than *Women have no need for men*.

When similes that might have been notable when first coined are overused, they become cliches (*as brave as a lion, as red as a rose, as fast as the speed of light*) or colloquialisms (*As angry as a cut snake* [Australian English]). We have more to say about cliches and colloquialisms later, where we make the point that, when it comes to academic writing, they are best avoided.

Similes in academic writing

Similes are frequently used in academic writing to make difficult or abstract concepts, comprehensible. Here are some examples from a range of disciplines.

- *Both Mitchell and Laplace thought of light as consisting of particles, rather like cannon balls, that can be slowed down by gravity and made to fall back on the star.*
- *Falling through the event horizon is a bit like going over Niagara Falls in a canoe.*
- *It is like burning an encyclopedia. Information is not lost if you keep all the smoke and ashes, but it is difficult to read.*
- *The problem of what happens at the beginning of time is a bit like the question of what happened at the edge of the world, when people thought the world was flat.*
- *Energy is rather like money. If you have a positive bank balance, you can distribute it in various ways.*

(Jobs for Editors, 2018)

Metaphor

Metaphors can be categorized in different ways. In literary fiction, up to 15 different types have been identified. These include primary, complex, dead, creative, extended, absolute, complex, implied, mixed, and root. The most relevant of these for the purpose of our discussion is the primary metaphor. These are closely related to similes. While similes make the comparison between one object or action and another explicit, metaphors go further, collapsing the object of interest and the comparison. The metaphorical equivalent of the Bentley example above would be: *The Bentley, is the stately*

Queen of cars. Here the Bentley is no longer as stately as a Queen, it *is a* stately Queen. In addition to primary metaphors, we will look at personification and grammatical metaphor, concepts of particular significance in academic writing.

Metaphors in academic writing

Metaphors are common in academic writing. Personification is particularly pervasive – so pervasive that when you research academic articles, you may not be aware of them.

The aim of the following exercise is to draw your attention to personification as well as other frequently used expressions in academic writing.

Here are our comments on use of metaphor in the statements:

1. 'Leverage' is a verb derived from the noun 'lever'. The literal meaning of leverage is 'to exert force by means of a lever'. In this statement, there are two senses in which the term is used metaphorically. In the first place, it is an instance of personification. (Translanguaging is a teaching method not a person.) Second, it refers to a mental capacity/skill, not to a physical activity.
2. The literal meaning of 'unpack' is to open and remove the contents of a container such as a suitcase or a storage box. Here it refers to the researchers' work in analyzing and interpreting their data.

Making connections

Examine the following statements taken from several empirical studies. What is the literal meaning of the underlined words? What is the relationship between the literal and metaphorical meaning?

1. Translanguaging in language education, therefore, recognizes and <u>leverages</u> learners' entire repertoire for learning.
2. We will now <u>unpack</u> the data presented in the previous section of our report.
3. In my literature review, I <u>surveyed</u> the <u>terrain</u> covered by the previous studies into the <u>efficacy</u> of the different vaccines current available.
4. This study <u>employed</u> a conceptual frame <u>borrowed from</u> a range of theoretical models.
5. In our pilot study, we analyzed the data through the <u>lens</u> of the analytical procedure described in the methodology section of the paper.

---

3. Here the terms 'surveyed' and 'terrain' are used metaphorically. As with statement 1, there are two senses in which the terms are used metaphorically. Both are instances of personification. In addition, they are both appropriated from the physical activity of land surveying. 'Efficacy' is a noun formed from the adjective 'effective'. This is an example of a grammatical metaphor, which we discuss below.

4. 'Employed' and 'borrowed from' are both personifications. Had the statement read "The researchers employed and borrowed from ...." the words would not be instances of personification but are still used metaphorically. (The researchers did not pay or borrow anything from the theoretical models.)

5. The literal meaning of 'lens' is 'a piece of curved glass for magnifying the size of an object over which it is placed'. Metaphorically, it means using a procedure or artifact for analyzing data.

Grammatical metaphor

The concept of 'grammatical metaphor' was first described by Halliday (1985). We have introduced it because it is "… one of the most important characteristics of academic, bureaucratic and scientific discourses …" (Devrim, 2015). It is also extremely complex. For this reason, we will describe only one type of metaphor. This is the process of turning actions (verbs) into things (nouns), a process called nominalization. This transformation makes a piece of writing increasingly abstract and difficult to process. Texts with lots of nominalization are difficult, if not impossible to process for many readers who are unfamiliar with the subject or whose command of academic English is less advanced (and this holds for first as well as second-language speakers of English).

Halliday uses the following example to illustrate this point.

1. Because technology is getting better, people are able to write business programs faster.
2. Because technology is advancing, people are (becoming) able to write business programs faster.
3. Advances in technology are enabling people to write business programs faster.
4. Advances in technology are making the writing of business programs faster.
5. Advances in technology are speeding up the writing of business programs.

The statement becomes more metaphorical from version 1 to version 5. By version 5, the processes (verbs) in version 1 (*getting better* and *to write*) become things (nouns) in version 5 (*advances in technology* and *the writing of business programs*). The conjunction *because*, which makes the relationship between improvements in technology and the ability of people to write faster business programs has disappeared completely. It is now replaced by the phrase *are speeding up*. (The example could be made even more challenging by substituting 'accelerating' for 'speeding up'.) If the message in version 5 is the same as version 1, what's the point of creating a version that is more difficult to process? Basically, version 5 expresses the message in a more abstract and generalized fashion. The question of whether it is 'better' depends on the audience, as we discussed in Chapter 4. According to Halliday, readers unfamiliar with the subject matter will find sentence 1 easier to process and therefore 'better'. (For a detailed discussion of this, and other types of grammatical metaphor, see Devrim, 2015. See also Halliday & Martin, 1993; Halliday & Matthiessen, 1999; Martin, 1992.)

Making connections

Here are two versions of a statement. The first is from Martin (1992). The second was written by us to make the statement easier to process. What modifications did we make? Was it easier to process?

Version 1

The enlargement of Australia's steel-making capacity, and of chemicals, rubber, metal goods, and motor vehicles all owed something to the demands of war.

Version 2

Wartime demanded that Australia's steel makers enlarge their capacity to produce chemicals, rubber, metal goods, and motor vehicles.

In version 1, the processes, *to enlarge* and *to demand*, are nominalized, that is turned into things *the enlargement* and *the demand*. We turned them back into processes and made the necessary adjustments to the rest of the statement. This adjustment resulted in the grammatical metaphor *the demand* into an instance of personification. It also means changing the theme of the statement from *enlargement* to *wartime*. Of course, within the content, this change of theme may make the original paragraph more difficult to process if the rheme of the preceding sentence is *enlargement*.

Idioms, colloquialisms, cliches, and slang

In this section, we describe and provide examples of idioms, colloquialisms, clichés, and slang. Like similes and metaphors, these have a figurative meaning which differs from their literal meaning of the individual words. Similes and metaphors are widely used and acceptable in academic writing. Idioms and colloquialisms vary in their degree of acceptability. Colloquialisms and slang are best avoided. Some are restricted to a particular speech community or country, and many are ephemeral, lasting no more than a generation or two. All four figures of speech are more common in speech than writing.

Dictionary definitions of 'idiom' are not particularly helpful. For example: "a group of words established by usage as having a meaning not deducible from those of individual words. (e.g., *over the moon, see the light*)". This definition holds for all figures of speech. The major difference between idioms and similes/metaphors is their widespread currency. Truly memorable similes and metaphors are unique. A good example would be the Irish poet Oscar Wilde's depiction of the sky as *a little tent of blue* in his poem *The Ballad of Reading Gaol*.

> *I never saw sad men who looked*
>
> *With such a wistful eye*
>
> *Upon the little tent of blue*
>
> *We prisoners called the sky*
>
> *And at every happy cloud that passed*
>
> *At such strange freedom by*

Well-chosen similes and metaphors have a place in academic writing. When it comes to idioms, however, you need to exercise caution. Some are acceptable, some marginally so, and some are unacceptable. The degree of acceptability will depend to a certain extent on the audience, purpose, and genre. The idiom *up in the air* might be acceptable in a departmental memo (*The health and safety committee was up in the air over whether to ban smoking on campus.*) In an assignment, thesis, or formal report, it would not be. In any of these genres we'd prefer *undecided* to *up in the air*. While the idiom might be more nuanced, implying perhaps a degree of confusion on the part of committee members, *undecided* is unambiguous and perfectly adequate.

In a graduate seminar on figurative language, a group of our highly proficient L2 students completed the exercise. The idioms they didn't know were: *pull the wool over someone's eyes, cross the bridge when you come to it, cut the mustard,* and *back to the drawing board*. Not surprisingly, they were unable to adjudicate on the acceptability or otherwise of the idioms they didn't know.

Making connections

Which of the following idioms do you know?

- The research report's conclusion was extremely vague. One reviewer had to <u>read between the lines</u> to interpret the findings. Another accused the author <u>of sitting on the fence</u>.
- According to Denny, psychometric research is not the <u>only game in town</u>.
- Smith's (2015) article into political conspiracy theories was an elaborate attempt at <u>pulling the wool over readers' eyes</u>.
- Many young researchers investigating child cognitive development <u>look up</u> to Alice Gopnik's <u>ground-breaking</u> work in the area.
- Although the research team <u>cut corners</u> in certain respects, they should be given the <u>benefit of the doubt</u> when it comes to the conclusions they reached.
- The journal editors wanted the <u>best of both worlds</u>.
- I don't want to be <u>a devil's advocate</u> but having your article rejected could be <u>a blessing in disguise</u>.
- I know you can't <u>judge a book by its cover</u>, but Arnold's recent work seems <u>a far cry</u> from his best.
- I doubt that your proposed topic will be acceptable to the research advisory committee, but you <u>can cross that bridge when you come to it</u>.
- A piece of writing that is full of idiomatic expressions just won't <u>cut the mustard</u>. The student will certainly be told by her advisor to <u>go back to the drawing board</u>!
- <u>At the end of the day</u>, the nature of the question should determine research paradigm to be used.

How would you express the above ideas in non-idiomatic English?

Here are two examples:

- A piece of writing that is full of idiomatic expressions just won't <u>cut the mustard</u>. (meet the required standards)
- The student will certainly be told by her advisor to <u>go back to the drawing board</u>! (start again from the beginning)

Which of the idioms would you consider to be acceptable in academic writing? Which would be unacceptable?

This exercise was designed to demonstrate that idioms vary in their acceptability in academic writing. Most students deemed these acceptable: *reading between the lines, sitting on the fence, ground breaking, benefit of the doubt, best of both worlds,* and *not being hard and fast*. It was generally agreed that these should never be used: *cutting the mustard, pulling the wool over someone's eyes, straight from the horse's mouth,* and *jumping on the bandwagon*. This doesn't mean that colloquialisms will never appear in formal writing or speech. In his inauguration as President of the United States, Joe Biden promised the American public that he would "level with you". While this idiom would generally be considered unacceptable on such a formal occasion, it packs a greater punch than the literal phrase "tell you the truth". It also shows an attempt by Biden to connect with his audience. We'll say a little more about degrees of acceptability later in the chapter.

Like the figures of speech we have already discussed, colloquialisms, clichés, and slang express meanings that can't be understood by the words that make them up. With few exceptions, however, they have no place in academic writing, but belong to everyday spoken language. Some are only used in certain speech communities. Others are generational, going out of fashion as abruptly as they have come in.

The exercise above also shows that the distinction between the different types of figurative language is not clear cut. Idioms such as *cut the mustard*, which we have identified as being unacceptable in academic writing, could also be classified as colloquial or even slang. Other expressions that could be classified as either idioms or colloquialisms include *hit the books* (put in extra study for an upcoming exam); *hit the sack/hit the hay* (go to bed); *on the ball* (competent and alert); *stirring the pot* (causing trouble in a mischievous way). (In our opinion, all of these examples are colloquialisms, even though some can be found in published lists of idioms.)

Clichés are everyday expressions that that have lost their communicative impact through overuse. Many began as similes and metaphors: for example, *as quiet as a mouse, as white as a ghost,* and *as blind as a bat,* but have lost their power over the years. Others entered everyday speech by way of literature. Shakespeare is the source of numerous present-day clichés such as *there's method in his madness* and *a rose by any other name would smell as sweet*. They weren't clichés when Shakespeare coined them of course, but over the centuries, they have been used thousands of times in speech and writing and are among the best-known clichés in the English language. Use them in everyday speech if you wish, but not in your writing. They certainly have no place in academic writing where their use reveals either lack of thought or ignorance on the part of the writer.

For those who advise others on the art and craft of writing, clichés are to be avoided at all costs. In his advice to would-be writers, Stephen King, one of the most successful authors in the world, had this to say about figurative writing.

> The most common [potential pitfall of figurative writing] is the use of clichés, similes, metaphors, and images. He ran **like a madman**, she was pretty **as a summer day**, the guy was **a hot ticket**, Bob fought **like a tiger**…don't waste my time (or anyone's) with such chestnuts. It makes you look either lazy or ignorant. Neither description will do your reputation as a writer much good.
>
> (King, 2000, p. 209)

We agree with King on clichés but not about similes and metaphors, with the caveat that they be well chosen. (King himself is not above using similes, metaphors, idioms, and even clichés.)

Slang refers to expressions that are extremely informal. As with colloquialism and clichés, they belong almost exclusively to spoken discourse and have no place in academic writing. Many slang expressions are specific to one variety or dialect of English but not to others. They also tend to last for a single generation. Some terms survive from one generation to the next, although their meaning can change. In the East End of London, the locals speak a variety of English known as cockney. It's an extremely colorful variety in which figurative language features prominently.

David on speech community slang

In 2012, I published a memoir of growing up a tough, working-class, minting township in the arid interior of Australia. The memoir took the form of short stories of critical incidents that had marked my path from infancy to young adulthood. In it, I tried to capture the colorful nature of working-class Australian English. The manuscript was accepted by an American publisher. When it was being prepared for publication, the editor wrote to me with a list of colloquialisms and slang expressions she found incomprehensible. "*He was flat out, like a lizard drinking*", she wrote, "What on earth does that mean?"

"It means that the person in question was extremely busy", I replied.

"But that doesn't make any sense".

"It would if you ever saw a lizard drinking. It makes furious, short, sharp motions of its head, and it scoops up water with its tongue". Having to explain these expressions, sucks all the life out or them, I though. It was like having to explain the punch line of a joke.

In due course, the book appeared. When I received an advance copy, I discovered a glossary of terms at the back of the book prefaced by the following statement:

This glossary provides a 'translation' from Australian English to American English of some of the words that may be unfamiliar to readers in North America.

Here are a few of the glossed terms, to give you a flavor of Australian slang.

arse-over-tit – head-over-heels

arvo – afternoon

bushie – a person who lives in the Outback (the 'Bush')

dipso – an alcoholic a dipsomaniac, i.e., a drunk

drongo – an idiot, person who doesn't something foolish

dunny outhouse – outdoor toilet

esky – an ice chest

to wag – to skip school

(Nunan, 2012, pp. 205–252)

Degrees of acceptability

As we have already indicated, there is no unanimity when it comes to the acceptability of figurative language in academic writing. Attitudes change over time and vary from one academic discipline to another. What is unacceptable to one generation is perfectly acceptable to the next. In the course of this book, we have provided examples of these changes, particularly the growing acceptance of the author's personal voice. Using personal pronouns no longer brings retribution. Attitudes toward the use of figurative language are also changing.

The following statements have been taken from assignments submitted by university students. Each contains a figure of speech that would be considered unacceptable by many academics, although there is no uniformity of opinion on this. Opinion also varies on the degree of acceptability. In a workshop on academic writing, a group of graduate students from a range of disciplines was asked to rate the acceptability of the underlined phrases on a scale from 1 – completely acceptable to 5 – completely unacceptable.

- I found this article to be over the top.
- We were able to delve deeply into our data.
- There was a bunch of theories in the papers we had to review.
- The teacher gave one group of students the third degree.
- Going forward, I want to investigate ways of getting my students up to speed on their listening.
- To start out, I wasn't really into working with young kids.
- Coming up with a research problem had me really bamboozled.
- The school had an English only policy. Use of the L1 was a complete no-no.
- I thought the lesson I had developed for my teaching practice as cool, but when I taught the class, it really backfired.
- The new online support opened a window of opportunity for those students who were prepared to go the extra mile.
- My supervisor was very critical of my research question. He said that it just didn't cut it. I had no idea what he was talking about.

Participants in the workshop completed the task individually and then worked in groups to compare their ratings and come to a consensus on the degree of acceptability of each. Although there was consensus on several items ('a complete no-no' was universally deemed a 'no-no'!), there was lack of agreement on items such as 'delve deeply', 'going forward, and 'a window of opportunity'. Some participants found them acceptable. Others did not.

Terry Denny, whom you met briefly earlier in the book, is one qualitative researcher who has developed a distinctive voice by using idioms, colloquialisms, and even slang. Here's an extract from an article he wrote in defense of storytelling in academic writing. The extract describes his method of doing fieldwork, which required him to travel around the country, spending his days interviewing informants and his evenings recording his data on index cards.

Making connections

As you read the piece below, underline the instances of figurative language.

Terry Denny breaks the rules

Rosalie Wax [is] my ideological patron saint. ... Successful fieldwork involves a lot of crazy little things that I learned the hard way; such as giving precise cleaning instructions to motel and boarding house service people, and getting the motel manager's permission to tape notes, maps on the wall. I promise swift and permanent injury to anyone who disturbs my bedspread's 3 × 5 card matrix... [you need] antidotes for going native... hit the library early on site ...go to the board of education and check out the last three years of board minutes (they'll think you're nuts) ... visit at least three neighbourhood bars and get the bartenders' view ... begin a series of Dutch-treat luncheons ...get out of the administrators office as soon as possible [and] set up shop in the open if at all possible ... give your informants a chance to check you out.... It's when I'm jiving, lying and exaggerating that the fieldwork gets hard ... The next topic is a bag full of tricks – the act of interviewing ... most books on interviewing techniques are devoted to fact finding, number crunching ... Therein lies the rub ... interviewing is the fatal flaw of many a field study .... Myopia runs a close second. (Denny, 1978/2015, pp. 48–52)

Denny's piece is crammed with all manner of figurative expressions: metaphors (*Rosalie Wax is my ideological patron saint*), colloquialisms (*going native, crazy little things, runs a close second*), clichés (*set up shop, number-crunching, fatal flaw, therein lies the rub* – the last item being a Shakespearean creation), and slang (*they'll think you're nuts, hit the library, jiving*). He flouts a core principle of this chapter to avoid colloquialisms or at least to treat them with caution. He does so, not only because it's become a feature of his own personal voice but also because it fits the audience, purpose, and context of the article.

Denny's chapter was originally delivered as a conference presentation. The breezy, informal style was appropriate given the context. Adopting the voice of a storyteller was also appropriate to the topic of the talk. This is not to say that the paper was insubstantial. On the contrary, it deals with the conceptually challenging issues, defining and teasing out the interrelationships between ethnology, ethnography, case study, and storytelling and "addressing issues of validity; of theory contribution, of completeness, of generality, of replicability" in academic writing. He gets away with it because he's a master storyteller and illustrates the truism that if you want to break the rules, you must master them first. Denny was acutely aware of the tone he wanted to strike – and strike it well he does.

This is in contrast with the students who produced the sentences we shared with you earlier. Most were unaware that some were unacceptable, or marginally acceptable at best, otherwise, they wouldn't have used them. All but one was first-language speakers of English. Second-language speakers rarely use colloquialisms or slang. They're either unaware of their existence, or don't know what they mean. 'Cut it', the last item on the above list underscores this point. It was deemed acceptable because it was used by her supervisor when giving oral feedback on a draft of her research proposal.

To summarize: use figurative language, and idioms – it's difficult not to – but be aware of how, when, and why you are doing so. In this book, we deliberately adopted a relatively informal style, evident in our use of contractions and idioms (e.g. *gets away with it*, in the paragraph above). We did so because the book introduces complex and unfamiliar concepts and we wanted it to be as accessible (*reader friendly*) as possible. In discussing the Biden example, it was no accident that we used *packed a greater punch* rather than the literal *had more impact*. However, our advice to you remains avoid colloquialisms and clichés and do not use slang.

Questions from readers

Q: I'm still not sure about the difference between similes, metaphors, and idioms. Could you elaborate a little more about the distinction between these figures of speech?

A: As we said earlier in the chapter, there is overlap between the figures of speech we discuss. All are made up of words that have a literal meaning. However, the figurative meaning can't always be determined directly from its literal meaning (although this is sometimes possible from the context). The idiom *he's on the ball*, which originated in the 18th century, had its origin in sports involving a ball. These days, the idiom refers to someone who has initiative and competence and gets things done without being directed to do so. Idioms are widely used within a given speech community and are generally more common in spoken rather than written language. This is not always the case with similes and metaphors. When Wordsworth likens himself to a cloud (*I wandered lonely as a cloud, that floats on high o'er vales and hills* …) the personification creates a powerful image. However, the expression never became idiomatic. Nor did Wilde's metaphorical depiction of the sky as a '*tent of blue*'. Many of Shakespeare's figures of speech did. The example we cited earlier: *a rose by any other name would smell as sweet* is so widely used it's now considered a cliché; so common, in fact, that it often goes unfinished:

> *What are you going to call that fabulous pasta sauce you created last night?*
>
> *Doesn't matter. A rose by any other name* … (shrug of the shoulders.)

Q: As a second-language speaker, I'm frequently confused by figures of speech. Some I can figure out, both most I can't. I'm not sure about using them in my own writing.

A: If you have any doubts about a particular expression, you can ask your interlocutors whether the expression you are thinking of makes sense or if there is a better or more accurate expression in English. Our past students, who have knowledges of many different languages, sometimes try out figurative language from languages they are more familiar with and ask us if there is an equivalent in English. We often get into rich discussions comparing the different characterizations of things. Of course, this kind of negotiation is not always possible in written work, but you can always try translating and looking up words online to see whether there are similar expressions. Longman Publishing and Oxford University Press both publish dictionaries of idioms. There are also online glossaries of idioms.

Summary

Initially, we had planned to cover the topic of figurative language in Chapter 1, where we introduced you what we consider the basics of what every writer of academic English should know about language. However, as we started drafting the chapter, we realized that the topic was so rich, and the use of figurative language is so pervasive that it demanded a chapter of its own. (Just look at the two instances of figurative language in the preceding sentence!) As a writer it's useful to know the differences between different types of figurative language even though particular expressions can migrate from one type to another. What does matter is to be aware of which expressions are acceptable in academic language, which are marginal, and which are unacceptable. Similes and metaphors that illustrate a concept or assertion can add life to your prose. If you have a doubt, leave it out, or get a second opinion. As we demonstrated in the chapter, idioms occupy a figurative middle ground. We also said that times change, acceptability is not immutable. Expressions that are unacceptable to one generation become acceptable to the next. Audience and purpose are also important as the Biden speech, and the Denny extract demonstrate.

Figures of speech, particularly idioms and colloquialisms, are often signs of confusion or lack of thought on the part of the writer. Before submitting a piece of work, you should scan it for figures of speech. Get rid of clichés and slang. In relation to other colloquialisms and idiomatic expressions, ask yourself whether these reflect confusion or uncertainty about what you really want to say. If so, rephrase them. This is not always an easy process, but it's worth the effort. As we have intimated throughout this book, writing is hard work and, in Clive James' words, writing clearly is the hardest thing of all.

Further reading

Lakoff, G., & Johnson, M. (1980). *Metaphors we live by*. The University of Chicago Press.
This book has been around for many years, and for good reason. It's a classic. If you can get hold of a copy, at the very least, read the opening chapter.

References

Denny, T. (1978/2015). Story-telling and educational understanding. *Case Study Evaluation: Past, Present and Future Challenges, 15*, 41–61.

Devrim, D. Y. (2015). Grammatical metaphor: What do we mean? What exactly are we researching? *Functional Linguist, 2*(3), 1–15. https://doi.org/10.1186/s40554-015-0016-7

Halliday, M. A. K. (1985). *Introduction to functional grammar*. Edward Arnold. Halliday, M. A. K., & Martin, J. R. (1993). *Writing science: Literacy and discursive power*. The Falmer Press.

Halliday, M. A. K., & Matthiessen, C. M. I. M. (1999). *Construing experience through meaning: A language-based approach to cognition*. Cassell.

Jobs for Editors. (2018, November 12). *Similes in writing*. https://web.archive.org/web/20220723044330/https://jobsforeditors.com/blog/similes-in-writing.html

King, S. (2000). *On Writing: A memoir of the craft*. Hodder & Stoughton.

Martin, J. (1992). *English text: System and structure*. John Benjamins.

Nunan, D. (2012). *When Rupert Murdoch came to tea: A memoir*. Wayzgoose Press.

7

Seeking and providing meaningful feedback

Getting meaningful feedback is an essential step in improving a piece of writing. As the author, you will be too close to your writing regardless of whether it's an assignment, a piece for a student newsletter, or an article for a refereed journal. One way we gain distance is to put it aside for a while – a few days, weeks, or even a few months. We do this when we finish the first draft of a book and again as we complete successive drafts of individual chapters. Of course, you won't have the luxury of abandoning your piece for weeks or months. However, when working on an assignment, you should plan to finish the draft leaving enough time to put it aside for a few days at the very least. If you're adept at time management, you'll leave enough time to get feedback from a 'critical' friend.

In this chapter, we discuss some of the practicalities of seeking feedback on our own work and providing meaningful feedback to others. Questions addressed in the chapter include: What is feedback? Who should provide feedback? How should it be provided? At what point in the drafting process should it be provided?

What is meaningful feedback?

We frame this section by looking at feedback in educational contexts in general and in academic writing in particular. Let's begin by considering it in everyday life where it's ubiquitous. When we're in contact with other people, we constantly monitor and evaluate the signals they send and adjust our behavior accordingly. Much of the feedback is non-verbal, subconscious on their part, and barely conscious on ours. How do we interpret the raised eyebrows on the face of a colleague as we enter a meeting? Did we slap on too much makeup in a rush to make the meeting on time? Why does our supervisor purse her lips and pluck at her chin as we present to our seminar

DOI: 10.4324/9781003179092-8

group the conclusions we draw from a literature review? Does it signal disagreement or dissatisfaction? At a more conscious level, think of the many contexts in which the word 'feedback' is used:

- *Can you adjust your microphone? We're getting too much feedback out here.*
- *I think we're on the right track – the feedback from the focus group was extremely positive.*
- *Can you take notes while I rehearse my talk and give me feedback on how I can improve the presentation?*
- *My boss gave me several pages of feedback on the draft report, so now I have to redo it from scratch.*

Despite the range of contexts, whether the feedback was verbal or non-verbal, formal or informal, spoken or written, they have a similar pattern: action > reaction > response. Let's now look at how this pattern also plays out in educational contexts. We begin with some examples of feedback.

1. *You applied the wrong statistical procedure to your data.*
2. *Overall, I really liked the design of your study. Unfortunately, you applied the wrong statistical procedure to your data.*
3. *Overall, I really liked the design of your study. Unfortunately, you applied the wrong statistical procedure to your data. The good news is that you still have the raw data, so you can rerun the analysis.*
4. *Overall, I really liked the design of your study. Unfortunately, you applied the wrong statistical procedure to your data. The good news is that you can rerun your data. You need ANOVA – analysis of variance – not a whole bunch of t-tests.*

While these are concocted examples, they're representative of the kinds of feedback that we've observed in different settings from classroom observations to teacher education workshops and student consultations. The first exemplifies negative feedback. The advisor bluntly informs the student that there is a basic flaw in his research design. The burden of the second statement is also to deliver bad news, but the advisor mitigates the news by providing some positive feedback. In the third example, the bad news is sandwiched between two pieces of good news. Hyland and Hyland (2001) refer to this as 'sugaring the pill'. They point out that, while this could minimize the negative effect of the bad news, the student might miss the real intent of the feedback, which is to deliver bad news. Example 4 demonstrates the good news, bad news, good news pattern, but also suggests a solution. So, the aim of all four pieces of feedback is to deliver bad news, but two mitigate the bad news by giving the student something positive to take away from the consultation. Example 4 goes one step further by offering the student a solution.

The standard definition of feedback is to provide information on the performance of a product (*In general, your sentences are far too long, and overburdened with information which makes them difficult to process.*), a procedure (*The ideas in your report are all over the place.*), or an individual or group of individuals (*The choir was off-key on the high notes.*). This definition is fine as far as it goes, but for our purposes, it doesn't go far enough. It's problematic for two reasons. In the first place, it fails to distinguish between formative and summative feedback. Summative feedback is provided at the end of the instructional process when there are no second chances. The judgment is final. The aim of formative feedback is to provide recipients with information or advice to help them improve the product or process. They get a second chance. In this chapter, we focus on formative feedback, that is, on advice or suggestions from teachers, peers, and others intended to help you improve your writing. The statements would have been improved with the addition of a suggestion on improving the product or process, for example:

- *In general, your sentences are far too long and overburdened with information which makes them difficult to process. When you revise the essay, try cutting these longer sentences into two or even three shorter ones.*
- *The ideas in your report are all over the place. It's fine as a first draft, when you're developing your ideas, but next time use it to sketch out an overall plan to guide you as you produce a final draft.*
- *The chorus was off-key on the high notes. In future, the conductor should rehearse those sections separately.*

Another problem with the 'standard definition' of feedback is that it isolates the product, the process, and the person. This might be justified if the focus is a piece of electrical hardware, or an aspiring Olympic gymnast, but not if the focus is a piece of academic writing where all three are in play.

Like motherhood, positive feedback is a 'good thing'! It motivates us to continue. According to the beautician Mary Kay Ashworth, we value recognition and praise even more than money and sex! Well, that's her opinion. As with negative feedback, it can be helpful to the writer if the statement indicates why the writing is good. Negative feedback can be dispiriting and therefore demotivating. Effective feedback will contain positive comments as well as indicating areas for improvement. As already noted, the best feedback also suggests a solution, or where a solution might be found. Least useful are negative comments that are vague and imprecise. You've probably had a piece of writing returned with comments such as: *I didn't really get the argument you were trying to make. Your points need to be better organized. This essay is very vague. You could do better. You need to put more effort into your writing.* If you receive comments such as these, which provide no indication of the nature of the problem, or negative feedback with no suggestions on how the piece might be improved, you have every right to schedule a meeting with your assessor and ask for further clarification.

The question framing this section contains the adjective 'meaningful'. You might think the word is redundant. It should be. While it might be meaningful to the person giving the feedback, this is hardly the point. If it is vague, fails to pinpoint the aspect(s) of writing needing improvement, and/or doesn't include *how* perceived problems might be addressed, then it will not be meaningful to the author. For all writers, meaningful feedback will deal with substantive issues, such as the content, strengths or weaknesses in argumentation, and so on. But it will also focus on the linguistic issues dealt with in earlier chapters. (This should come as no surprise, given the subtitle of this book.)

Sean Wang, one of Julie's current master's level students studying to become a teacher, shares his views on feedback.

Sean's voice on feedback

When I entered my bachelor's degree at a university in Australia, I realized teachers normally will not tell us what they want to see in our assignments. They release some basic requirements and criteria and let us think individually. Most teachers in the undergraduate programs will not let students share their 'essay plans' with them. They may listen to my basic ideas of argument or thesis statement but many times, the feedback I received from them was "this statement is interesting, your argument is good, the topic is heated, I think you have a clear idea, just keep going". But after I received my grade, I always felt unsatisfied. The feedback I received was only a few words, usually a kind of "summary statement" on my assignment. During the three years of my undergraduate study, I just got tired of such "useless" feedback. Before the assignment, they make everything seem like it all looks perfect. However, after I receive the feedback, I feel like everything needs to change. It seems to me, the problem is, the feedback is never clear enough. I have no idea where the specific problem is and how I can improve next time. I understand each teacher has many assignments to mark and it is impossible for them to give detailed feedback. However, from a student's perspective, it just looks like they are lazy and shirking their responsibilities.

When I received Julie's feedback on my essay, I was shocked. The feedback was detailed, clear, and simple to understand. She put a lot of annotations on my paper to let me know where the mistakes were (e.g., grammar, spelling, wrong typing, and unclear ideas). At the end of the feedback, she gave me a long paragraph to summarize. As a student in Education who is studying to become a teacher, I think this type of feedback is what I really need.

Another of Julie's students Francesca Lo Presti reflects on an experience of receiving meaningful feedback and the impact this had on her to reflect on what she had written. It is also possible to see how meaningful feedback isn't just related to the content or how to improve the work but can have an affective impact, making students feel valued, inspired about the profession they are writing about, and these feelings in turn motivate them to take their studies and writing more seriously.

Francesca's voice on feedback

In my experience as a university student, I have received much feedback on my assignments. Most of them did not have any particular impact as they would only point out the problem without effectively helping me understand how I could have done better. I did not receive feedback for other assignments, which made me feel like I was not even worth an explanation. After all, I am the student, just a number among other numbers. There is no time for me, nor anyone else.

Then, one day, I received feedback for one of my assessments, and to my surprise, this was different. In reading it, it was like my tutor was speaking to me. A few simple but powerful words made me feel valued not only as a student but also as a person. I sat back and reflected for a while. I reread it more than once, and I thought that this time, my tutor had spent some time writing to ME, FOR me, and about MY work. That is when I thought: WOW! She has read my paper and has given up her time FOR me to write what she thought about it, in a way that made me stop and reflect on what I had written myself.

This experience was highly impactful for two reasons. First, from meaningful feedback came meaningful reflection of my work and organization of thoughts. I was forced to stop and think about what I had written and appreciate it from another point of view. Second, this feedback was pouring passion and appreciation for the teaching profession. I could feel how much dedication and attention my teacher put into her job, and this awareness impacted my motivation as a student.

Responding to feedback

There are various ways of responding to feedback depending on the nature of the piece of writing and the purpose of the feedback. If you receive summative feedback from an unknown assessor, for example, an examiner's report on your master's thesis or a capstone project, you obviously won't be able to respond directly. You may complain to your supervisor or advisor that the examiner has 'misunderstood me', which may be your fault because as a writer, the onus is on you to present your case as clearly and coherently as possible to minimize the possibility of misunderstanding. You shouldn't dismiss such unidirectional feedback out of hand. While you can't contest the comments with the author, you can learn from them. External examiners are generally highly experienced. They put considerable time and effort into their work and their comments shouldn't be taken lightly. Once you've recovered from the disappointment of receiving a negative evaluation or a lower grade than you'd hoped for, take time to reflect on the comments and consider how you can use at least some of them to improve your writing.

Numerous studies have looked at how students respond to teacher feedback. There is no space here to provide a detailed overview of this research. What we'd like to do is return to a piece of research that featured in Chapter 4. In that chapter, we provided the backstory to a study carried out by Kailin Liu. The study was written up and co-published by Kailin and her supervisor, Neomi Storch. Here, we provide a summary of the study because the context and focus are directly relevant to this chapter. Two research questions were investigated by the researchers:

- How do L2 learners respond to teacher written feedback given on different aspects of their writing?
- What individual and contextual factors influence L2 learners' engagement with teacher-written feedback? (Liu & Storch, 2021)

The context for the research was an advanced academic writing course for L2 graduate students at a large Australian university. The focus was student responses to written feedback on the first draft of one of their assignments. The data included student drafts, teacher-written feedback, and transcripts of semi-structured interviews in which students reported their perceptions and feelings about the feedback and described the changes they made to the draft in light of the feedback. Four main dimensions which aligned with the assessment criteria emerged from the data: Language (written corrective feedback (WCF)), Ideas (development and clarity), Structure (cohesion and coherence), and Citation conventions. Feedback points were designated as either direct or indirect. (We describe and give examples of these feedback later in the chapter.)

Most of the teacher's feedback points focused on WCF in the form of direct reformulations and indirect suggestions. Incorporation of the feedback into students' revised draft was very high (97%). This was the case even when the feedback was not totally understood or agreed with by the students. Evidence from the interviews suggested that this was because the teacher was the one who would be grading the final draft of the assignment. Despite this, the researchers noted that there were "signs of resistance and an emerging sense of agency, particularly when responding to ideas and structure compared to WCF" (p. 18). Reasons students reported resisting suggestions included feeling that the original was clear enough, and that the suggested change did not reflect the students' intended meaning. Some students wanted direct feedback because they were able simply to copy the reformulated sentences. Others preferred indirect feedback because it stimulated them to process the feedback more deeply and to come up with their own correction or solution to the error. This is not to say their solution was the correct one, particularly when it came to ideas and structures which are more abstract and there may be more than one solution, in contrast with language (i.e., grammatical and lexical errors). Liu and Storch argue that if there is follow-up discussion with the teacher and/or peers of the problem indicated in the feedback a possible solution to it, this can be a valuable learning opportunity.

Seeking critical feedback from others can also be important. 'Critical' is the operative word. Relative and close friends are notoriously unreliable and are to be avoided. Having a teacher provide comments on a draft would obviously be helpful as she will be marking the assignment. However, don't be disappointed of your invitation to preview your piece is politely but firmly rejected. If the teacher accepts your invitation, she will be under a moral obligation to provide formative feedback to the other students in the class. Peer feedback, in which you exchange drafts with a fellow student and give each other comments, can also be helpful for improving the clarity of your work. In the next section, we'll provide more details on this procedure.

Making connections

Think of a recent situation in which you received feedback.

- What was the context?
- Was it formal or informal, formative or summative?
- Who provided the feedback?
- Was it oral or written?
- Was it to the group or to individuals?
- Was the feedback positive, negative, or both?
- How did you react?
- Did you find it helpful or unhelpful, motivating or demotivating?
- What, if anything did you do as a result of the feedback?

Peer feedback

In our own teaching, we have used a peer feedback procedure successfully. In the procedure, students form pairs, exchange draft assignments, and give each other feedback. From the teacher's point of view, the procedure can be a time-saving way of students getting feedback on early drafts of their work and improving the quality of their written work. For it to be successful, a number of caveats are in order. Participation must be optional. Choice of partner by those students who volunteer to take part must be by mutual consent. Feedback and discussion should focus on those parts of the text that are unclear to the reader. Critiquing the content, and negative comments are to be avoided, although it's acceptable to point out errors of spelling and punctuation. These caveats were negotiated and agreed to over time by students themselves as we experimented with the procedure. The Liu and Storch (2021) study deals, among other issues, with peers as a potential source of feedback.

David's experience with peer feedback in his classroom

Some years ago, I introduced peer feedback in my undergraduate academic writing classes at the University of Hong Kong. Students initially resisted this form of feedback. When I discussed their reluctance, several issues emerged. Students didn't feel that their peers would have the knowledge to give informed feedback. They didn't want to be put in the position of receiving negative feedback or giving it themselves. They wanted feedback directly from me.

I pointed out that peer feedback was one of the techniques I used to encourage a more reflective and independent attitude to learning on their part. It wasn't my intention that they should criticize each other or make judgments, but that they could get feedback on parts of their piece where the ideas were unclear or could be elaborated. I pointed out that this review process was not a waste of time, but an important part of the learning process and of becoming a better writer. I also stressed the fact that I would certainly be providing detailed feedback on the final draft of their assignment, but that, given the number of students in my classes, it wasn't feasible to provide detailed formative feedback on initial drafts. I then worked collaboratively with the students to develop a peer feedback procedure in the form of a set of non-judgmental questions to guide the review process. Once the procedure was implemented, students came to accept its value.

Corrective feedback

In addition to documenting graduate students' reactions to written feedback, Liu and Storch (2021) investigated the contextual factors that led to great engagement by their informants with the feedback. Engagement is important. If students are disengaged, it's unlikely that they will benefit from the feedback. The literature on corrective feedback indicated that contextual factors might include:

- whether the feedback was verbal or written
- whether it was directed to an individual student or the class as a whole
- whether it was indirect or direct
- the focus of the feedback (This could include any of the aspects of writing that we have introduced in this book such as grammar, vocabulary, punctuation, cohesion, coherence, thematization, overall structure, paragraph structure, figurative language, and appropriateness to the audience.)

Liu and Storch found direct versus indirect feedback to be a primary distinction in the feedback provided by the teacher (Storch) in their study. In direct feedback, the teacher reformulates the students' error. In some cases, the reformulation was accompanied by an explanation, and in others it was not. In indirect feedback, the teacher indicates the existence of a problem but leaves it to the learner to figure out what it is. (We prefer the word 'problem' to 'error', because occasionally, the issue is not an 'error', but something problematic such as an inappropriate choice of vocabulary. In the Liu and Storch study the indirect feedback was made as a suggestion. Again, in some cases the suggestion was accompanied by an explanation, and in others was not. According to their learning styles, students varied in their preference for direct or indirect feedback and whether they wanted an explanation for the teacher's intervention.

In the case of indirect feedback, the teacher can draw attention to the existence of an error or a problem and then give a suggestion as to the nature of the problem in the form of an 'error guide sheet':

For example:

sp – spelling

mc – no main clause

pl – plural

ic – incomplete sentence

ap – apostrophe

ca – comparative adjectives

t – tense

th – thematization

co – cohesion

ch – coherence

vc – vocabulary choice

Student's sentence: The focus of the interview was international students from China who had experience living in two different geographic.

Direct reformulation: The focus of the interview was international students from China who had experience living in two different geographic regions.

Reformulation plus explanation: "Geographic is an adjective. Its purpose is to describe a quality or attribute of a noun. In your sentence, there is no noun". (This explanation is wordy. It's unrealistic to expect teachers to reply at such length. Also, the writer may be unfamiliar with the distinction between attributive and predicative adjectives. More succinct would be "Incomplete sentence. The adjective (geographic) needs to be followed by a noun".)

Indirect: The focus of the interview was international students from China who had experience living in two different geographic.

Indirect suggestion: The focus of the interview was international students from China who had experience living in two different geographic. (ic)

Some researchers argue that indirect feedback is more effective than direct feedback because it requires a greater depth of cognitive processing than when the students is simply given the correct form. In other words, the student has to think harder. In the Liu and Storch study, some learners prefer direct feedback, while others prefer indirect feedback.

Making connections

- If you are currently studying, which strategies do your teachers use when giving feedback on your writing?
- What kinds of errors do they correct?
- Do you prefer direct or indirect feedback?
- Do you like having explanations of problems of grammar or would you rather figure out the nature of the problem yourself?
- Do different teachers prefer to give written feedback, oral feedback, or a combination?
- What could you ask more for?

Here is what Kailin Liu had to say about direct versus indirect feedback. These comments were made in relation to her classes of secondary school students, not the graduate students who provided the data for her study with Neomy Storch.

Kailin's voice on direct versus indirect feedback

Students tend to react more (and sometimes only) to direct feedback that gives them the answer and tells them what needs to be fixed in a succinct manner. Yet, whether and to what degree students understand the feedback and learn the knowledge involved is often unknown. In many situations, students do not seem to be asking the 'why' of the feedback or to acquire a new understanding or skill, as they just simply revise the teacher-highlighted parts strictly as instructed without examining their writing as a whole. They may also not be able to articulate why changes need to be made in a certain way.

As for indirect feedback that are often posed as questions for students to think about their development of ideas in writing, many seem to have little engagement with it on their own and they do not really understand its meaning or what to do with it. This is often observed through the follow-up individual writing conference, where students seem to be reading and thinking about this feedback for the first time and then often relying on the teacher to give them the solution to their development of ideas in writing.

For a comprehensive review of corrective feedback, see Ellis (2010).

Computer-mediated feedback

Much of the first draft of this book was completed during the Covid-19 pandemic. During this time, institutions around the world were in lockdown, and teaching at all levels, from elementary to postgraduate, had to be conducted online. The quality of instruction ranged from abysmal to inspirational. (The only people who were truly happy were those who had shares in Zoom!) Every challenge brings opportunities, and creative teachers found opportunities to extend their professional skills. Learners also found new ways of developing their language skills through the resources offered on the Internet.

Of course, computer-aided instruction (CAI) predated the appearance of Covid by many decades. It's not our intention to rehearse the story of CAI here. In this section, we want to take a selective look at the use of digital resources for providing feedback. (For a compact and accessible history of computer assisted language learning, see Beatty, 2010.) When it comes to writing, millions of users rely on the autocorrect function of Microsoft Word (MS Word) to correct errors of spelling, punctuation, and grammar. Teachers recommend, and students rely on the feedback offered by the software. More recent versions also suggest changes to the text to improve the clarity of a sentence. In general, these suggested changes are helpful, but in many instances, they are not. The feedback either removes the nuances from the original, or the suggestions are just plain wrong.

MS Word's correction in Example 1 is incorrect. The 's' on the end of 'thing' indicates plurality, not possession. We rejected the correction out of hand. Example 2 requires deeper consideration. If you've been reading this chapter as carefully as we hope you have, you will know we accepted the advice. Our original sentence was not incorrect, but MS Word's was better. While there's nothing wrong with 'take a' removing the words results in a sharper statement. (We had overlooked the advice we offered you in Chapter 4, and elsewhere, on wordiness.) Example 3 is similar to Example 2. Our original sentence and MS Word's suggested amendment are both grammatically correct. In this case, we rejected the feedback. 'Actually' serves an important communicative function within the sentence. It acts as an intensifier to the

Making connections

Here are four examples of MS Word corrections, one of which we accepted and one we rejected. Which would you reject, and which would you accept? Why?

Example 1

We wrote: *There are two things people want more than sex and money …*

MS Word suggested: *There are two things' people want more than sex and money …*

Example 2

We wrote: *Let's take a look at these four examples…*

MS Word suggested: *Let's look at these four examples…*

Example 3

We wrote: *What she didn't know was that the assignment had been double marked, and that the second teacher had actually argued for a lower grade.*

MS Word suggested: *What she didn't know was that the assignment had been double marked, and that the second teacher argued for a lower grade.*

Example 4

In an article on research methods, David cited the following sentence from Donald Freeman (2018, p. 25): *The meaning is the substance; it is what you have to work with, what travels from the situation itself in time and space to other settings.*

MS Word suggested: *The meaning is the substance; it is what you must work with, what travels from the situation itself in time and space to other settings.*

point we are making and strengthens the original teacher's assessment that the essay was inadequate. If the sentence had been spoken, the stress would fall on 'actually'. Use of past perfect rather than simple past also strengthens the argument being made, highlighting the relevance of a prior event (a second teacher's assessment) to a more recent past event (the objection of the student to her grade). Example 4 is another example of a suggested amendment that is perfectly grammatically correct and makes sense. The difference between 'have to' and 'must' is in the strength of the suggestion. By changing 'have to' to 'must', MS Word is suggesting that Freeman is telling the reader that it is imperative that your work with meaning. However, there is another interpretation, Freeman might be telling the reader that meaning is the only resource available. Under this interpretation, 'to' belongs to the prepositional phrase 'to work with', not to 'have'. Given the broader context of the text from which the sentence is taken, it is clear that this is the interpretation Freeman intended.

Accepting corrective feedback from a machine presents challenges for both first and second-language writers. While the challenges are more acute for L2 writers, their first-language counterparts are not above reproach, as Lynne Truss reminds us in relation to the apostrophe. If L1 writers randomly insert an apostrophe when it signals plurality rather than possession, they are more than likely to accept MS Word's correction (Truss, 2005).

In recent years, online software packages for improving written texts have become popular. One such tool is *Grammarly*, which is more sophisticated than MS Word, being able to do all that Word can do, and more. For example, it can provide explanations for corrections and so can function as an instructional tool. The package claims to be free, but this is a marketing 'hook', as the free feedback it provides is limited. If you want more detailed feedback, you have to pay for it. In addition to 'correctness', it offers feedback on 'clarity', 'engagement', and 'delivery'. Consider the following paragraph from a graduate student's essay.

> Identity construction is not stationary, but the culture of a particular community influences it. It is perceived to be a continuous process, being influenced by several external factors, such as interaction with the people. Language change the identities, and the identity shaped by varied languages used daily. The statement states that one can be born in a particular country, and their character linked to a different culture from where they were born. Derakhshan (2019) notes that language is not static, and there exist different languages spoken in the world.

If you are using the free version of *Grammarly*, the text receives an overall score of 94. For 'correctness', two errors are highlighted, and the following advice is provided in a side box (see p. 157):

We like the approach taken here. The first error is explained deductively. A second error is highlighted, and the writer is left to figure how to correct it inductively. The other characteristics of good writing, 'clarity', 'engagement', and 'delivery' are vague and subjective, and the writer is provided with

> ## is shaped
>
> It seems that you are missing a verb. Consider changing it.
>
> Learn more.
>
> **Linked** – Add a missing verb.

vague and subjective feedback: 'clarity' receives a 'very clear', 'engagement', 'engaging', and for 'delivery', the text is considered to be 'just right'. The writer is then informed that there are three other problems with the text. These are highlighted (see below), but if the writer wants feedback, he/she will have to pay for the Premium service. Otherwise, they will have to figure out the problem for themselves. (Other problems are missed. These include the imprecise 'stationary', in sentence 1, which should more accurately be 'static' – which the author is clearly aware of as she uses it in the final sentence. More seriously, lack of subject–verb agreement 'language change', which even MS Word picked up, is also missed.)

Tharanga, one of the Julie's doctoral students recently completed her doctoral research into multilingual MOOC students' online writing practices in higher education environments. Here is what she had to say about two of her informants' experiences with feedback from text editors.

> ## Tharanga's voice: L2 writers' experiences with text editors
>
> L2 students bring with them myriad meaning-making resources to self-scaffold their writing compared to their L1 counterparts. These included linguistic resources such as their mother tongue, other languages, meta-linguistic knowledge (cognate words between mother tongue and L2), and digital resources, for instance, digital translators (Google Translate), online dictionaries (monolingual and bilingual), and text editors (MS Word, Grammarly) to facilitate writing in English. In general, they reported mixed feelings about the usefulness and effectiveness of these tools.
>
> A common practice was to draw on their metalinguistic knowledge of true cognates or words that have a similar meaning in their L1 and L2. For example, Gloria, an L1 speaker of Portuguese pursuing doctoral studies in English in a Brazilian university wrote the word 'transmite' in

her text. This was immediately underlined by Word's spellchecker. She replaced it with 'transmit', one of the three options offered. In a stimulated recall interview, she admitted that she frequently juxtaposed Portuguese spelling when writing in English. Mastering the conventions of English spelling takes years of practice. She and another informant found the instant feedback, during the course of writing, was extremely helpful. However, when it comes to false cognates, this feature is not so helpful. When Bianca, an L1 Spanish speaker wrote 'ilustration', the spellchecker altered it to 'illustration'. In our interview, when I asked her why she wrote 'illustration', she said she thought it meant 'enlightenment' as it does in Spanish.

These examples show that a text editor can be useful in providing immediate feedback during the composing process. However, for multilingual writers whose proficiency is not advanced enough to enable them to differentiate between true and false cognates, it can lead them astray.

When it comes to feedback on the coherence of written texts, a major disadvantage of computer-mediated feedback such as MS Word and software like *Grammarly* is that they are confined to sentence-level corrections of punctuation, spelling, and grammar, and even at this level, the feedback is by no means infallible as we have seen. Analyzing and correcting problems beyond the sentence have, at the point of writing this book, been a challenge for technology. In earlier chapters, we have presented extracts from students' writing showing that problems at the discourse level cause far greater challenges than sentence-level errors. We use the word 'problems' rather than 'errors' because the individual sentences making up a longer stretch of discourse such as a paragraph may be error-free but lack coherence. In Chapter 2, we introduced the notion of cohesion. We pointed out that cohesive devices such as reference, substitution, conjunctions, and lexical cohesion can assist readers in making links between the sentences in a text, but they don't create coherence because coherence is an inside-the-head factor.

> While cohesive devices provide helpful pointers to connectivity, they do not create the connectivity. So, where is the source of the coherence? If it does not reside in the language itself, it must reside in the individuals who process the language – the reader and listener. In other words, while cohesion resides in language, coherence resides in the person processing the text.
>
> (Nunan, 2010, p. 115)

Making connections

Download the free version of *Grammarly* and use it to evaluate a paragraph or two of your own writing.

- How useful is the feedback?
- What did you learn about your writing?
- Would you consider buying the Premium version of the program? Why or why not?

It would be unwise, arrogant in fact, to dismiss the ability of technologists to devise programs for providing feedback to writers (and teachers) for dealing with discourse-level problems. Theme/rheme patterning in which the rheme of one sentence becomes the theme of the next would be one area where this might be possible. Of course, if texts adhered relentlessly to this patterning, the result would be writing that puts readers to sleep. In a meticulous piece of linguistic scholarship published over 30 years ago, Hoey (1991) showed the remarkable intricacy in the patterning of authentic written texts. He demonstrated that while cohesion makes an important contribution, it does not constitute coherence. This remains a central challenge for technology.

When should feedback be provided?

Timing is an important factor when it comes to the effectiveness of the feedback. Closing the gap between the occurrence of the error and the feedback increases the impact it is likely to have. 'Impact', of course, is susceptible to interpretation. It can range from students noticing the error to incorporating the correction into their productive repertoire. Immediate feedback is feasible in the case of spoken errors but not for written ones. The teacher can halt an activity and correct the spoken error – although opinion is divided as to whether such an intervention should be taken when the learners are engaged in a communicative task. There is a view that when the focus is on meaningful communication, the teacher should make a note of errors as they occur and only provide feedback when the task has been completed.

One advantage of computer-mediated feedback is that the corrections can be instantaneous. Both informants in Tharanga's study named immediate feedback as a major advantage of text editing software. However, not all software is equally useful. The feedback will only be potentially useful if the student notices it. In the case of autocorrect when the software makes the correction automatically, the student may not even be aware that an error had been made. For this reason, we favor software that highlights the error and indicates the action to be taken (e.g., 'delete repeated word'). The writer then has the opportunity to accept the correction or ignore it. Making an error salient by underlining or highlighting the word or phrase is one thing. Making the nature of the error explicit is quite another, as we discussed in the preceding section. More often than not, *Grammarly* only provides explicit feedback for customers who select the Premium subscription option. Their explanations can demand a level of language proficiency beyond the current capacity of the learner to comprehend. The feedback can also be presumptuous. (*Grammarly* once advised David to delete 'definitely' from a sentence beginning *I definitely recommend....* on the grounds that it made him seem assertive. "But I am assertive", he wanted to reply to the program. Unfortunately, there's just no arguing with software.)

Questions from readers

Q: My experiences of receiving general feedback at university are like Sean and Francesca's experiences. How should I approach my assessors for more meaningful feedback? What do I say? I am worried I may come across as pushy and insensitive.

Julie: I am thinking back to some students who have approached me in the past requesting not necessarily for more meaningful feedback but a discussion concerning a breakdown of their marks against the criteria. They are understandably anxious and upset when they are emailing me to request an appointment, but the most effective requests (at least for me) have been the ones where students have thanked me for the feedback and asked if we could arrange a time to meet so that they can clarify a few questions and ask other questions to improve their work in the future. Perhaps what also works for me is when the tone of the request doesn't have some kind of hidden anger but conveys a spirit of genuine desire to learn and improve one's work. Obviously, students can question and interrogate what they want to know at the meeting, but a dialogic stance or attitude is generally the best way forward not only for students to understand the assessor's feedback better but also to build relationships with their teachers.

Q: I'm often overwhelmed with assignment deadlines and find myself pumping out assignments all in the final week of submission which doesn't leave a lot of time for polishing the writing, proofreading, or asking others to have a look. What can I do about this?

Julie: This is a common issue that many students experience. In my own experience, I found Brian Paltridge's and Sue Starfied's (2019) recommendations very helpful. They are writing about thesis and dissertation writing but I think their advice can be extended to any scholarly writing activity. The gist of their advice is that you need to see writing as an integral part of the research process and make writing a habit rather than just think of it as something to be done. Here is an extract on what they say:

> … consider trying out what Murray (2013) calls *snacking* – that is regular writing but for defined, shorter periods of time. What causes problems for many writers, according to Murray, is the idea that they can only write if and when they have large chunks of time available for what she calls a writing *binge* – writing for extended periods of time, often in an attempt to meet a deadline, which can become unproductive and exhausting. While complex intricate thinking cannot be done in 15-minute 'snacks', she suggests that a combination of larger time slots combined with briefer 30-minute slots may be helpful. Scheduling regular writing times each week as recommended by Zerubavel has been found by many writers, both academics and novelists, to help productivity.
>
> (p. 67)

There are many other valuable and practical recommendations on how to go about thinking about writing and managing your time from Paltridge and Starfield's book *Thesis and Dissertation Writing in a Second Language*. (One of the chapters from this book can be downloaded from the Routledge Freebook *A Practical Guide to Academic Writing for International Students* which can downloaded from: https://web.archive.org/web/20220728075418/https://www.routledge.com/rsc/downloads/A_Practical_Guide_to_Academic_Writing_for_International_Students-A_Routledge_FreeBook-_FINAL_VERSION_.pdf)

Summary

Positive feedback is comforting. It reduces insecurity and boosts confidence. Best of all, it can motivate you to continue improving your writing skills. Another good thing about positive feedback is that no further action is required. However, while it might give you a warm, inner glow, the feeling will be temporary and won't indicate specific measures you can take to improve the quality of your writing. While no-one enjoys negative feedback, it has the potential to improve the quality of your writing. This doesn't mean you have to act on all the negative feedback you receive, but you shouldn't dismiss criticisms without carefully considering the suggestions.

We hope this chapter has given you an opportunity to think about the different ways in which you're likely to receive feedback on your written work and to reflect on the type of feedback that works best for you. Do you prefer direct or indirect feedback? Do you like to have your teacher provide you with detailed explanation of a grammatical errors, inappropriate word choices, or problems with the way you develop and link the individual sentences together in a paragraph?

Receiving and thinking about feedback is only the beginning of the process of improving the clarity and coherence of your writing. The next and more challenging step is to incorporate the feedback into second and subsequent drafts of your work. Issues and techniques for revising you work is the subject of the next chapter.

Further readings

Andrade, M. S., & Evans, N. W. (2013). *Principles and practices for response in second language writing: Developing self-regulated learners*. Routledge.
This useful book highlights various practical aspects of responses to L2 writers, with special emphasis on developing student independence and autonomy.

Zerubavel, E. (1999). *The clockwork muse: A practical guide to writing theses, dissertations, and books*. Harvard University Press.
The Clockwork Muse provides a way through 'writer's block' via an examination of the writing practices of successful writers. It challenges the romantic ideal of the writer dashing off a piece of writing when the 'muse' inspires him or her. Instead, writers are offered a simple yet comprehensive framework that considers such variables as when to write, for how long, and how often, while keeping a sense of momentum throughout the entire project. Routines and regularities facilitate 'inspiration'.

References

Beatty, K. (2010). *Teaching and researching computer-assisted language learning*. Longman.

Ellis, R. (2010). A framework for investigating oral and written corrective feedback. *Studies in Second Language Acquisition, 32*(2), 335–349. https://doi.org/10.1017/S0272263109990544

Freeman, D. (2018). Four approaches to teachers studying their own classrooms. In D. Xeri & C. Pioquito (Eds.), *Research literate: Supporting teacher research in English language teaching* (pp. 24–29). English Teachers Association of Switzerland.

Hoey, M. (1991) *Patterns of lexis in text*. Oxford University Press.

Hyland, F., & Hyland, K. (2001). Sugaring the pill: Praise and criticism in written feedback. *Journal of Second Language Writing, 10*(3), 185–212. https://doi.org/10.1016/S1060-3743%2801%2900038-8

Liu, K., & Storch, N. (2021). Second language learners' engagement with written feedback [Online-First Article]. *Australian Review of Applied Linguistics*. https://doi.org/10.1075/aral.20029.liu

Nunan, D. (2010). *What is this thing called language?* Palgrave Macmillan.

Truss, L. (2005). *Eats, shoots & leaves*. Profile Books.

8
The power of revising

In Chapter 7, we dealt with formative feedback. In this chapter, we look at ways in which you can use feedback for revising your work for public consumption. We say 'public consumption' because, when writing for yourself, revision may not be necessary. When writing for others, it's crucial. Despite its importance, it often gets glossed over or ignored altogether in books on writing.

This is a relatively short chapter. In it, we draw on and refer you to previous parts of the book that are relevant to the revision process. There is only one main section to the chapter. In it, we outline the steps you can take to turn a first draft into a piece that will be clear and coherent to your reader. We discuss the challenges involved in revising your work including time pressure imposed by submission deadlines. We also stress the importance of having a positive attitude toward this important final step in creating a clear and coherent piece of writing.

From first to final draft: steps along the way

The poet Robert Graves may have been stretching the truth a little when he asserted that there is no such thing as good writing, only good rewriting. His point is that getting to the end of your first draft doesn't mean that your journey is complete. You may be entitled to a decent latte or a modest glass of cooking sherry, but please leave the champagne on ice. The journey from first draft to your destination, which may be a distinction grade on an assignment or a publication of one sort or another, will take time and effort. There will be potholes along the way, but without emotional and intellectual investment, you won't receive your hoped-for payout. With hard work, and attention to the issues we have highlighted in this book, you'll reach your goal and deserve your glass of fizz. We're not suggesting that a first draft

DOI: 10.4324/9781003179092-9

doesn't matter. Quite the opposite. The stronger the foundation, the sounder will be the building on which it rests.

Revising your work involves massaging the text, and clarifying statements that, on re-reading, strike you as clumsy or imprecise. You will also need to prune your work. Cutting sentences, paragraphs, and even entire sections is a painful but necessary part of the process. Do not be tempted to skip it.

We've referred to William Zinsser's *On Writing Well* several times in the course of this book. Now in its umpteenth edition, it's rightly designated as "the classic guide to writing nonfiction". Like many good storytellers, Zinsser begins his book with an anecdote about being invited to a school in Connecticut to address the topic of writing as a vocation. When he arrived at the school, he discovered a second speaker had been invited, a surgeon who had recently taken up writing as a diversion from cutting people up. Here's an edited version of Zinsser's story.

Zinsser doesn't tell us whether or not Dr. Brock's easy-going approach to writing resulted in pieces that were publishable. Presumably it did, or he wouldn't have been invited to address an audience on writing as a vocation. Zinsser's acidic dig at the end on his conversation with the doctor reveals just what he thought of Brock's approach to writing. "Letting it all hang out" is fine for a first draft, but that draft is only a point of departure not a destination. In the following vignette, David described the steps he follows to progress from a first to a final draft.

William Zinsser on the hard graft of revising

Dr. Brock was dressed in a bright red jacket, looking vaguely bohemian, as authors were supposed to look, and the first question went to him. What was it like to be a writer? He said it was tremendous fun. Coming home from an arduous day at the hospital, he would go straight to his yellow pad and write his tensions away. The words just flowed. It was easy. I then said that writing wasn't easy and it wasn't fun. It was hard and lonely, and the words seldom just flowed. Next Dr. Brock was asked if it was important to rewrite. Absolutely not, he said. "Let it all hang out", he told us. … At the end [of the session] Dr. Brock told me he was enormously interested in my answers – it had never occurred to him that writing could be hard. I told him I was just as interested in *his* answers – it had never occurred to me that writing could be easy. Maybe I should take up surgery one day (Zinsser, 2006, p. 4).

David's voice on knowing when your piece is ready

Before the Covid epidemic had us all housebound, at a conference somewhere in Asia, I took part in a seminar on 'Writing for publication'. From the size of the audience, it seemed that getting published was a major goal for most of the conference participants. Six of us spoke, each addressing a different aspect of the writing process. The order of presentations mirrored what the organizers assumed was the order in which a piece progressed from bright idea to appearance in print. As 'Professor Polishing-your-piece', I was fifth on the panel, sandwiched in between 'Dr Feedback' and 'Ms Find-a-publisher'. At the inevitable Q&A session following the presentations, I drew gasps from the audience when, in answer to the final question posed to me, "When is a piece polished to perfection?", I replied "Never". On leaving the auditorium, I was approached by the young woman who had posed the question. She thrust her business card into my hand and requested an interview. Without waiting for my response, but assuming it would be yes, she guided me into a side room, sat me in a chair, and fished a phone from her bag to record our conversation. She asked me to elaborate on the one-word responses I'd given to her question. I replied that the process of revising a piece could go on *ad infinitum*, but it would never be perfect. Sooner or later, you have to say *enough's enough*. If you're writing a term paper or have a book under contract, someone else will set the deadline for you. I glanced at her business card and saw that she was an assistant editor for a prominent educational publisher. "You of all people should know that".

She laughed. "I haven't been in publishing all that long, but I've learned how stubborn authors can be when it comes to submitting their precious work. Some just can't let go. What's your writing process? How many drafts do you do? And how do you know when 'enough is enough'?"

I tell her that it depends. The last book I'd written *The Infidels Next Door* was a factional four-generation account of my maternal forebears. At the time of writing, I didn't have a publisher, so wasn't facing a deadline. It took seven drafts and consumed six years of my life before I said *enough's enough* and went in search of a publisher. Each draft focuses on different aspects of the writing process and makes different demands. The first is qualitatively different from subsequent drafts. For some writers, staring at a blank screen and winking cursor is enough to bring on writer's block. For others it provides an opportunity to draw on all their creative energy. Before I begin to write, I remind myself of the purpose or purposes I have for writing as well as my intended audience – real or imagined.

As words and sentences emerge and the first draft takes shape, you begin to discover in detail what you want to say and how you want to say it. For me, facing a blank screen is liberating – sometimes even exhilarating. In subsequent drafts, you progressively refine your project. Regardless of whether it's a thesis, a novel, or a magazine article, the aim is the same: to produce a piece of writing that's clear, coherent, and true to the purpose and audience. Getting to that point can be a painful process, as it requires rearranging and deleting pieces of text that had been so creatively crafted at the first draft stage. When he was once asked how he had created his astonishing masterpiece, *The Pieta*, Michelangelo replied that it was easy. The stature was there all the time. All he had to do was chip away at the block of marble until it was revealed. While not an exact analogy, that's what a writer has to do – chip away at the first draft, until the story reveals itself. My main task at the second draft stage is to work on large chunks of text. Then I work on individual paragraphs, deleting some sentences, and rearranging the internal structure of others using the devices of cohesion and thematization to improve the readability of the paragraph. When I'm satisfied that the paragraph says what I want it to say, I hunt through the manuscript for figures of speech. Are my metaphors apposite, or clumsy, mannered, or forced? Do I overuse colloquialisms? (In some cases, the occasional colloquialism can give the text a friendly tone.) Clichés and slang tell the reader – and should tell you – that you've become lazy. Replace them! Next, I go through the entire manuscript and root out superfluous phrases and words that have escaped earlier editing stages. At the word level, I'm particularly harsh on adjectives and adverbs. I also replace words and phrases that lack precision. (There are times when I spend the better part of an hour wrestling with a stubborn sentence.) Then, it's time for a final proof-read, something I'm notoriously poor at. In this, I'm not alone. Reading for meaning is a natural inclination. Try reading backwards. That will overcome the temptation to read for meaning. At various points along the way, I seek feedback from a colleague or fellow writer on bits of the text that I'm not happy with.

There comes a time when I give the manuscript a rest. Occasionally, if I'm not racing against a deadline, it can lie fallow for weeks and even months in a folder on my desktop. I need a vacation from my manuscript, and it probably needs one from me. When I return to the folder and open the file, I'm able to view the text somewhat more dispassionately. There are parts that please me, and parts that don't. Some paragraphs are particularly egregious. I highlight these and eject them, an act I could not have performed prior to our temporary separation. Finally, I send the entire manuscript to one of my critical friends for comment before giving it a final massage and submitting it to an editor or publisher.

In the above vignette, David describes the process he uses to take a manuscript from first to final draft. The process is one of progressively refining the manuscript. First, he works on larger chunks. In the case of a book, he might move entire chapters around. If it's a chapter within a book, or an article, paragraphs or entire sections might be moved around or even deleted. (In this book, we moved the chapters on figurative language and voice from the front to the back half of the book because as the content of these chapters evolved, we decided they'd be more challenging than we'd anticipated when planning the book.)

David then works at the level of the paragraph, ensuring that succeeding sentences flow coherently from the one before. Figurative language is subjected to critical scrutiny before he turns his attention to individual words and phrases. To tighten up the text, he deletes any that he deems redundant. To enhance coherence, he exchanges words and phrases that lack precision for ones that capture more explicitly the meanings he wants to express. Having proof-read the entire piece, he sends it to a colleague who can be trusted to provide an honest appraisal rather than telling him how brilliant he is. The 120,000-word manuscript is then ready to be sent off, hopefully for immediate publication, but more likely for further revision. Outright rejection is an outside possibility, but he pushes that thought aside. Has he polished the piece to perfection? Almost certainly not: there's no such thing.

In the voice chapter, we introduced you to Annie Lamott and her delightful book *Bird by bird: Some instructions on writing and life*. In discussing the revision process, Annie poses the rhetorical question: How do you know when you're done? She answers her own question as follows:

This is a question my students always ask. You just do. I think my students believe that when a published writer finishes something, she crosses the last t, pushes back from the desk, yawns, stretches, and smiles. I don't know anyone who has ever done this, not even one. What happens instead is that you've gone over something so many times, and you've weeded and pruned and rewritten, and the person who reads your work for you has given you suggestions that you have mostly taken – and then finally something inside you just says it's time to finally just get on to the next thing. Of course, there will always be more you could do, but you have to remind yourself that perfection is the voice of the oppressor.

(Lamott, 1994, p. 93)

A wise woman, Annie, and an exceptional writer, to boot.

Making connections

Think about the steps that would work for you and create your own revision template.

- Step 1 Create a first draft
- [Add up to four additional steps]
- Step X Final draft

Now 'road test' your template. Write a short piece (4–5 paragraphs, 400–500 words in total) on a topic that interests you or extract several paragraphs of approximately the same length from something you have as a first draft. It could be related to your academic study or work, or it could be a narrative about an incident that occurred at university or at work. Alternatively, use a draft you're currently writing for a school assignment. Don't worry about style, precision, or clarity; just get your ideas onto the screen. Now revise the piece, using the template you created.

Reflect on the exercise. Did you think that your first draft was so good, that it didn't really need further revision? Or do you agree with Zinsser, who says that when you reflect on a sentence or longer piece of writing you'll find that "… it almost always has something wrong with it. It's not clear. It's not logical. It's verbose. It's clunky. It's pretentious. It's boring. It's full of clutter. It lacks rhythm. It can be read in several different ways. One sentence doesn't lead out of the previous sentence. … The point is that *clear writing is the result of a lot of tinkering*." (p. 83-4).

Share the first and final drafts with a fellow student or critical friend. Don't tell them which version is which. Ask them which one they prefer. Can they tell you why? (In the spirit of what we said about peer reviewing in the previous chapter, offer to carry out the same exercise for your fellow student or friend.)

How effective was the template you created as a guide to revising your writing? Would you like to adjust the template, adding or deleting steps?

Questions from readers

Q: I was taught in school not to look at the first draft when rewriting, but to save it and open a new word document and write a different version. Is that wrong?

A: We think so. What you'll probably end up with is two first drafts. There's little point in doing that. It overlooks the point of rewriting. As we point out in the chapter, rewriting is a process of progressively refining the initial draft, not by rewriting it from scratch. The only exception to this statement is if you realize that your first draft is so ramshackle that you need to toss it out and start from scratch. However, this should be the exception, not the rule. If you do want to keep the first draft, copy and save it, and then work on the copy, making sure you rename it so the two versions don't get confused.

If a paragraph, or even a sentence within a paragraph can't be repaired, it probably reflects the fact that you don't really know what you want to say. As we pointed out in Chapter 3, there are two aspects to writing: the final product and the process of arriving at the final product. That process involves shaping, refining, and, if necessary, rethinking and rewriting parts of the initial effort. Many of our students dislike the revising process because it's hard work. It takes time and effort. As one student said, "I hate revising. It makes my head hurt". Often, they've left the writing of an assignment to the last minute and don't have time to revise and refine it. As we've pointed out numerous times, you, the author, should be doing the hard work, not the reader. The important thing is to be systematic in making your revisions. Don't go through the text making corrections at random or simultaneously trying to deal with grammar, thematization, paragraph placement, cohesion, vocabulary choice, typographical errors, and so on. Your revision template is designed to facilitate this systematicity.

Q: My professor really liked my last assignment. It was an account of an action research study I carried out last semester. She said that it was good enough to be published. Can you give me some advice about how I can revise it for a journal?

A: In relation to your question, you should review the academic conversation between David and Kailin in Chapter 4. Part of the conversation is devoted to the changes Kailin needed to make to her assignment to make it suitable for a different audience. She also had to make a compromise on the purpose of the piece, a compromise that she wasn't particularly happy with. Her process was different from the one you will have to go through in that she co-authored it with her supervisor who guided her along the path from assignment to journal article.

Given the time and effort involved, you should begin by reflecting on your motive for taking on the task. At the same time, you need to consider how the audience and purpose will need to change. Ask yourself: What would motivate anyone to read this article? What will they get out of it? To answer these questions, you need to identify publications that might be interested in taking on your article. If you haven't published before, we recommend non-referred journals/magazines. Your teacher should be able to advise you on these. Alternatively, you can do an online search. Many professional associations publish newsletters and magazine and are always looking for contributions. Most of these publish an online, open-access format. Once you've identified a potential publication, scan several recent issues. Look at the table of contents and read two or three articles. If the magazine has submission guidelines, estimate how much work might be involved in rewriting to assignment. If not, send a 200–300-word abstract to the editor with a covering note.

Conclusion

Revising is crucial to achieving clarity and coherence in your writing. If you are writing for a limited audience, such as a university assignment for a lecturer, it will be the last step in a process that that will involve reading, discussing the assignment with fellow students, and then drafting and redrafting to clarify you own thinking on the topic, and then polishing your effort for an audience of one. If it's for public consumption, such as an article in a refereed journal on non-refereed publication such as a teachers' newsletter, it will almost certainly not be the final step in the process. You will have to go through one final step to satisfy the concerns or criticisms of anonymous reviewers or editors.

All too often, students think of assignment writing as a thankless chore, forced on them by their teachers to display what they've learned and to reveal what they haven't. This may be partly true, but it's wrong-headed. Writing assignments is part of the learning process. Recall what we said about writing as a thinking process. Through producing an initial draft and progressively refining and adding to your initial effort you will be adding to your personal stock of knowledge. Embrace the challenge. Enjoy it. See it as an opportunity to grow as a writer and scholar. You might as well, you have to do it anyway. In short, it's important to adopt a positive attitude toward the challenging and 'head-hurting' task of redrafting your assignment. You should approach the task as a learning opportunity. Pause from time to time to reflect on the process and ask yourself: What have I learned today about the writing process and about the content of my essay? What were the problems? How did I solve them?

In revising your work, you will draw on perspectives we have presented in this book and on insights contained in the additional readings we have provided at the end of each chapter. You will bear in mind the purpose and audience of the piece you are working on as well as the nature of the writing as process, knowledge of grammar, sensitivity to figurative language and vocabulary, technical aspects of discourse such as thematization and cohesion, emerging sensitivity to your strengths and weaknesses as a writer, and more. At least, that's our intention and our hope. In the final chapter, we will pull together and elaborate on the major themes presented in the book.

Further readings

Despite its importance, books on academic writing don't have a lot to say about the process of revising. While the following books are no exception, they do have something to say. We've included them here because they have a great deal of sensible things to say about the practicalities of writing. Both guides complement the themes and perspectives we have presented here.

Crème, P., & Lea, M. (2011). *Writing at University: A guide for students* (3rd ed). Open University Press.

Morley-Warner, T. (2008). *Academic writing is … – A guide to `writing in a University context*. Sydney University Press.

References

Lamott, A. (1994). *Bird by bird: Some instructions on writing and life*. Anchor books.

Zinsser, W. (2006). *On writing well* (30th ed.). HarperCollins Publishers.

9
In a nutshell: ten thoughts to take away

A fundamental problem is representing the non-linear experiential world in linear form. Resources such as cohesive devices and thematization can help us solve this problem. As we say, solving problems is at the heart of the writing problem. Also important is receiving meaningful feedback and using this in the rewriting process. Through this work, and with the judicious use of other resources such as figurative language, you will find your own voice and your identity as a writer will emerge.

Two other themes we highlight in the final chapter are the fact that academic writing is no one's native tongue. This leads to the issue of standards, and who gets to adjudicate on which standards should apply.

Introduction

We began this book with a Clive James's sentiment that the most complicated thing there is in this world is expressing oneself clearly. A profound and troubling sentiment presented, paradoxically, with Clive's trademark clarity. Sure, he can bamboozle, confuse, and obfuscate when he's in the mood, but he does so with a purpose. Troubling, because there are no shortcuts to clarity and coherence. At some stage on your journey through this book, you would have come to see James's point.

Here are ten tangled thoughts for you to take away.

1. Detailed and explicit knowledge of language is fundamental to good writing
2. Muddle-headed prose is often a result of muddle-headed thinking
3. Defining your purpose and audience is essential
4. The paradox of representing the world in print (the challenge of linearity)
5. Standards aren't set in stone
6. Academic language is no one's native tongue

DOI: 10.4324/9781003179092-10

7.   Solving problems is at the heart of the writing process
8.   There is no good writing, only good rewriting
9.   Writing is a method of discovery (writing as a thinking process)
10. Finding your own voice can enhance the power of your writing

Detailed and explicit knowledge of language is fundamental to good writing

This is the central theme of the book. As the book is about academic writing, we restricted our focus to those linguistic features most pertinent to written rather than spoken modes. We also had to circumscribe what we meant by 'detailed knowledge'. An exhaustive description of all the linguistic features of written English would have run to many more pages than we had at our disposal and would have resulted in an audience of exhausted readers. We restricted our focus to those aspects of grammar, discourse, vocabulary, and punctuation which we felt would be most useful to you as a writer. For grammar and vocabulary, we presented the basic word classes (nouns, verbs, adjectives, adverbs, prepositions, pronouns, conjunctions, and determiners), the grammatical roles these could take (subject, verb, object, and complement) and the seven basic clause types constituted by mixing and matching these roles. At the level of discourse, we looked at cohesion (reference, ellipsis, substitution, conjunctions, and lexical cohesion), and thematization.

In putting these grammatical, lexical and discoursal elements to work, we advocated a functional approach. Such an approach stresses the intimate and intricate connection between linguistic form and communicative function. It sees linguistic elements as meaning-making resources. As Halliday, the 'father' of functional grammar said, "Language is what language does" (Webster, 2003, p. 267). An explicit knowledge of language enables you to make choices that are not based on intuition. The work of educators and linguists working in this tradition such as Debra Myhill, Beverly Derewianka, Jim Martin, and others we have cited demonstrate the positive benefits to writers who have this explicit knowledge. It also provides us with tools to think and talk about the choices we make as we create our texts. Throughout the book, we have provided examples of how we have used these tools to enhance the effectiveness of our own writing, as well as to provide explicit feedback to our students that goes beyond vague statements such as "*This paragraph doesn't hang together*", or "*Your ideas are all over the place*".

Other aspects of language dealt with in the book include figurative language. We showed how well-chosen metaphors, similes and idioms can enliven your prose. However, colloquialisms should be treated with caution. Our advice on a figure of speech you're uncertain about is, leave it out.

Muddle-headed prose is often a result of muddle-headed thinking

In the course of the book, we presented examples of writing that lacked clarity and coherence. In each instance, we identified the source of the problem, and indicated ways in which it might be addressed. In doing so, we were restricted to working with the linguistic resources offered by the English language. We pointed out that much confused and confusing prose reflects muddle-headed thinking. This is as true of our own writing as it is of anyone else's. More often than not, when we review a paragraph or longer piece that lacks clarity, we realize that we're confused about the thread of an argument we want to pursue, the claim we want to put before the reader, or the landscape we want to survey. If we're confused, how can we present a coherent argument to our readers? It's only through a painful and often prolonged process of rewriting that what we really want to say becomes transparent. This notion of writing as a thinking process is another central theme, and one to which we return later in the chapter. We can't do your thinking for you. The most we can do is share with you the resources you can draw on to express your own meanings.

Defining your purpose and audience is essential

These two factors will have a crucial bearing on your writing. Without clarifying why you're writing (and there may be more than one purpose), and for whom, your writing will lack focus. That's not to say that you will always begin with purpose and audience clearly articulated. As you begin to write, these may be vague prospects which only become clear as you draft and re-draft your piece.

In their guide to dissertation writing, Paltridge and Starfield identify purpose and audience, but go further, listing six other social and cultural factors that need to be considered. Here is their complete list:

- the setting of the text
- the focus and perspective of the text
- the purpose/s of the text
- the intended audience for the text, their role and purpose in reading the text

- the relationship between writers and readers of the text
- expectations, conventions, and requirements for the text
- the background knowledge, values, and understandings it is assumed that thesis and dissertation writers share with their readers, including what is important to their reader and what is not
- the relationship the text has to other texts

(Paltridge & Starfield, 2020, p. 3)

Although Paltridge and Starfield's handbook is intended for second language writers of theses and dissertations, these interrelated factors are relevant for all writers of academic texts regardless of whether they are writing in their first or an additional language.

In Chapter 4, on audience (who am I writing for?) and purpose (why am I writing this?), we make the point that, although the 'why' and the 'who' represent different dimensions of the writing process, they are intimately entwined. This intimate relationship is a key feature of the academic conversation between David and Kailin. In discussing her term papers, Kailin points out that although her audience is her course lecturers, they don't constitute a homogeneous group. With some, she develops an affective bond. They become mentors and guides. While obtaining good grades matters, it's not her overweening motive. She wants to engage with them on the substantive issues at the heart of her work. Others are remote. In class, and from the (often superficial) comments on her work, she feels a lack of engagement. From them, all she is interested in is a good grade.

From a general discussion of purpose and audience relating to assignments, the conversation focuses on the empirical study Kailin was required to carry out and present as a thesis in her Master of Applied Linguistics course. The topic of her thesis was how L2 students engage with and learn from different kinds of feedback. Initially, her purpose of selecting this topic was to gain insights into how she could improve the quality of the feedback she gave her own students. During the interviews that provided data for her study, her purpose shifted. She now wanted informants' voices to be heard and hoped that they might have an impact on the university lecturers who read it.

Impressed with the quality of her work, one of the examiners suggested she turn the thesis into an article for publication. This required the purpose and audience to shift yet again. She was now writing for an audience of external journal reviewers. The suggestion also brought another shift in purpose: if the article were accepted, it would strengthen her application for a place in the doctoral program, a path she planned to pursue once she had completed the master's program.

To be accepted for publication, the reviewers argued that the study needed a conceptual/theoretical framework. This necessitated major revisions and another change in the purpose of the piece. As Kailin says in her interview, she had to 'weave' her data into the theoretical framework. In the course of doing this, the strength of her informants' voices was lost.

The paradox of representing the world in print (the challenge of linearity)

Another major point in the book concerns the linearity of prose. As lived time unfolds the external world assails all of our senses. I (David) am working on an initial draft of this chapter in a coffee shop, waiting to meet my colleague to discuss the reviews of an article we submitted for publication. My ears are assailed by myriad sounds, the clutter of cups and plates, the hiss of the espresso machine, an altercation over a disputed check, piped music, the irritating whine of a passing motor scooter, conversations at adjoining tables, the buzzing of my phone informing me of an incoming text message.

In the experiential world, all of these sounds (and numerous others – I didn't report the police siren in the next street or the slammed door) occurred simultaneously, but it took me several minutes to represent (re-present) them. The linearity of language required me to report sequentially events that occurred simultaneously. I had to decide which sounds to include and which to leave out and the sequence in which to report them. A comprehensive account of that split second would have to include my other senses: sight (the shaft of like light with its motes of dancing dust), touch (the roughness of the tablecloth), taste (the lingering bitterness of the espresso), physical sensations, etc. And then there's the interior monologue or self-talk that accompanies us as we experience the physical world: irritation in a meeting at a colleague's prolixity, and how we should respond to an unfavorable journal reviewer.

Reducing the physical world to a line of print is one thing. Doing the same to an abstract argument or some other academic genre is quite another. In the book, we introduced you to the linguistic resources that enable you to do so. Within the sentence level, these include ways of introducing two or more pieces of information and indicating the relationship between them through clause types such as coordination and subordination. Beyond the sentences, resources include cohesion, and theme/rheme structuring.

Solving problems is at the heart of the writing process

At the beginning of this chapter, we said that there was a good deal of overlap between the ten 'takeaways' with which we conclude the book. This is true of writing as problem-solving. The principle relates particularly to Chapter 4 on audience and purpose where, in the section on the 'art and craft of writing', we give a detailed example of problem-solving from our own writing. Hopefully, the example, and many others in the book have been sufficient to convince you that writing is both an art and a craft. It requires the skilled deployment of linguistic tools as well as creativity (see Casanave, 2010; Nelson, 2018; Sword, 2012; Tardy, 2016).

As we have mentioned at several points in the book, and summarized in the preceding section, the basis of the challenge is to represent the non-linear experiential world in sequential lines of print. This process is reductive. We are constantly faced with decisions about what to leave out and what to leave in, and how to stitch the latter together using linguistic resources so they tell a story that makes sense to the reader.

Of course, solving problems isn't peculiar to writing a thesis. Daily life constantly confronts us with problems to be solved. Some are relatively trivial and readily solved. Your three-year-old misplaces her favorite doll and sets up a wail that wakes the neighbors. It needs to be found before there is a knock on the door from Welfare Services. You get the child to retrace her steps, and there's the doll wedged behind the sofa. Problem solved. Others are not so easily dealt with. Spending most of the night to finish an assignment in advance of a looming deadline to find on waking bleary eyed in the morning that your computer has crashed and the assignment has disappeared into the ether. Daily life revolves around solving problems. Plumbers, carpenters and electricians no less than the brain surgeon in the operating theatre and the barrister in the courtroom face challenges requiring creativity and ingenuity that go well beyond the application of well-rehearsed routines. The outward manifestation of these problem-solving practices may seem a world away from the writer's work but the mental processes are not so different.

Finding your own voice can enhance the power of your writing

We've introduced some challenging concepts and terminology in this book. Some linguistic terms such as sentences, nouns and verbs, would have been familiar, others such as clauses and complements, less so. You had probably heard of them but would be challenged to define them or find examples in a text. There are many terms that would be known to you in an everyday sense, but are used to name complex, abstract concepts in linguistics. These included cohesion, coherence, field, tenor, mode, genre, identity, and voice.

Most students find the concept of identity and voice particularly challenging. We looked at the relationship between the concepts and followed Paul Matsuda's defining of voice as a unique configuration of linguistic (discursive) and non-discursive features. Given the abstract nature of the definition, we augmented it with examples from texts produced by authors writing across a range of genres.

We suggested several techniques you can use to further your understanding of voice and to develop your own. One of these was imitating the style of a writer you admire. However, we also warned against following another author's voice so slavishly that you never find your own. As Annie Lamott said, you have the writer's voice on loan, and eventually have to give it back. William Zinsser voices a similar sentiment when he says:

> … we eventually move beyond our models; we take what we need and then we shed those skins and become who we are supposed to become. But nobody will write well unless he gets into his ear and into his metabolism a sense of how the language works and what it can be made to do.
> (Zinsser, 1989, p. 15)

Writing is a method of discovery (writing as a thinking process)

Writing as a method of inquiry is another thread that's woven into the fabric of the book. This doesn't mean we start out with a mind that is as blank as the screen in front of us. Very often, the opposite is the case. Our mind is teeming with ideas. However, it's only by writing that we can unravel and develop them. As we write, new ideas will percolate into our consciousness and connections between separate ideas begin to coalesce. Developing abstract ideas and arguments require the written word. Only an exceptional few can mentally tease apart an argument that has many moving parts.

This view of writing has its own purpose and audience. The purpose is to use writing as an instrument to take an initial idea on a topic and develop it in a variety of ways such as presenting a coherent argument, solving a problem or telling a story. As already indicated, new ideas and the relationship between them will emerge. In this process, we have an audience of one – ourselves. In some cases, we will remain the sole audience. In others, the piece will be developed for a wider audience. That audience may be a single individual, such as your teacher, or multiple individuals.

You can use this approach, not only to produce an entire text, but also parts of a text. For example, if you run short of ideas in a subsection of an assignment, you could adopt a procedure recommended in Chapter 3. In the final substantive section of the chapter is a *Making connections* box. The box contains a task for trying out and evaluating writing as a thinking process. This task would be ideal for generating ideas for your troublesome subsection.

There is no good writing, only good rewriting

Revising your work is not only desirable, it's essential if you want to produce quality writing. The number of drafts you produce will depend on the amount of time you're able to allow yourself, and this will depend on timelines and deadlines set by others. In your case this will most likely be your teachers. In our case, it's publishers for books and journal editors for articles. As an absolute minimum, you need to plan on two drafts. Your second draft should be guided by feedback from another reader. Ideally, this would be your teacher, but few teachers have the time to provide individual feedback. Successive drafts are subject to the law of diminishing returns.

If you do have the luxury of time, successive drafts should focus on different aspects of your writing and become more fine-grained as you work from moving sections and paragraphs around to sentences, and then to words.

Academic language is no one's native tongue

You may be reassured to know that all writers, regardless of their first language, struggle when it comes to mastering academic writing. Years ago, the

French sociologists Pierre Bourdieu, Jean-Claude Passeron and Monique de Saint Martin (1994) made this point:

> Academic language is a dead language for the great majority of French people, and is no one's mother tongue, not even that of children of the cultivated classes. As such, it is very unequally distant from the languages actually spoken by the different social classes. To decline to offer a rational pedagogy is, in this context, to declare that all students are equal in respect of the demands made by academic language.
>
> (p. 8)

In general, reading and writing are unnatural acts. Unless we have some form of disability, we all acquire the ability to understand and speak the language(s) of the speech community into which we're born. Learning to speak is an astonishing feat, achieved without formal instruction. It doesn't occur effortlessly and automatically, but with considerable effort and a great deal of frustration as all parents know. Parents, primary caregivers, and older siblings play an important social role in supporting, scaffolding and encouraging a child's oral language development.

Learning to read and write is another matter. Apart from a few exceptional children who teach themselves the rudiments of reading, developing basic literacy requires formal schooling. Many emerge from 12 years of school with only rudimentary literacy skills. In the United States, over half the population of adults are unable to read above the 6th grade level, and 4% remain functionally illiterate (National Center for Educational Statistics, 2019). We should add that what counts as 'being literate', is constantly changing. In this digital age, the ability to process the printed word is no longer considered an adequate way of characterizing literacy. "The evolving and dynamic nature of communication in the 21st century calls for an expanded understanding of what it means to be literate" (Rajendrum, 2021, p. 520).

Academic language, particularly academic writing, is a highly specialized genre. In this book, we have described the genre as well as its evolution so that you can appreciate and take seriously the challenge of becoming adept academic writers. Regardless of your first language, throughout your schooling, and particularly in your high school years, you will have been increasingly exposed to academic language. Only a minority graduate as skilled academic writers without explicit instruction. As Bourdieu, Passeron, and Saint Martin (1994) imply in their statement, "[not] all students are equal in respect of the demands made by academic language" not even offspring of the "cultivated class". All writers, regardless of whether they are functioning in their first or second language, struggle with academic writing. This is true of us, it's true of highly accomplished authors we have introduced to you in these pages such a Laurel Richardson and William Zinsser who share their struggles with the written word.

If you're an L1 speaker of a language other than English, John Flowerdew's words will resonate with you. He says:

> While there may be discipline-specificity, there will also be some sort of broad general competence. And of course, the development of such a general competence is likely to be more challenging for the EAL writer than the native writer, because the native writer will have likely developed such general competence in the home, reading media materials, and during schooling.
>
> (Flowerdew, 2019, pp. 251–252)

Flowerdew's argument makes sense. The linguistic knowledge acquired by L1 speakers through everyday social interaction and also more formally through schooling, provides an initial advantage over L2 speakers. However, the implication that the 'native speaker' represents a homogeneous body of language users is simply not the case. Even when it comes to everyday, non-academic language, native speakers can be ranged on a continuum. This is true of both spoken and written modes. At one end of the continuum, there are users who struggle to express themselves for a range of linguistic, educational, and affective reasons. At the other, are those who can speak coherently and convincingly in multiple settings and for a range of purposes, from entertaining guests at a dinner party, to selling second-hand cars and getting elected to parliament. The ability to use written language in non-academic settings also exists on a continuum.

We accept the general proposition that native speakers have an advantage when it comes to academic writing, but the potential to develop high-level skills is not evenly distributed. Some show marked improvement over the course of their studies, while others don't. Of course, not all native speakers have the capacity or desire to master one or more discipline-specific genres that exist in academic and professional writing. In post-colonial countries where English remains the dominant/official language, high-level literacy skills are comparatively rare. We've already cited data from the United States, where less than half the population achieve literacy skills beyond elementary grade level. While those who progress to higher education are advantaged by the massive amount of implicit knowledge acquired by virtue of their L1 statues, with very few exceptions, those who do gain acceptance into graduate programs, are challenged by the demands of academic writing.

We agree that there are no native speakers of academic English, and that academic writing belongs to no one as a birthright. We also concur with Flowerdew that being born into any speech community confers certain advantages when it comes to using that language for a range of social and educational purposes. These advantages relate to tacit knowledge of morphosyntax, core lexis, and idiomatic expressions acquired through social interaction in everyday life as well as thousands of hours exposure to formal learning of academic spoken and written language in school. These provide a baseline advantage for first-language speakers over speakers of other languages in post-secondary educational and professional contexts.

That said, as we have argued, the development of advanced literacy skills, challenges everyone, regardless of their first language. The more you write and reflect critically on what you produce, the greater the facility you develop. However, every time you sit or stand at your desk to write, you will be challenged. We certainly are. We found it reassuring to read Debra Myhill's statement that writing is never easy. In a similar vein, Bazerman et al. (2017) point out that the development and maintenance of high levels of academic writing (indeed all writing) is a 'lifespan' endeavor. They remind us of the multidimensional nature of this development which includes linguistic, cognitive, affective, sensorimotor, motivational, and technological factors. In this endeavor, there is no single path and no single endpoint.

The challenges facing first, and second language writers are similar in some respects and dissimilar in others. However, first-language background is just one of the factors implicated in and determining the trajectory of each person's writing development. In addition to the dimensions listed above, personal interests and abilities are also strongly implicated. Research based on language portraits and language learning trajectory grids reveal the complexity and uniqueness of each person's learning histories (Choi, 2022; Choi & Slaughter, 2020). It supports the fact that, "for writers who write in multiple languages, the aspects of literacy that can be transferred from one language context to another are variable, and the transfer is not always direct" (Bazerman et al., 2017, p. 355). Kramsch and Lam (1999) also highlight the role that producing written texts can play in shaping second language learners' social and cultural identities. Drawing on texts produced by bi/multilingual writers, they state that while such writers face challenges that are different from L1 writers, the opportunity to write in a second language can be a source of creativity and innovation. Those who teach L2 writers, "need to develop both an insider's and outsider's view towards English, realizing the tension between the standardized forms of English and ways in which NNS see through these forms and test their limits as they develop their 'textual identities'" (Kramsch & Lam, 1999, p. 57).

Standards aren't set in stone

When it comes to academic writing, standards, or 'rules of the game' are constantly being challenged. Rules of the writing game, as well as rules of the research game vary from discipline to discipline. The hard sciences have generally been resistant to change, particularly in allowing the personal to creep into academic discourse. Accepting a subjective voice in scholarly writing subverted objectivity, a key rule of the positivist research game. As we shall see later in the section, there have been, and continue to be, members of a hard science persuasion who are quite prepared to challenge the notion of objectivity and the primacy of deductive logic.

The debate over 'standards' is a long-running one in education in general and language education in particular. In the debate, the term is used in two senses: as an adjective (standard English) and as a noun (English standards). Standard English refers to a variety of English in which all the key features of the language such as grammar, spelling, pronunciation, and punctuation have been codified. The need for standardization emerged in the wake of the invention of the printing press, which made print materials widely available. In the United Kingdom, the dialect of the educated, ruling class in southern England became the standard. Access to certain occupations and institutions was restricted to those who possessed the dialect. Globally, there are numerous standard Englishes: standard American, Australian, Singaporean etc. Although they are codified, they are not immutable to change.

> In her book on World Englishes, Jennifer Jenkins (2009) notes that:
>
> Standard language is the term used for that variety of a language which is considered to be the norm. It is the variety held up as the optimum for educational purposes and as a yardstick against which other varieties of the language are measured.
>
> (p. 33)

Discussions of standard language are bound to arouse controversy. The obvious question arises: considered to be the norm by whom? As we indicated earlier in relation to standard English, the dialect that was considered the norm for education and other specialized purposes, was that spoken by the community holding the greatest wealth and political power. Used as a noun, the word can also be contentious, particularly in educational contexts. The shibboleths of 'falling educational standards' and the imperative to 'get back to basics' are commonly heard from conservative politicians and their backers in the media.

When it comes to language, numerous scales exist to specify standards at different levels of ability from novice to expert. One widely used scale is the Common European Framework of Reference for Languages (CEFR). The CEFR specifies language performance standards for general and specific purposes. The CEFR for academic and specific purpose writing begins at B2, the middle range of the generic scale. The self-assessment standard/descriptor reads:

> I can write clear, detailed text on a wide range of subjects relating to my interests. I can write an essay or report, passing on information or giving reasons in support of or against a particular point of view. I can write letters highlighting the personal significance of events and experiences.
> (Council of Europe, 2001)

Performance-based standards such as these are criticized on numerous grounds. Terms such as 'clear' and 'detailed' are vague and imprecise. What constitutes a 'wide' range of subjects? The range of genres is restricted to essays, reports, informative and argumentative texts, and personal letters. In addition, genres, as well as linguistic features such as grammar and lexis are specific to particular academic subjects. As a self-assessment tool, it's probably of dubious value to students. (How useful would *you* find it?) (For a discussion, see Nunan, 2007, 2015).

As we noted at various points throughout the book, standards are not immutable, but change over time and can vary according to the purpose and audience for which the text is being written. Early in our careers, we were admonished for using contractions, first-person pronouns, for admitting the personal into our writing. These days, such features are increasingly accepted. While we advised you to treat colloquialism and certain idioms with caution and to avoid slang, a degree of informality may be acceptable, again depending on your audience and purpose.

The issue of standards permeates all levels and areas of education. Standards are promulgated by ministries of education, and there is much handwringing by politicians and the media when they are not achieved. Languages constantly change. The rate of change is compounded by globalization and technology. Variation and change are the rule, not the exception. In the case of English as a major contact language between cultures since the 18th century, this variation has been particularly marked and has resulted in pidgins and creoles in different parts of the world. If there were no variation and change, we would have fixed standards and immutable rules.

David's voice: the 'Gold Standard'

Some years ago, I was invited by the Minister for Education in Singapore to act as External Advisor to the English Language Institute of Singapore (ELIS). The Institute was newly established with, the 'Founding Father' of modern Singapore, Lee Kuan Yew, as its patron. Singapore was a place I knew well, having visited it for work and pleasure over many years. I had spoken at numerous International Language Seminars, taught on the master's program, and served as a member of the Governing Board of the Regional Language Centre (RELC). I also had close connections with key institutions of higher education including the National University of Singapore, and Nanyang Technological University. I was delighted to accept the position.

On my first advisory visit, I had a briefing session with the Director of ELIS. When I asked about ELIS's mission, she told me that it was to enhance the English language skills of content teachers in secondary schools, that is, teachers of science, history and so on, not only English teachers. There's far too much use of Singlish (colloquial Singaporean English) in the classroom. "We have to stamp it out Singlish", I was informed.

She looked puzzled when I asked what would count as success as far as ELIS was concerned. I elaborated.

> At the end of the day, you and I will be evaluated by the Singaporean Government, which is funding the Institute, on their perception of whether it had succeeded in its mission. What concrete evidence would convince them that their money had been well spent?

"Oh," she replied, "if all subject teachers spoke as clearly, and accurately as newsreaders on Singaporean television. They would have to speak British English of course, not American English. Singapore is a Gold Standard country, and British English is the Gold Standard".

I was tempted to ask her whether Australian English would do, but discretion prevailed. Besides, I figured that I already knew the answer.

Some genres are more resistant to change than others. Legal and academic language are obvious examples. When it comes to academic language, some of the reasons for this conservatism has already been spelled out. Conspiracy theorists argue that rigid rules, standards, and practices are maintained to restrict access to higher education to a privileged, educated elite. Having spent most of our adult lives within the academy, we are not so sure. Neither of our backgrounds, as different as they are, could be characterized as educated or elitist.

A major source of conservatism in academia stems from the dominant positivist, paradigm. As we wrote about earlier in the book, this paradigm evolved over several 100 years. The procedures and principles for developing and testing knowledge became known as the scientific method. Rules of the game for researchers working within the paradigm included reliability, validity, and objectivity. The researcher had to be rendered invisible, a ghostly presence in the machinery of the method. These rules had to be adhered to not only in the research process but also in its reporting.

The positivist approach was challenged by scholars working within the naturalistic paradigm. They rejected the rules of objectivity and impersonality in academic writing. Laurel Richardson is particularly severe on those who separate the research process from the writing process. The two are inseparable. She writes to discover perspectives and insights that can only emerge through the writing itself. For her, the static writing model of the positivists is a product of 'mechanistic scientism', 'quantitative research' and 'entombed scholarship'. Reading this lifeless prose puts her to sleep.

Her struggle to promote an alternative approach to academic writing, to reimagine the relationship between research and writing, and to apply standards other than objectivity and impersonality came at a cost. She faced rejection from editors, reviewers, and publishers. In the end, however, she prevailed.

Not all scholars of a positivist persuasion are guilty of 'mechanistic scientism' and 'entombed scholarship'. One of our favorite writers on academic research and writing is Peter Medawar, who won a Nobel Prize for medicine. Although he has been dead for over 30 years, his words continue to resonate. In his paper *Is the scientific paper a fraud?*, he challenged the notion that scientific hypotheses were the product of logico-deductive thinking, stating that,

> scientists should not be ashamed to admit, as many of them are ashamed to admit, that hypothesis appear in their minds along unchartered byways of thought; that they are imaginative and inspirational in character; that they are indeed adventures of the mind.
>
> (Medawar, 1999, p. 31)

A good scientist possessed the combined qualities of a free-flowing imagination and creativity on one hand and skepticism and criticality on the other. "There is a sense in which he must be free, but another in which his thought must be very precisely regimented; there is poetry in science, but also a lot of bookkeeping" (Medawar, 1996, p. 63). His autobiography, published in 1986 just a year before his death, was playfully titled *Memoir of a Thinking Radish*. No, there was nothing entombed about Sir Peter's scholarship and definitely not a hint of the mechanistic about his writing.

We don't want to give the impression that proponents of the personal in academic writing are sweeping all before them. Resistance remains, particularly among those working within a quantitative paradigm. As a graduate student, Diego Mideros writes of being sanctioned for employing first-person pronouns.

> I prefer to use "I argue that ..." However, I was encouraged to avoid the use of "I" by one of my assessors who comes from a quantitative paradigm ... [so] I managed to do without it in my dissertation. Although it was an interesting writing exercise, I did feel constrained as I was unable to express certain ideas more comfortably using "I", which I strongly see as part of the language of qualitative research.
> (Botelho de Magalhães, Coterall, & Mideros, 2019, p. 10)

Do we believe that 'anything goes' when it comes to academic writing? Presumably, the answer is 'no'. If it's 'yes', then that's the end of the conversation, and of our book. A 'no' answer requires the application of some kinds of standards and the vexed question of 'whose standards'? The question brings us back to purpose and audience, which we dealt with earlier in the chapter. The standards applied by anonymous reviewers and the editors of a top ranked journal will not be the same as those applied to an M.A. student's term paper. This, of course, doesn't solve the 'standards' issue – just makes it more complicated.

Conclusion

In a world where there is increasing multilingual and multimodal complexities in making meaning and communicating one's intended meanings, it may seem odd that we are writing yet another book that focuses on writing and language. There is indeed growing inclusion of multimodal texts and possibilities to present one's work through multimedia platforms as forms of assessments in formal educational contexts. Such possibilities also mean there is more than just 'language' and 'writing' to think about when communicating meaning through some form of visual media. However, building one's linguistic knowledge to write clearly and coherently are not irrelevant even in the production of multi-modal/-media texts. A great deal of work that happens behind the scene involves stitching a coherent narrative together, which often happens through writing, is used to build the final product. The more knowledge one has about language, the more they have at their disposal to create the representations they wish to create.

As Julie's process and product dissertation writing experience in Chapter 3 of coming to understand the role that explicit knowledge of language as tools for meaning-making shows, such metalinguistic awareness not only transformed the way she came to see writing as a thinking process but also helped her to realize her sense of power and agency as a writer to write in ways that made sense to her. Such life changing experiences have an impact on her pedagogical approaches with her own graduate level students. She is guiding her students to develop and explicitly demonstrate their content knowledge as well as the language and literacy expectations in relation to the genre, purpose, and audience of their work. Her most recent international student, named here as XT, who Julie supervised to develop her 13,500-word capstone research project, created a booklet for Julie at the end of the semester documenting her own transformational journey into coming to see writing differently. The booklet includes eight key versions of her drafts based on the numerous feedback Julie gave on the content, language, and writing from February to June 2022 and some personal diary entries on what XT was learning about writing throughout her journey. On each of the dividers, XT wrote some brief reflection notes of how she reflects on those different drafts in the present moment. With her permission, we have included her reflective notes here to show how powerful learning to write and learning to write clearly and coherently are for learners who have been well-educated but never experienced writing as a method of discovery and thinking process. As they experience such a process they realize how much more they need to improve their knowledge about language to be able to clearly and coherently communicate their message (Figure 9.1).

We hope that XT's journey resonates in some ways with the one you have taken with us throughout this book. In one of his marvelous TED Talks, *Do schools kill creativity?*, Ken Robinson says that the whole propose of education is to turn out university professors. He notes a curious fact about professors: they live entirely inside their heads. They see bodies as transportation systems for their heads. The sole purpose of the body is to get

Figure 9.1 XT's booklet on her experience of coming to think about writing differently through her capstone writing project.

their heads to meetings. XT's journey is a reminder that making progress as writer is not a simple thing, that as our friend Clive James said, writing clearly is the hardest thing there is. But it tells us more than that. It requires persistence and dedication, but also creativity and imagination. Along the way there will be tears of frustration. However, with guidance and encouragement, it can be an adventure, not solely of the mind, but of the whole person.

Making connections

Having come this far, you will be aware that throughout our writing journey, we've taken bearings from students. This is consistent with our ideological commitment to learner-centeredness. Our students also helped to keep us honest. It therefore seemed fitting to share with you diary extracts from one of Julie's students. As you read the extracts, consider what it takes to help students develop the kind of transformation XT experienced, captured in her title as *'From heartless to heartful academic writing transformation'*. Knowledge of language and writing are a given, but they alone cannot sustain the hard work that is required to develop the writing muscle. As XT states, "Writing is not a simple thing, it needs persistence and dedication. 加油! [jiāyóu!: literal translation: 'Add oil' meaning 'Do your best!'] ☺". Consider what is needed to persist (Table 9.1).

Table 9.1 Diary extracts from XT: from heartless to heartful academic writing transformation

20 Feb 2022	About the first draft... I have to say I'm still stressed when I see it now. How could I have written every single paragraph without a topic sentence? Thx Dr Julie for not giving up on me lol.
01 Apr 2022	Ok... this time I briefly read the samples that Dr. Julie sent to me. So I changed the title and research question. I'm now feeling ashamed reading this omg... Must think carefully before every single word before writing. Be consistent!
04 Apr 2022	From here I stared to write a diary. It's absolutely an effective way to reflect myself on my writing. I did the diary after I got feedback from Dr. Julie and tried to figure out how to improve.
17 Apr 2022	This version was still problematic in the methodology and the focus was still on intercultural communication which we agreed would not lead to an interesting angle.
25 May 2022	My face is exactly the same as the girl in the meme when I sent this draft to Dr. Julie. I must have brought her some tough time with my draft. Sorry ☺ From here I started to think about another research question about translanguaging. We began sharing some memes about writing in our email. **Figure 9.2** Translation of Chinese text: Tutor, this is my thesis.
14 Jun 2022	Milestone: Dr. Julie and I had a face-to-face meeting!! My methodology still needed improvement; the lit review also needed to be reorganized. I was happy to know the problems & afraid of what I should do at the next stage because there are only 8 days left!!! Btw, after the meeting I went home and slept for 12 hours...

Table 9.1 (*Continued*) Diary extracts from XT: from heartless to heartful academic writing transformation

18 Jun 2022	Dr. Julie emailed me to ask me about the Chinese translation for "collective storytelling". The time I received the email I was like: "What is this? I've never heard of it before". Then I jumped out of my bed and started to search ☺. I also asked my other Chinese friends what do they think about this word. Dr. Julie is really good at building relationship with students. This is the first time I met a teacher who took the initiative to discuss issues outside of the subject with students. I also feel it is meaningful to pay attention to nuances in different languages. Thx Dr. Julie for letting me know the difference ♡	
24 Jun 2022	Finally! I finished my proposal by the support of Dr. Julie. Yah🎉 I have so much to say and I need 10 mouths to express my feelings and gratitude to my supervisor Dr. Julie. How did I get so lucky ☺ Thank you, my role model Dr. Julie and then thank you to myself ♡ (I cried for 2 minutes after I saw my mark and cried for another 2 minutes after I saw Dr. Julie's comments.) Writing is not a simple thing, it needs persistence and dedication. 加油! (jiāyóu: Do your best!) ☺ About the miserable face ⇒ : Yes that is me in both March & April… I've never cried for any assignment before. But I can't stop crying for this one.	 **Figure 9.3** XT's text message to her friend during the writing journey telling her she is crying and writing every day.

References

Bazerman, C., Applebee, A., Beringer, V., Brandt, D., Graham, S., Matsuda, P., Murphy, S., Rowe, D., & Schleppegrell, M. (2017). Taking the long view on writing development. *Research in the Development of Writing, 51*, 351–360.

Botelho de Magalhães, M. B., Coterall, S., & Mideros, D. (2019). Identity, voice and agency in two EAL doctoral writing contexts. *Journal of Second Language Writing, 43*, 4–14.

Bourdieu, P., Passeron, J.-C., & Saint Martin, M. (1994). *Academic discourse: Linguistic misunderstanding and professorial power.* Polity Press.

Casanave, C. (2010). Taking risks?: A case study of three doctoral students writing qualitative dissertations at an American university in Japan. *Journal of Second Language Writing, 19*(1), 1–16. http://dx.doi.org/10.1016/j.jslw.2009.12.002

Choi, J. (2022). Learning about multilingual language learning experiences through language trajectory grids. In J. Purkarthofer & M. Flubacher (Eds.), *Speaking subjects – Biographical methods in multilingualism research* (pp. 163–172). Multilingual Matters.

Choi, J., & Slaughter, Y. (2020). Challenging discourses of deficit: Understanding the vibrancy and complexity of multilingualism through language trajectory grids. *Language Teaching Research, 25*(1), 81–104. http://dx.doi.org/10.1177/1362168820938825

Council of Europe. (2001). *Common European framework of reference for languages: Learning, teaching, assessment.* Council of Europe, European Language Portfolio. https://rm.coe.int/168045b15e

Flowerdew, J. (2019). The linguistic disadvantage of scholars who write in English as an additional language. *Language Teaching, 52*(2), 249–260. https://doi.org/10.1017/S0261444819000041

Jenkins, J. (2009). *World Englishes: A resource book for students* (2nd ed.). Routledge.

Kramsch, C., & Lam, W. S. E. (1999). Textual identities: The importance of being non-native. In G. Braine (Ed.), *Non-native educators in English language teaching* (pp. 57–72). Lawrence Erlbaum.

Medawar, P. (1996). *The strange case of the spotted mice and other classic essays on science.* Oxford University Press.

Medawar, P. (1999). Is the scientific paper a fraud? In E. Scanlon, R. Hill, & K. Junker (Eds.), *Communicating science: Professional contexts* (pp. 27–31). Routledge.

National Center for Educational Statistics. (2019). *Adult literacy in the United States.* U.S Department of Education, National Center for Educational Statistics. https://nces.ed.gov/pubs2019/2019179/index.asp

Nelson, R. (2018). *Creativity crisis: Toward a post-constructivist educational future.* Monash University Publishing.

Nunan, D. (2007). Standards-based approaches to the evaluation of ESL instruction. In J. Cummins & C. Davison (Eds.), *International handbook of English language teaching* (pp. 421–438). Springer.

Nunan, D. (2015). Standard English, English standards: Whose standards are they in English language education? In L. T. Wong & A. Dubey-Jhaveri (Eds.), *English language education in a global world: Practices, issues and challenges* (pp. 3–12). Nova Science Publisher.

Paltridge, B., & Starfield, S. (2020). *Thesis and dissertation writing in a second language: A handbook for students and their supervisors* (2nd ed.). Routledge.

Rajendrum, S. (2021). A pedagogy of multiliteracies and its role in English language education. In P. Vinogradova & J. Kang Shin (Eds.), *Contemporary foundations for teaching English as an additional language* (pp. 151–187). Routledge.

Sword, H. (2012). *Stylish academic writing.* Harvard University Press.

Tardy, C. (2016). *Beyond convention: Genre innovation in academic writing.* University of Michigan Press.

Webster, J. (2003). (Ed.). *The language of early childhood: M.A.K. Halliday* (Vol 4.). Continuum.

Zinsser, W. (1989). *On writing well: The classic guide to writing nonfiction.* HarperCollins Publishers.

Glossary

abstract noun: a noun that represents an abstract concept or quality (*e.g., complexity*) cf. *concrete noun*

active voice: A sentence or utterance in which the doer of the action is the subject of the sentence.

Example: The research team – put their study on hold due to lack of funds.

adjective: A major word class whose members modify or define more clearly a noun or pronoun.

adverb: A class of words that modify or qualify *verbs, adjectives,* or other *adverbs.*

affix: A bound *morpheme* that is added to the beginning (prefix) or the end (suffix) of a word.

anaphora (anaphoric reference): Within a text, a cohesive device in which the second and subsequent references to an entity or event is marked by a pronoun.

antonym: A word having the opposite meaning of another word.

article: The *determiners the, a/an* preceding a noun or noun phrase.

background knowledge: The knowledge of the world that the reader or listener utilizes in interpreting a piece of spoken or written discourse.

bilingualism: The ability to speak two languages fluently.

bound morpheme: A morpheme that does not have its own existence but must be attached to another morpheme. (See *morpheme* for more information.)

clause: A major grammatical building block containing a main verb. Independent clauses can stand alone as a sentence in their own right. Dependent clauses, marked by **conjunctions**, must be attached to a main verb.

Example: If the procedure goes as planned (dependent clause), we should have the results by morning (independent clause).

coherence: The extent to which the sentences in a text are perceived by the readers as 'hanging together' and making sense. Coherence is a psycholinguistic rather than a linguistic phenomenon, although linguistic phenomena such as **cohesion** and **thematization** can facilitate the perception of coherence by the reader.

cohesion: Linguistic links existing between clauses and sentences that mark referential, logical, and lexical relationships.

collocation: A form of lexical cohesion in which two or more words are related by virtue of belonging to the same semantic field.

compound word: A word which is constructed from other words. Compound words usually begin life as two disconnected words (*data base*), then become joined by a hyphen (*data-base*), and then merge into a single word (*database*).

Computer-mediated feedback: Feedback on your writing provided by software packages such as Grammarly and the MS Word correcting function. While these can be useful, the feedback needs to be treated with caution as the advice is sometimes incorrect.

concordancing: A procedure for identifying patterns, regularities, and associations between words and word groups in large computerized databases (*corpora*).

concrete noun: A noun describing a physical entity (*the team, the procedure*). Concrete nouns contrast with **abstract nouns**.

conditional clause: A **dependent clause** expressing a condition and marked by a conjunction such as *if* or *unless*.

Examples:

If the procedure succeeds, the funding is almost certain to be renewed.

Unless the procedure succeeds, it's unlikely that the funding will be renewed.

conjunction: A cohesive device that makes explicit the logical relationships between the ideas in two different sentences or clauses. There are four types of logical relationship in English: additive (marked by conjunctions such as *and* and *also*); adversative (marked by words such as *but* and *however*); causal (marked by words such as *because*); and temporal (marked by conjunctions such as *firstly, then, next,* and *finally*).

connotation: A meaning implied by a word that goes beyond its literal meaning.

constituent structure: When one linguistic element is made up of lower-order elements, we say they have a constituent structure. For example, the constituent structure of the word *watched* are the morphemes *watch* and *-ed*.

content word: A word that refers to a thing, quality, state action, or event. (Content words contrast with function words.)

context: The linguistic and experiential environments in which a piece of language occurs.

coordination: The joining of two different ideas with a coordinating conjunction. Use of coordination signals that the ideas have the same status within the discourse. It contrasts with **subordination** in which the ideas have unequal status.

culture: The (often implicit) norms and rules and practices that govern the interactional and personal behavior of groups and individuals.

declarative knowledge: Knowledge that can be stated (or 'declared') such as a grammatical rule.

definite article: The word *the* which precedes a noun or noun phrase.

demonstrative: The words *this, that, these,* and *those,* which indicate the proximity of objects to the speaker.

descriptive grammar: A grammar that sets out to describe the way people use language without prescribing what is correct or incorrect.

determiner: Words that modify nouns to limit their meaning. Common determiners in English include articles (*a/an, the*), demonstratives (*this, that, these, those*), possessives (*his, their*), and quantifiers (*some, much, many*). Determiners are important elements in cohesion.

direct object: An object that is directly affected by the main verb in a sentence. Direct objects contrast with **indirect objects**. In the sentence "*Lyn handed her assignment to the teacher*", "*her assignment*" is the direct object, and "*the teacher*" is the indirect object.

discourse: Any stretch of spoken or written language viewed within the communicative context in which it occurred.

discourse analysis: The systematic study of language in context. Discourse analysis is sometimes contrasted with **text analysis**, which focuses on analyzing the formal properties of language.

ellipsis: The omission of clauses, words, or phrases that, strictly speaking, are required to make an utterance grammatical, but that can be recovered from the preceding sentence.

existential subject: (also known as *empty* or *dummy subject*) Use the *there* or *it* in existential sentences.

Examples:

There will be a seminar on Friday.

It's surprising how often graduate students apply the wrong procedure to the analysis of their data.

exophoric reference: Referring expressions such as 'he', 'this', and 'here', which point to entities and events in the world outside the text.

feedback: Providing information on the performance of a product, procedure, or individual/group of individuals. Summative feedback is provided at the end of the instructional process. Formative feedback is designed to help the individual or group improve a product, such as an assignment, or a procedure such as an oral examination.

figurative language: Expressions whose meanings can't be deduced from a literal knowledge of the words that make them up.

field: In systemic-functional linguistics, the subject matter of a text. (See also **ideational meaning.**)

first language: An individual's native tongue.

function word: A 'grammatical' rather than 'content' word, belonging to one of the closed word classes such as **determiners**, prepositions, pronouns, modals, and conjunctions.

genre: A purposeful, socially constructed oral or written text such as a narrative, a casual conversation, a poem, a recipe, or a description. Each genre has its own characteristic structure and grammatical forms that reflect its social purpose.

grammar: The study of how words are formed and combined to enable the communication of meaning.

grammatical metaphor: The process of turning actions into things.

Example: They are <u>constructing</u> a new building next to our school which has increased the amount of noise in the area considerably. → The <u>construction</u> of the new building next to our school has increased noise in the area considerably.

grammar word: A word belonging to a closed grammatical class such as prepositions or articles. They are also called *function words* or structural words.

grapheme: The smallest meaningful unit in the writing system of a language.

homonym: Words that are spelled or sound the same but have different meanings.

Examples:

'*study*' (a room, to examine carefully)

'*Write*', '*right*'

hyponym: A word that is the subordinate of a more general word.

Example: '*physics* and '*chemistry*; and hyponyms of '*science*'.

ideational meaning: The experiential content or subject matter of a text.

indefinite article: The word *a/an* used before singular count nouns or noun phrases to refer to an entity that is either unknown or has not previously been mentioned.

indirect object: A noun phrase that usually comes between the main verb and **direct object** in a sentence or utterance.

Example: *I gave <u>my boyfriend</u> a really cool t-shirt for his birthday.*

inductive reasoning: The process by which a learner arrives at rules and principles by studying examples and instances. Inductive learning contrasts with deductive learning, in which principles, rules, or theories are applied to understand an example or instance.

instantial relationship/meaning: A meaning or relationship between entities, events, and states-of-affairs that only make sense within the spoken or written context in which it occurs.

interpersonal meaning: That aspect of a written or spoken utterance that reflects the speaker's feelings and attitudes toward the topic of the utterance. In systemic-functional linguistics, the term '*tenor*' is also used.

lexicon: All of the words in a language.

lexical: To do with the words in a language.

lexical cohesion: Lexical cohesion occurs when two or more content words in a text are related. The two major categories of lexical cohesion are reiteration/repetition and collocation.

Examples:

Reiteration/repetition: The <u>information explosion</u> has greatly <u>facilitated</u> the development of <u>technology and globalization</u>. In fact, these three factors, the <u>information explosion, technology,</u> and <u>globalization</u>, are interrelated and mutually reinforcing.

Collocation: Our <u>garden</u> looks best in <u>spring</u>. By <u>summer</u>, the <u>flowers</u> are past their best.

lexical density: The ratio of content words to grammar/function words in a text. Generally speaking, written texts have a higher lexical density than spoken texts.

lexical relationship: The relationship between content words in a text. (See also *lexical cohesion.*)

lexicography: The study of words.

linguistics: The systematic study of language. Linguistics is divided into a series of sub-disciplines, including *phonetics, phonology, morphology, syntax, semantics,* and *pragmatics.*

literacy: The ability to read and write a language.

logical connectives: Conjunctions such as *therefore, however, in addition, firstly, and,* and *but* that mark textual relationships such as causality, temporality, and adversity.

metalinguistic awareness: Developing an awareness and understanding of language as an abstract phenomenon as well as the ability to 'step back' and reflect on the underlying processes of your own language use.

metaphor: Words and phrases used to describe things they do not physically resemble.

modal verb: A closed set of verbs (*can, could, have to, may, might, must shall, should, will, would*) that express attitudes such as certainty, permission, and possibility.

modality: That aspect of a sentence or utterance that reveals the attitude of the writer or speaker toward the content of what has been said or written. The most common way of expressing modality is through modal verbs and adverbs.

mode: One of the three register variables in systemic-functional linguistics. Mode refers to the means of communication, e.g., written versus spoken and face-to-face versus Zoom.

morpheme: The smallest meaningful element into which a word can be analyzed.

Example: The word *walked* consists of two morphemes: *walk* which signifies an action and *-ed* which signifies the fact that the action took place in the past. *-ed* is *a bound morpheme*. It can't exist as a meaningful unit in its own right.

morphology: The study of the internal structure of words.

morphosyntax: The combined study of the internal structure of words (morphology) and the rules that govern the arrangement of words into clauses and sentence (syntax).

nominalization: The process of turning verbs into nouns. (See also ***grammatical metaphor.***) Nominalization has a number of purposes, including that of removing the doer of the action. It also allows for a process to be topicalized.

Example: *The home team won which excited the crowd.* → *The team's win excited the crowd.*

notions: General concepts expressed through language such as time, duration, and quantity.

nouns: Probably the largest class of content words in any language, nouns refer to persons, objects, and entities. There are various ways of classifying nouns, for example, countable (people, planets, movies) versus uncountable (food, noise, water), and concrete (houses, statues, ant) versus abstract (enmity, eternity, eccentricity). New nouns are being created as quickly as new entities are entering our universe.

object: That part of a sentence or utterance that follows the main verb and is affected or 'acted upon' by the subject.

object complement: A word or phrase that describes or modifies the object of a sentence.

Example: I used to call her my best friend.

parse: To divide a sentence into its component parts and label these grammatically as subject, verb, object, etc.

passive voice: A sentence or utterance in which the result of an action rather than the performer of the action is made the subject. The passive voice contrasts with the *active voice* and has a number of important discourse functions such as to emphasize or *thematize* an action or result of an action or to refer to the result of an action with the doer is unknown.

Example: The book was finally finished. The hotel room was totally trashed.

phoneme: The smallest meaningful unit of sound in a language.

phonetics: The description and analysis of the ways in which speech sounds are produced, transmitted, and understood by speakers and hearers.

phonology: The description and analysis of the distinctive sounds in a language and the relationship between sound and meaning.

phrasal verbs: The phrasal verb consists of two parts, a verb + a preposition or adverb

Examples: Put up, look after, shut down, carry on, come across

pragmatics: The study of the way language is used in particular contexts to achieve particular ends.

procedural knowledge: The ability to use knowledge to do things. It is sometimes informally known as 'how to' knowledge and contrasts with declarative knowledge which has to do with the ability to declare rules and principles.

process writing: This term is used in several senses in the book. In the first place, it describes a method developed is the 1980s as an antidote to the mechanistic copying of models that was considered to be sterile and discouraged creativity. The process began by guided discussion and brainstorming to generate topics on the theme of the writing followed by free writing, teacher conferencing of initial drafts, and progressively shaping the writing. It was also seen as a several step procedure of initial drafting of ideas, revising and redrafting, incorporating new content that arise during the writing process, inserting new ideas as a result of feedback, and then drafting of a final product. The third, and most extensive discussion, was the notion of writing as a thinking process.

pronominalization: The process of substituting a pronoun for an entire noun phrase.

Example: I went to the seminar on how to be a better writer last night. It was better than I expected.

pronoun: A word that substitutes for a noun or a noun phrase.

proposition: A statement about some entity or event.

psycholinguistics: The study of the mental processes underlying language acquisition and use.

purpose: The reason(s) form *why* you are writing a piece (whether it be an assignment, an article, or even a book). Keeping purpose in mind goes hand-in-hand with audience as you consider the effect you want to have on the reader.

recount: A *genre* consisting of a sequence of events initiated by an introduction and orientation and ending with a comment and conclusion.

reference (cohesive): Those proforms (largely pronouns and demonstratives) in a text that refer to and can only be interpreted with reference to some other part of the text or to some entity or event in the experiential world.

register: The kind of language used by discourse communities for particular communicative purposes. In systemic-functional linguistics, register is described in terms of *field* (the subject of the communication), *tenor* (the relationship between the interactants), and *mode* (the means of communication, e.g., written versus spoken and face-to-face versus Zoom).

reiteration: A form of lexical cohesion in which the two cohesive items refer to the same entity or event. Reiteration includes repetition, synonym or near synonym, superordinate, and general word. In the following example, the underlined words refer to the same entity and are therefore an example of reiteration.

Example: My *computer has been playing up ever since I installed that new software. The thing has been driving me crazy.*

relative clause: A subordinate clause that modifies or provides additional information about the subject of a sentence. Relative clauses provide a level of 'delicacy' not possible with coordinate clauses because they can indicate the relative status of the additional information.

Example: The following statement contains two pieces of information about the President of the University of Hong Kong. *The president of the University of Hong Kong comes from Shanghai and he is a microbiologist.* Both pieces of information have relatively equal status. (It could be argued that his place of origin is more important than his academic discipline because it occurs first, but that's probably splitting hairs!) If the author of the statement wants to prioritize place of origin, she could make it part of the main clause and 'relativize' the academic field:

The president of the University of Hong Kong, who's a microbiologist, comes from Shanghai. Or, she could elevate his status, as follows: The president of the University of Hong Kong, who comes from Shanghai, is a microbiologist. By placing either place of origin or academic discipline at the end of the sentence, the author is giving the information the status of 'new' (i.e., important information), as this typically comes at the end of the sentence. (See entries on theme and rheme below.)

repair: The correction of clarification of a speaker's utterance either by the speaker (self-correction) or by someone else (other correction). These corrections serve to avert communication breakdowns in conversation.

reported speech (or indirect speech): Language used to report what someone else said. Reported speech involves a tense shift.

Examples:

I am sorry I missed the seminar. → Jake said that he was sorry he missed the seminar.

I finished my assignment early. → Jane said that she had finished her assignment early.

I'll be there at six. → John said that he'd be there at six.

I've seen that movie five times. → Wendy said that she had seen the movie five times.

rheme: (see *theme/rheme,* below)

schema theory: A theory of language processing based on the notion that past experiences lead to the creation of mental frameworks that help us make sense of new experiences.

second-language acquisition: The psychological and social processes underlying the development of proficiency in a second language.

semantic network: A network of words in which individual words belong to a particular 'family' such as 'the weather', 'linguistics', and 'education'.

semantics: The study of the formal meanings expressed in language without reference to the contexts in which the language is used.

sentence: A unit of language containing a subject and a finite verb. Sentences can be simple, containing a single clause, or complex, containing more than one clause. The basic elements of a sentence are **subject, verb, object, complement,** and **adverbial.**

sociolinguistics: The study of language in its social context.

standards: In the book, we discuss two terms: **standard language** and **language standards.** All languages come in different varieties: 'Standard language' is that variety considered to be the norm, the yardstick against which other varieties are to be judged. The term is controversial, as is the term 'language standards' as the questions immediately arise: Considered to be the norm by whom? and Who is to arbitrate on standards of acceptability? As we indicate in the book, standards are constantly changing as is degrees of acceptability.

subject complement: A word or phrase that describes or modified the subject of a sentence.

Example: I am really tired.

subordinate clause: a clause that is part of another clause. Subordinate clauses are labeled according to the way they function in relation to the main clause.

(a) Nominal clauses take on functions associated with noun phrases, e.g., subject or object in the main clause.
(b) Adverbial clauses take the function of adverbials.
(c) Relative clauses take an 'adjectival' function, as modifiers in a noun phrase.
(d) Comparative clauses take a modifying function in an adjective phrase, an adverb phrase, or a noun phrase, following a comparative word or construction. (Leech, 1992, p. 108.)

subordination: The process of 'downgrading' one clause in a sentence in order to show that the information it contains is less significant than the information in the main clause. (See *relative clause* above.)

substitution: A category of cohesive device in which proforms stand in for earlier mentioned nouns, verbs, and clauses.

synonym: Two word or phrases having the exact or almost exact meaning as each other. Some linguists argue that no two words have exactly the same meaning, that, for example, while *run* and *sprint* are very similar, they have different shades of meaning.

syntax: The study of the rules that govern the formation of grammatical structures and the ordering of *words* into *sentences*. *Grammar* consists of *syntax* and *morphology*.

systemic-functional linguistics: A theory that sees language as sets of interrelated systems, that stresses its social nature, and that attempts to account for grammatical features in terms of their communicative functions.

text: The written record of a communicative event which conveys a complete message. Texts may vary from single words (e.g., 'EXIT') to books running to hundreds of pages.

text analysis: The analysis of textual features such as cohesion, text structure, and information focus. The focus is on formal rather than functional features of language, and the analysis generally makes little reference to the extra-linguistic context that gave rise to the text in the first place.

text structure: Rhetorical patterns within texts such as problem-solution.

theme/rheme: In terms of message structure, Halliday divides sentences/clauses into two. At the beginning of the message, is the **theme**. The writer is saying to the reader: *I want to tell you something about X.* The rest of the sentence is the **rheme**. Here the writer is saying: *This is what I want you to know about X. Please pay attention, this is news!* This process of giving prominence to certain elements within a sentence by placing them at the beginning of the sentence or utterance is known as thematization.

top-down processing: The use of background knowledge, knowledge of text structures, etc., to assist in the interpretation of discourse.

topic: The experiential subject of a text, that is, what the text is about.

topicalization: Very closely related to the concept of **thematization**, topicalization is the process of giving prominence to certain elements in a sentence or utterance by shifting them to the beginning. The following sentences express the same propositional content, but each is topicalized differently.

Examples:

I will finish this glossary tonight.

This glossary will be finished tonight.

Tonight, I will finish this glossary.

transactional language: Language that is used to obtain goods and services. This use of language contrasts with **interpersonal language** where the purpose is primarily social.

transcription: The written record of a piece of spoken discourse.

verb: A word class denoting actions and states.

voice (1): When it comes to grammar there are two forms of voice: active and passive. Voice enables the speaker or writer to focus on the person performing the action or the result of the action.

voice (2): Given the focus of this book, the second, and more significant sense in which voice is use is in terms of the development of your own voice as a writer. We suggested that you make your voice heard by your choice of what to write about and how you choose to tell the story. Your voice will reflect your identity. It will be revealed in the discursive (linguistic) and non-discursive resources you draw on.

word: A single meaningful unit consisting of one or more **morphemes**.

Reference

Leech, G. (1992). *Introducing English grammar*. Penguin.

Index